# Inclusive Finance India Report 2015

**Bulk Sales**

SAGE India offers special discounts
for purchase of books in bulk.
We also make available special imprints
and excerpts from our books on demand.

*For orders and enquiries, write to us at*

Marketing Department
SAGE Publications India Pvt Ltd
B1/I-1, Mohan Cooperative Industrial Area
Mathura Road, Post Bag 7
New Delhi 110044, India

*E-mail us at* **marketing@sagepub.in**

**Get to know more about SAGE**

Be invited to SAGE events, get on our mailing list.
*Write today to* **marketing@sagepub.in**

# Inclusive Finance India Report 2015

M.S. Sriram

**SAGE** www.sagepublications.com
Los Angeles • London • New Delhi • Singapore • Washington DC

*Copyright © ACCESS Development Services, 2016*

All rights reserved. No part of this book may be reproduced or utilised in any form or by any means, electronic or mechanical, including photocopying, recording, or by any information storage or retrieval system, without permission in writing from the publisher.

*First published in 2016 by*

 **SAGE Publications India Pvt Ltd**
B1/I-1 Mohan Cooperative Industrial Area
Mathura Road, New Delhi 110 044, India
*www.sagepub.in*

**SAGE Publications Inc**
2455 Teller Road
Thousand Oaks, California 91320, USA

**SAGE Publications Ltd**
1 Oliver's Yard, 55 City Road
London EC1Y 1SP, United Kingdom

**SAGE Publications Asia-Pacific Pte Ltd**
3 Church Street
#10-04 Samsung Hub
Singapore 049483

**ACCESS Development Services**
28, Hauz Khas Village
New Delhi 110 016
*www.accessdev.org*

Published by Vivek Mehra for SAGE Publications India Pvt Ltd, Phototypeset in 10/12 pt Minion Pro by Diligent Typesetter, Delhi and printed at Saurabh Printers Pvt Ltd, Greater Noida.

**Library of Congress Cataloging-in-Publication Data Available**

**ISBN:** 978-93-515-0866-3

**SAGE Production Team:** Shambhu Sahu, Alekha Chandra Jena and Rajinder Kaur

**Disclaimer:** The views expressed in this publication are those of the authors and do not necessarily reflect the views and policies of ACCESS Development Services.

**Cover photograph courtesy:** ACCESS.

# Sponsors & Partners

BILL & MELINDA
GATES *foundation*

Rabobank

# Contents

# List of Tables, Figures, Boxes, Appendices and Abbreviations

## *Tables*

## Figures

## Boxes

## Appendices

## *Abbreviations*

| | |
|---|---|
| AEPS | Aadhaar-Enabled Payment System |
| ANBC | Adjusted Net Bank Credit |
| ATM | Automated Teller Machine |
| BMB | Bharatiya Mahila Bank |
| BC | Business Correspondent |
| BSBDA | Basic Savings and Bank Deposit Account |
| BSNL | Bharat Sanchar Nigam Limited |
| CASA | Current Accounts Savings Accounts |
| CBS | Core Banking Solution |
| CDC | Commonwealth Development Corporation |
| CRAR | Capital to Risk-weighted Assets Ratio |
| CSP | Customer Service Point |
| DBT | Direct Benefit Transfer |
| DEG | German Development Finance Company |
| DFI | Development Financial Institution |
| DFS | Department of Financial Services |
| DPO | Departmental Post Office |
| eIPO | Electronic Indian Postal Order |
| eKYC | Electronic Know Your Customer |
| FMO | Netherlands Development Finance Corporation |
| FY | Financial Year |
| G2C | Government to Customer |
| GCC | General Credit Card |
| GDS | *Grameen Dak Sewak* |
| GLP | Gross Loan Portfolio |
| GNPA | Gross Non-Performing Assets |
| GoI | Government of India |
| GSM | Global System for Mobile Communication |
| ICT | Information and Communication Technology |
| IFC | International Financial Corporation |
| IFIF | India Financial Inclusion Fund |
| IIN | Issuer Identification Number |
| IMPS | Immediate Payment System |
| IRLT | Institute of Livelihood Research and Training |
| IT | Information Technology |
| JAM | Jan-Dhan, Aadhaar and Mobile |
| JLG | Joint Liability Groups |
| KCC | Kisan Credit Card |
| KVP | Kisan Vikas Patra |
| KYC | Know Your Customer |
| LAB | Local Area Bank |
| LPG | Liquefied Petroleum Gas |
| MFI | Microfinance Institutions |
| MFIN | Microfinance Institutions Network |
| MGNREGA | Mahatma Gandhi National Rural Employment Guarantee Act |
| MoRD | Ministry of Rural Development |
| MUDRA | Micro Units Development and Refinance Agency (Bank) |

| | |
|---|---|
| NABARD | National Bank for Agriculture and Rural Development |
| NBFC | Non-Banking Financial Company |
| NBFC-MFI | Non-Banking Financial Company–Microfinance Institution |
| NGO | Non-Governmental Organisation |
| NMI | Norwegian Microfinance Initiative |
| NPA | Non-Performing Asset |
| NPCI | National Payments Corporation of India |
| NPS | National Pension Scheme |
| NRLM | National Rural Livelihoods Mission |
| NSC | National Savings Certificate |
| NSS | National Savings Scheme |
| NULM | National Urban Livelihoods Mission |
| NUUP | National Unified USSD Platform |
| PAR | Portfolio at Risk |
| PB | Payments Bank |
| PIN | Personal Identification Number |
| PLI | Postal Life Insurance |
| PMJDY | Pradhan Mantri Jan Dhan Yojana |
| PMO | Prime Minister's Office |
| POS | Point of Sale |
| PPI | Prepaid Instruments |
| PSL | Priority Sector Lending |
| PSLC | Priority Sector Lending Certificate |
| RBI | Reserve Bank of India |
| RPLI | Rural Postal Life Insurance |
| RRB | Regional Rural Bank |
| RTI | Right to Information |
| SFB | Small Finance Bank |
| SGSY | Swarnajayanti Gram Swarozgar Yojana |
| SJSRY | Swarna Jayanti Shahari Rozgar Yojana |
| SHG | Self-Help Group |
| SHGBLP | SHG Bank Linkage Programme |
| SIDBI | Small Industries Development Bank of India |
| SMS | Short Message Service |
| SRMS | Scheme for Rehabilitation of Manual Scavenger |
| SRO | Self-Regulatory Organisation |
| SSA | Sub Service Area |
| UCB | Urban Cooperative Bank |
| UIDAI | Unique Identification Authority of India |
| USB | Ultra-Small Branch |
| USSD | Unstructured Supplementary Services Data |
| YoY | Year on Year |

# Foreword

One hundred eighty million is a very large number. This is the number of new bank accounts that have been opened in the last one year since the Prime Minister Jan Dhan Yojana (PMJDY) was launched. Governments are usually very good at accomplishing numerical targets, but the challenge often is to assess and understand the underlying outcome and impact that these numbers will have. This is an important initiative of the National Democratic Alliance (NDA) government to build an inclusive financial system and provide social protection to a large unreached vulnerable population of the country. It augurs well that beyond headline-grabbing announcements, there is a whole big major effort within the Government to make the PMJDY a success.

This is an exciting year for financial inclusion advancement in India. Several path-breaking initiatives were taken at various levels during the year. The PMJDY is the biggest story of the year; perhaps the largest effort in financial inclusion globally, seeking to bring universal access to finance in a country where 21% of the world's unbanked reside. While in the first phase, the focus was on the opening of bank accounts, the second phase efforts seek to activate these accounts and enable transactions and access to entitlements. This year, three new social protection schemes were announced under PMJDY on micro-insurance (life and accident) and pension. Although a high percentage of these accounts, ironically, despite a mission-like effort, continue to be dormant, the differences within the Government to make PMJDY succeed is very evident, at every level.

The programme is still in its early days, and, perhaps, one year down the line will be a more appropriate time to assess the success of the programme. Strikingly, when the previous government launched the Swabhimaan campaign, the Reserve Bank of India (RBI) was entrusted with the leading responsibility of ensuring its implementation. For the PMJDY, the Government of India unequivocally retains the primary responsibility for pushing the programme. This has both positive and negative implications.

During the year, the RBI took several important initiatives as well. While the country does have a fairly impressive as well as diversified institutional infrastructure, the response of these institutions to financial inclusion challenges has remained skeptical, since they just don't see small ticket transactions as a viable business segment. Since over 75% of banking infrastructure is owned by the Government of India, the public sector banks are regularly pushed to participate in the Government's social sector programmes. To supplement this, even if reluctant, with the participation of the current Foreign Financial Institutions, the RBI issued guidelines for two types of differentiated banks last year: small finance banks (SFBs) and payment banks, and fairly swiftly announced 10 in-principle licences for SFBs and 11 for payment banks in a very short time. ACCESS ASSIST played an important role in influencing the guidelines for these banks by organising stakeholder consultations in which the RBI too was associated and shared key recommendations with the regulator. This was done as a part of ASSIST's role in the Department for International Development (DFID)-supported 'Poorest States Inclusive Growth Programme'. It is expected that these new generation niche banking institutions, given the operational framework within which they are mandated to operate, will be far more effective in serving the unreached and low-income clients.

Interestingly, of the 10 SFBs that were given in-principle licences, 8 are large microfinance institutions (MFIs). In some manner, this is historic, as the MFIs for a very long time have struggled to gain legitimacy in India for a variety of reasons. Now with the large ones getting banking licences, they have moved from the periphery to mainstream. Given their track record of viably and profitably dealing with small ticket loans, they are bound to introduce new products, new processes and institutional innovations to demonstrate that banking with the poor can be a viable proposition. Importantly, with these MFI banks now being able to collect savings, perhaps, over time, their lending rates, for which they have been castigated in the past, may come down sharply.

RBI Governor Raghuram Rajan feels that the payment banks will be a game changer. Through leveraging technology, these banks will significantly help in last-mile access. Most of these licensees are either in payment or in Telco space with deep pockets and they know their business niche well. Payment banks will essentially rely on technology to reach payment services to all customers, using mobiles as a vehicle of banking. Mobile phones will become the virtual ATM and the cheque book for small payments. Payment banks are expected to be key enablers. Interestingly, India Post too has been given a payment bank licence. While it has the infrastructure and outreach, it will need to harness best technologies to be in the race, and perhaps beat the competition.

Earlier, two new universal banks were licensed and both are now operational. Contrastingly, while one is an infrastructure financing company, the other is an MFI. Granting of a universal banking licence to Bandhan is truly a transformational story from an NGO MFI to a full-fledged bank. Several other MFIs are already aspiring that some day they too will be eligible for a full bank licence.

Another interesting initiative of the Government was to launch the MUDRA Bank during the year, targeting the missing middle–small businesses and micro-enterprises in the informal sector. MUDRA is expected to refinance this segment, besides playing a supervisory and regulatory function for MFIs. This jumbled mandate will take some time before the true purpose of MUDRA gets settled.

With the launch of PMJDY, the self-help group bank linkage programme (SHGBLP) story has taken a bit of a backseat, as its numbers no longer excite policymakers. National Bank for Agriculture and Rural Development (NABARD) and National Rural Livelihoods Mission (NRLM) continue to be the principal promoters of the programme. The year-on-year growth has slowed and in certain pockets the high incidence of non-performing assets (NPAs) is keeping the bankers from proactive lending to SHGs. The SHG version 2 does not seem to have revitalised the programme with no significant innovations being integrated into the strategy. Given the great promise that the programme holds, it is critical to design strategies for its revitalisation. The convergence of strategies with NRLM is critical. There is also a need to explore on how SHGBLP can be integrated within the PMJDY scheme and contribute to its outcomes. NABARD has begun a pilot project on digitising the SHG accounts. This is likely to help SHGs to integrate with PMJDY, to provide clearer picture on the health of SHGs, provide real-time information to banks and so on. A good development has been coming forward of a few private banks like ICICI to link SHGs on their own accord, without the need for a nudge.

Finally, on the MFI front, there is both cause for concern and cheer. Bandhan's becoming a universal commercial bank is the biggest accomplishment within the sector. The Bank was formally launched with great fanfare in August this year with over 500 branches and a loan book of ₹100 billion. Eight other large MFIs have been given 'in-principle' licences for SFBs. This opened up pathways for MFI graduation and opportunities for several others to strive to move to become banks. With nine large MFIs becoming banks, over 50% of the total MFI portfolio has moved out of the sector. The causes for concern are related to the blistering pace of growth and multiple lending among others. Many fear that there is another bubble in the making. Micro Finance Institutions Network (MFIN) and Sa-dhan, the two industry associations, which have also been designated as self-regulatory organisations (SROs), will need to be watchful, while this aggressive growth is taking place.

This has been an exciting year in India for advancing financial inclusion, with several initiatives at the policy as well as the operations level. Capturing the entire action and assessing short- and long-term implications and impact needed an adroit and astute commentator. Despite the related challenges, over the years, ACCESS has been fortunate in getting the right people to author the Report. With an expanded ambit, the 2015 Inclusive Finance India Report needed an author who had a full understanding of the financial ecosystem in India. I am particularly happy and feel privileged that Professor M.S. Sriram agreed to take up the challenge. Given his several priorities and commitments, it did take an effort to convince him to author the 2015 Report. Having been on the Board of a Commercial Bank just when banks were entrusted with the responsibility of rolling out Swabhimaan, having been a member of several committees of the RBI and the Government, having extensively written on financial inclusion and microfinance and having been a keen observer of the sector, there was no one perhaps more appropriate to take on this complex task. I am glad that Professor Sriram agreed. The 2015 Report is a bit of a departure from previous reports, as in addition to reporting on current trends, the author has provided the historical backdrop on all institutions that form a part of the formal financial architecture, and in some manner creating a baseline for tracking the future advancement of financial inclusion in India.

Several stakeholders have supported this effort. I would like to thank the Governor, Reserve Bank of India, for giving precious time to the author to give his perspective on several issues. I would also like to thank the Secretary DFS, Ministry of Finance and Chairman NABARD for their precious time. I would particularly like to thank Anurag Jain in the Prime Minister's office, who agreed to meet us late at night and spoke extensively on the challenge of rolling out PMJDY, when he was leading the campaign in the DFS, Finance Ministry. I would like to thank NABARD, particularly Chintala, for hosting an important consultation on SHGBLP, and Mohan Tanksale and IBA for a similar consultation with bankers. I also take this opportunity to thank MetLife Foundation, Bill & Melinda Gates Foundation, Rabobank Foundation, SIDBI, IFC, NABARD and Dia Vikas for sponsoring the Report. Their continued faith in the value of this effort helps us in continuing and building on this effort.

I also take this opportunity to thank my small dynamic team in facilitating the Report writing. While Radhika, the Executive Director ACCESS ASSIST, ably led the team, the anchor support to the entire process was provided by the little champion Anshu. Lalitha, as always, was the go-to person for all logistical support. I would also like to thank the Inclusive Finance India Advisory Group who provided useful suggestions to the author. I would particularly like to thank Nanda ji, Mr Brij Mohan and N. Srinivasan for their thoughtful insights.

This has been a complex task, particularly with so much action. While I am sure that the author has not missed out any important initiative, I hope that, as always, the Report will be of value to policymakers, practitioners as well as others who have interest in tracking financial inclusion advancement in India. The Report will be released at the Inclusive Finance India Summit, as per convention.

**Vipin Sharma**
CEO
ACCESS Development Services

# Preface

The year 2015 has been an interesting year for inclusive finance not only in terms of policy initiatives that bring in more of private sector into the inclusive banking fold, but also in terms of the implementation of some of the initiatives in the public sector. Initiatives taken during the year will have long-standing implications. These initiatives have laid down a foundation for newer initiatives. My predecessors have been doing a great job in writing the report, and it is not easy to step into their shoes and write something that matches up the benchmarks set by them.

This report not only represents a fair amount of continuity, but also some change. While the report largely focusses on the inclusive finance sector, I have tried to expand the scope by adding chapters on India Post and urban cooperative banks. I would have loved to include a chapter on the rural cooperative sector as well, but the non-availability of ready data and constraints of time did not permit me to do so. Similarly, while I have tried to look at the savings and credit side of the financial inclusion in its entirety, I have not touched upon insurance, risk mitigation and social security aspects. However, the idea this year has been to provide a stable and evolving template so that the users of the report could look forward to the basic coverage as we go forward, while we add more chapters. Similarly, the attempt is also to provide data formats that would be continuing in order to enable comparisons across years.

A report of this nature cannot be accomplished without the inputs of various people, and it is futile to try and acknowledge each one and associate each of them with the specific contribution they have made. I have made a list of people and their organisations with whom I interacted in the process of writing the report. However, the list does not capture the types of inputs that each of these individuals has provided me. Writing a report of this magnitude is a lonely activity, but has to be necessarily undertaken in a crowded place, while listening to various voices, opinions and also simultaneously perusing data. I have tried to be as dispassionate and objective as possible and have made all attempts to gather as much data as possible.

In addition to the people listed in the acknowledgements, I would like to especially thank the following personalities:

- Governor Raghuram Rajan of the Reserve Bank of India for readily agreeing to an interview for the report and also turning back the edited manuscript very quickly. It was a pleasure interacting with him.
- Anurag Jain, Joint Secretary with the Prime Minister's Office, who in spite of his busy schedule and the high security place of work agreed to spend more than an hour late one evening to give a detailed description of how the Pradhan Mantri Jan Dhan Yojana (PMJDY) was rolled out when he was with the Department of Financial Services.
- Hasmukh Adhia, (then) Secretary Department of Financial Services, for spending time in explaining the importance of PMJDY and Mudra Yojana.
- Harsh Bhanwala, Chair National Bank for Agriculture and Rural Development (NABARD), who gave time and a perspective on how NABARD is working on the digitisation of Self Help Group (SHG) data as well as the initiatives with regard to primary agricultural co-operatives.
- G.R. Chintala of NABARD for being so proactive in providing the updated data on SHGs and also for organising a consultation of the bankers with a specific focus on SHG Bank linkage programme.

- M.V. Tanksale, CEO of Indian Banks' Association (IBA), who, amidst multiple commitments, organised a consultation with the bankers to understand the field-level issues in not only rolling out PMJDY, but also other initiatives in inclusion. Similarly, M.V.N.K. Prasad also facilitated an informal consultation with grass-roots managers of Regional Rural Banks (RRBs) at the Institute for Development and Research in Banking Technology.
- Ratna Vishwanathan of Microfinance Institutions Network (MFIN) for being supportive in data and in providing insights about the work of MFIN.
- Smt Kalpana Tewari, Member Postal Services Board, Department of Posts (since retired), who spent precious time explaining the strategy of India Post vis-à-vis inclusive finance.

I am thankful to ACCESS for providing me with the opportunity to write this report and for all the logistical support. In particular, I would like to acknowledge the support of Anshu Singh who was the person to turn to for any support and Lalitha Sridharan who was always forthcoming in supporting me.

**M.S. Sriram**

# Introduction

## OVERVIEW

The focus on financial inclusion has been getting increased attention. As the report gets into its 10th year, there are exciting developments in the inclusive finance space. In keeping with the broadening of the definition of financial inclusion, this report also expands its canvas to broaden the sub-segments of inclusion to be covered.

Globally financial inclusion has moved away from looking at specialised interventions (like microfinance) towards the dynamic of financial inclusion comprehensively. Even in India the policy discourse has moved from credit dispensation (replacing the evil and oppressive money lender) to provision of a bouquet of services from the formal financial system. There are global benchmarks to measure the achievements on financial inclusion. The data put out by the World Bank Group on the Global Findex for 2014 (published in June 2015) gives a good idea of the level of inclusion achieved globally. In keeping with the expanded definition of inclusion, the measurements are moving beyond just ownership of accounts.

There has been a significant progress between the last round of the Findex survey and the current round. The overall percentage of adults having an account was 62% of the worldwide adult population (age above 15 years), while the percentage for India was 53%. However, the unbundling of these numbers (Table 1.1) gives the quality of inclusion and goes beyond opening of accounts.

According to the report, India is home to 21% of the world's and two-thirds of South Asia's unbanked population (Demirguc-Kunt et al., 2015). While these statistics are staggering and help the nation in its resolve to achieve greater inclusion, the Findex also notes the significant progress achieved between

2011 and 2014 where 18% of the adult Indian population were brought into the banking fold. With recent initiatives such as the Pradhan Mantri Jan Dhan Yojana (PMJDY), some of these numbers are expected to significantly increase, particularly after the roll-out of Phase II of PMJDY.

As the Global Findex is based on a sample survey (with some regions in the country completely left out due to law and order problems) resulting in a mismatch between the official data given out by the state, it is still useful to engage with this data as a benchmark. That is because a similar methodology is applied for data collection and therefore these numbers are comparable with the global averages. This also gives an idea of the quality of inclusion. As can be seen from the select parameters of Global Findex database, while there is significant progress in account opening, there are large gaps in borrowings from the formal sector, access to technology-enabled banking instruments (debit and credit cards) and the usage of the technology products, when available.

When Table 1.1 is examined with the global benchmarks, it is evident that even while the penetration of banking in terms of opening accounts could be deep, using the accounts for two-way transactions—both receiving payments and making payments have gaps, indicating that there is only that much a 'push' strategy could do—that is to help people open accounts. Eventually the account holders should see a meaning in operating these accounts. Some of the recent developments in India of 'pushing' direct benefit transfers (DBTs) into the accounts of the beneficiaries could ensure that the usage of accounts could potentially be habit forming. While this initiative has started in right earnest in the Government to Customer (G2C) payment in subsidy given for cooking gas, in the future years,

**Table 1.1** **Select inclusion parameters from India from the Global Findex**

| Parameter | % in 2011 | % in 2014 |
|---|---|---|
| Individuals having accounts with financial institutions | 35 | 53 |
| Women having accounts with financial institutions | 26.00 | 43.00 |
| Individuals from the bottom 40% of the poorest households who had accounts | 27.00 | 44.00 |
| Individuals who borrowed any money | | 46.33 |
| Individuals who borrowed money from formal institutions | 7.70 | 6.37 |
| Individuals who borrowed money from informal money lender | 6.43 | 12.53 |
| Individuals from the bottom 40% of the poorest households who borrowed from a private informal lender | 6.36 | 15.72 |
| ATMs (per 100,000 adults) | 9.00 | (Global average 9) |
| Commercial bank branches (per 100,000 adults) | 10.54 | (Global average 11) |
| Individuals who had credit cards | 1.77 | 4.18 |
| Of those who had credit cards, proportion who used them | | 3.35 |
| Individuals who had debit cards | 8.40 | 22.07 |
| Individuals who used mobiles for transactions | | 6.13 |
| Used ATM for deposit | 1.57 | |
| Used bank agents for deposit | 3.08 | |
| Used tellers for deposit | 89.29 | |
| Main mode of withdrawal: ATM | 18.43 | 33.11 |
| Main mode of withdrawal: bank agent | 3.18 | 2.04 |
| Main mode of withdrawal: bank teller | 69.71 | 54.07 |
| No deposit and no withdrawal in the past year | | 43.34 |
| Received domestic remittances in the past year | | 9.79 |
| Received domestic remittances in the past year, from poorest 40% | | 6.44 |
| Received government transfers in the past year | | 9.82 |
| Saved any money in the past year | 22.42 | 38.28 |
| Saved at a financial institution | 11.60 | 14.36 |
| Sent domestic remittances in the past year | | 9.94 |

*Source:* Data extracted from the Global Findex 2014 database. Available at http://datatopics.worldbank.org/financialinclusion/home, accessed on 31 August 2015.

there would be penetration of this channel when payments spread to the 26 centrally sponsored programmes that involve payments cutting across eight departments of the government. When this happens, the infographic (Figure 1.1) would reduce the white portion as far as India is concerned.

While India does not feature in the top countries in the world that have taken to mobile money, with the 11 new payment banks coming up in the next 18 months will fill in the gap on mobile-based transactions as well as payments. In the future years, there would be something different and interesting to report. The infographic (Figure 1.2) gives an overview of the big picture and the place of India in comparison to some of the peers.

## INCLUSIX

Apart from the global benchmarks, CRISIL has been measuring the progress of India's efforts in financial inclusion through an index, and the progress is monitored annually and published by them. CRISIL defines financial inclusion as 'The extent of access by all sections of the society to formal financial services, such as credit, deposit, insurance and pension services' (CRISIL, 2015). The report

**Many account owners are using their accounts to make or receive payments**
Adults with an account by its use for payments in the past year (as % of all adults), 2014

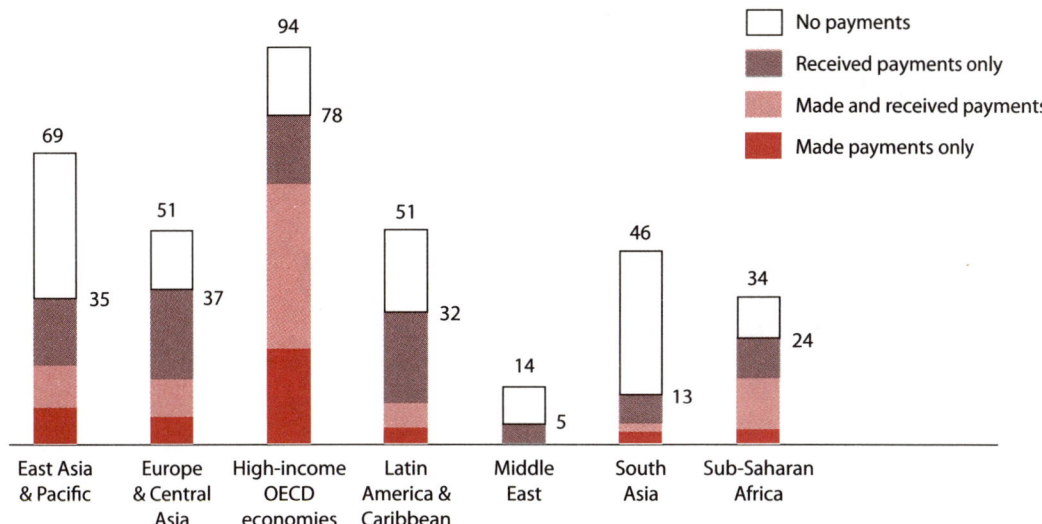

**Figure 1.1** How people use bank accounts

*Source:* Demirguc-Kunt, Asli, Leora Klapper, Dorothe Singer, and Peter Van Oudheusden. 2015. 'The Global Findex Database 2014: Measuring Financial Inclusion around the World.' Policy Research Working Paper 7255, World Bank, Washington, DC.

for 2013 (published in June 2015) indicated a significant progress from the past. A large part of the increase in score from 42.8 to 50.1 is due to the fact that data on microfinance was included in the index for the first time (Figure 1.3). Therefore, the numbers between 2012 and 2013 are not strictly comparable. With the new initiatives launched this year, the index is expected to further strengthen and also contribute towards reduction of the regional disparity.

While CRISIL has included bank and microfinance institution (MFI) data, the data on both post offices and cooperative societies are left out. While MFIs add to one side of the inclusion story by adding to the measure of both branch penetration and credit penetration, the postal network adds richness by providing data on both increased number of outlets and deposit penetration. Given the fact that the postal savings has limitations on the size of deposit it can take, this would well be treated as 'small deposit accounts'. The data of the postal network also would show the evenness of the spread of outlets across the various regions of the country. Again, while CRISIL uses insurance and pension services in its definition, it is not evident that these two services have been included in the computation of the index. With the PMJDY being linked to both insurance and pension and with the department of posts getting a payments bank (PB) licence, there is

every likelihood that when these data are added to the index, it would show a sharp growth in the next few years. While this might not help in sophisticated year-on-year comparison, it is well worth the effort to make the index comprehensive.

The inclusion scores broken up region wise show (Figure 1.4) that the penetration of financial services is deeper in the southern region and there is significant amount of catching up to do by the north-eastern region. The south shows a lower variability indicating that the services are available across the region uniformly while in the case of north-east, this was highly variable. While most of the data in this report consider figures for the year ending 2014–15, the Inclusix data are coming in with a lag of 2 years. This does not add to the quality of discussions.

From the preceding data it is important to note that while the southern region has high scores on all parameters, the scores for credit penetration are higher than the scores for branch and deposit penetration, indicating a more evolved credit market which may be addressing both the consumption smoothening and the enterprise finance needs. In all other regions, the branch and deposit penetration numbers are higher than the credit penetration numbers. While the incorporation of the microfinance data (which adds only to branch penetration and credit penetration index and not to the deposit

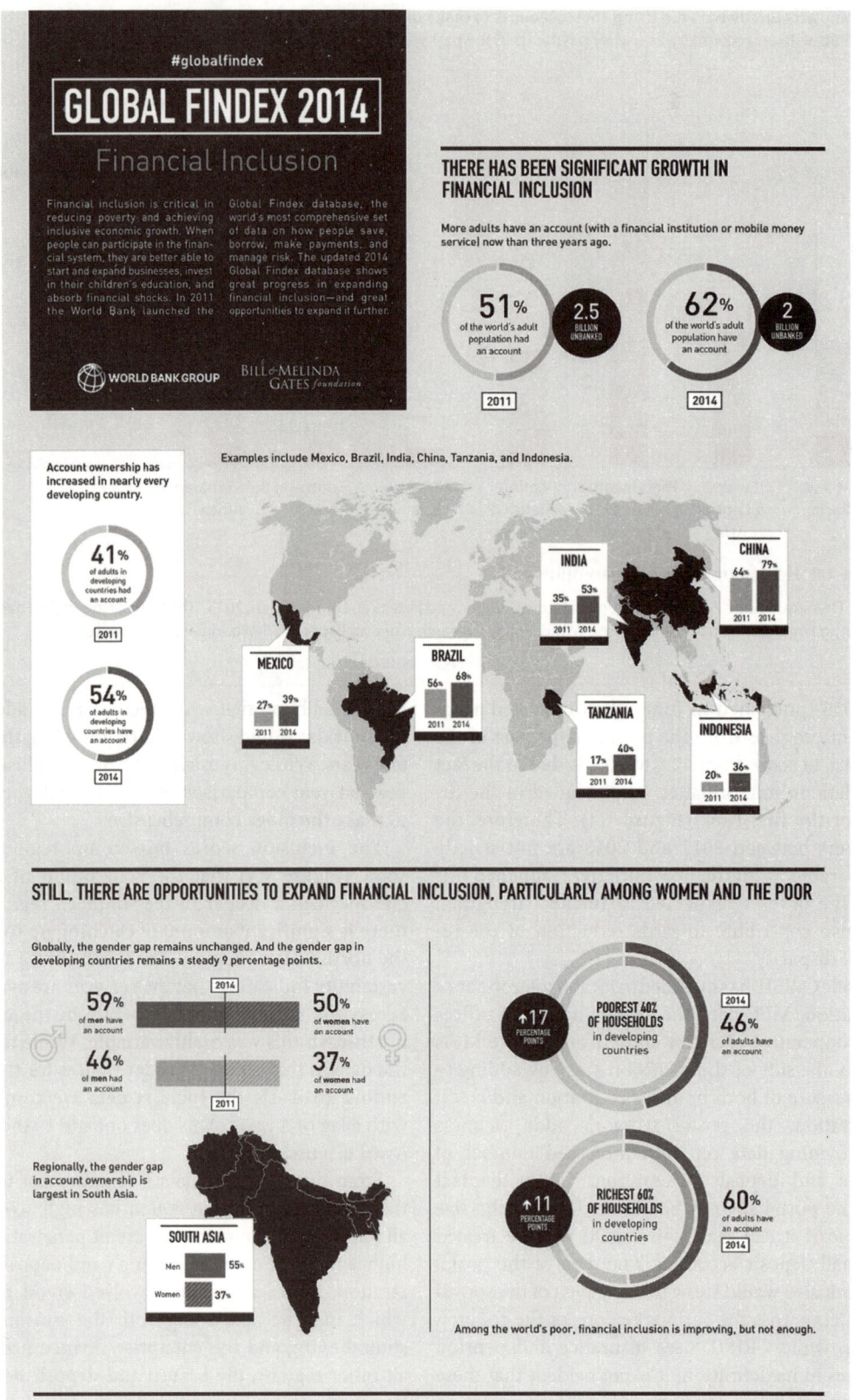

**Figure 1.2** Global Findex: meta numbers

*Source:* Global Findex website http://www.worldbank.org/en/programs/globalfindex/infographics/infographic-global-findex-2014-financial-inclusion, accessed on 4 September 2015.

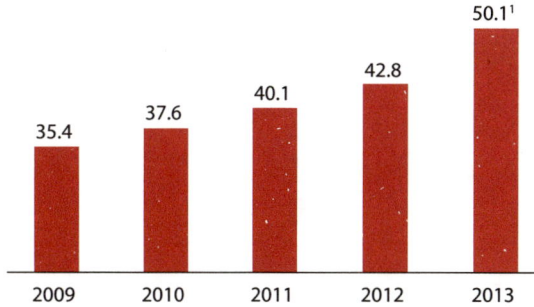

**Figure 1.3** CRISIL Inclusix scores over the years

[1]The index value of 50.1 for 2013 is not comparable with the index value of 42.8 for 2012 as data for MFIs is available only for fiscal 2013.
*Source:* Crisil Inclusix volume III. June 2014. Mumbai: CRISIL Limited.

index) shows the numbers are significantly higher in the low-penetration regions, there is much more catching up to do. If we were to incorporate the savings data from the postal system, the difference between the deposit and credit penetration will become sharper.

The progress of the individual states is captured in the map in Figure 1.5. From the map it is clear that while the northern region is lagging behind, there are pockets in the north that have a high penetration (Punjab, Himachal, Chandigarh and Delhi); there are other states that are below average (Rajasthan). It is only in south that all the states are exhibiting a high level of inclusion not only on the overall parameters, but also on all the individual physical and business parameters.

The top and bottom states as well as districts in the financial inclusion for 2012 and are given in Table 1.2. Unlike 2012, in 2013 the top nine districts have a score of 100, and all of them belong to Kerala.

There are some changes in the top states, and districts, while the bottom states remain unchanged. While the 2013 index includes access to financial services through microfinance as well, microfinance activities do not seem to have penetrated into the districts scoring low on Inclusix to make a difference in the score. However, since the Inclusix scores are only for 2013, it can be said that the bottom states would possibly show a significant improvement in the coming years. Chapter 9 on microfinance records the phenomenal growth that MFIs have shown in the eastern and north-eastern sectors. This aspect will be discussed in Chapter 9 in greater detail.

Apart from the larger figures that pertained to clients, the physical outreach and the delivery of financial products, there were changes happening in the overall ecosystem with regard to regulation of the financial inclusion space and the drastic changes in the roll-out of technology.

## A COMPREHENSIVE LOOK AT ALL THE PROVIDERS

While the Findex score looks largely at banks and the Inclusix looks at banks and MFIs, it is important to realise that there is a range of institutions operating in the country. When all the touchpoints are added together, the network is formidable. The data show that physically there is a formal sector touchpoint for every 4,100 persons and a self-help group (SHG) for every 156 persons (Table 1.3). However, the quality and the range of services that these touchpoints offer vary widely. For instance, more than half the formal sector touchpoints are those of the postal network which offer only savings, remittance and insurance services, but not banking and credit services. Similarly, the MFIs offer only some types of loans and not comprehensive services.

| Region | BP | | CP | | DP | | Inclusix | |
|---|---|---|---|---|---|---|---|---|
| | 2013 | 2012 | 2013 | 2012 | 2013 | 2012 | 2013 | 2012 |
| ■ Southern Region | 69.7 | 57.1 | 88.7 | 80.8 | 83.1 | 71.8 | 76.0 | 66.1 |
| ■ Western Region | 54.1 | 45.4 | 37.3 | 30.6 | 60.5 | 52.5 | 48.2 | 40.9 |
| ▫ Northern Region | 49.0 | 42.4 | 32.8 | 29.2 | 59.1 | 53.2 | 44.0 | 39.5 |
| ■ Eastern Region | 43.1 | 31.0 | 35.1 | 24.3 | 44.8 | 39.5 | 40.2 | 30.8 |
| ■ North-eastern Region | 41.2 | 30.9 | 35.8 | 24.1 | 45.9 | 41.0 | 39.7 | 30.9 |
| ▫ India | 52.4 | 42.7 | 45.7 | 38.7 | 60.3 | 53.2 | 50.1 | 42.8 |

| Region | 2013 | 2012 | 2011 | 2010 |
|---|---|---|---|---|
| Southern Region | 0.18 | 0.21 | 0.22 | 0.23 |
| Western Region | 0.29 | 0.32 | 0.34 | 0.37 |
| Northern Region | 0.28 | 0.32 | 0.36 | 0.35 |
| Eastern Region | 0.33 | 0.32 | 0.32 | 0.34 |
| North-eastern Region | 0.41 | 0.42 | 0.44 | 0.46 |
| India | 0.38 | 0.40 | 0.42 | 0.43 |

**Figure 1.4** Region-wise Inclusix scores

BP branch penetration; CP credit penetration; DP deposit penetration
*Source:* CRISIL Inclusix volume III, 2015.

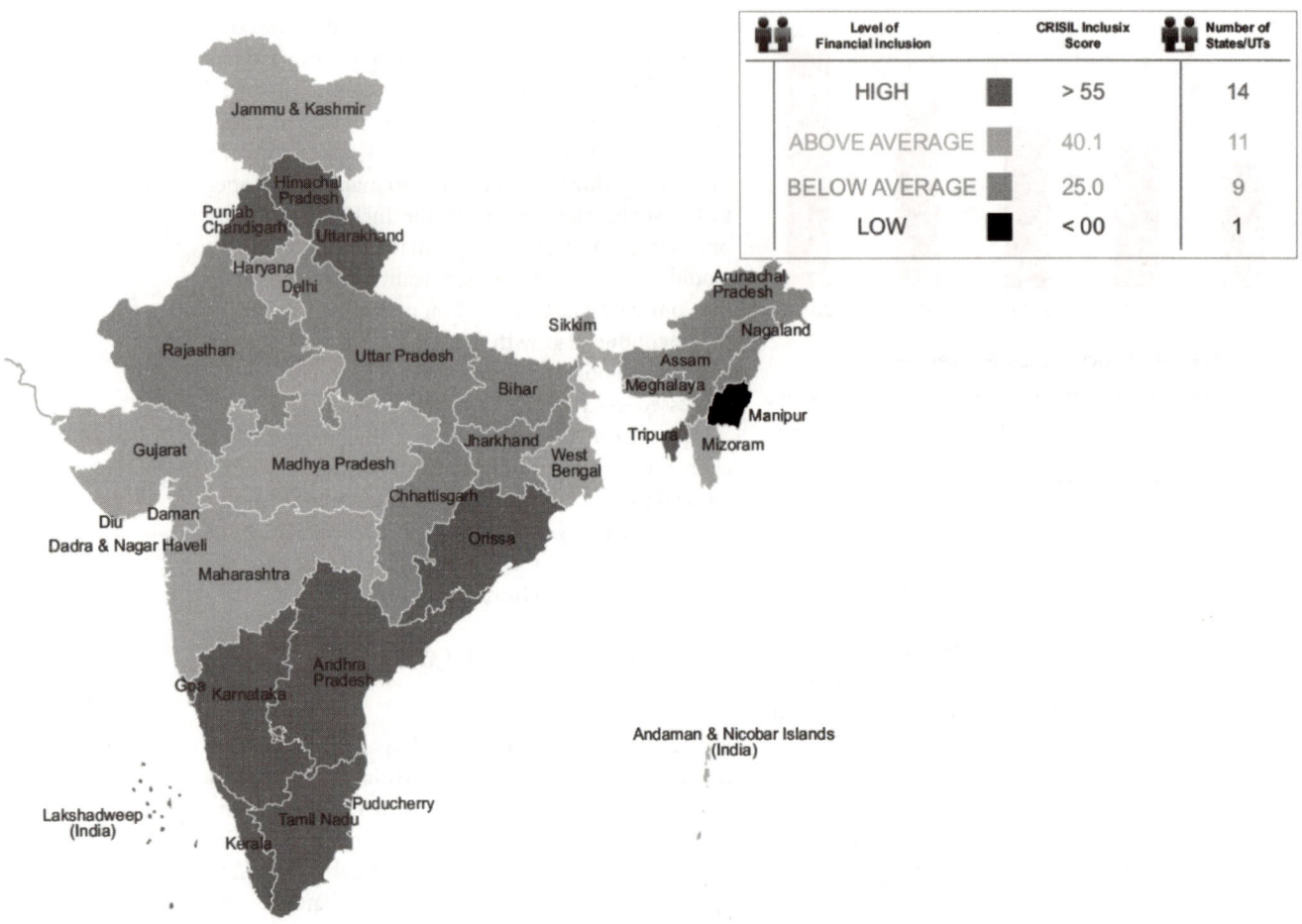

| | Level of Financial Inclusion | | CRISIL Inclusix Score | | Number of States/UTs |
|---|---|---|---|---|---|
| | HIGH | | > 55 | | 14 |
| | ABOVE AVERAGE | | 40.1 | | 11 |
| | BELOW AVERAGE | | 25.0 | | 9 |
| | LOW | | < 00 | | 1 |

**Figure 1.5**  Level of financial inclusion across the states

*Source:* CRISIL Inclusix volume III, 2015.

**Table 1.2   CRISIL Inclusix: top and bottom states and districts**

| 2012 | | 2013 | | 2012 | | 2013 | |
|---|---|---|---|---|---|---|---|
| **State** | **Score** | **State** | **Score** | **District** | **Score** | **District** | **Score** |
| **Large States: Top Three** | | | | **Districts: Top 10** | | | |
| Kerala | 80.4 | Kerala | 88.9 | Pathanamthitta (Kerala) | 100 | Alapuzha (Kerala) | 100 |
| Andhra Pradesh | 64.8 | Tamil Nadu | 79.2 | Karikal (Puducherry) | 99 | Ernakulam (Kerala) | 100 |
| Tamil Nadu | 64.8 | Karnataka | 74.4 | Thrissur (Kerala) | 97.2 | Kottayam (Kerala) | 100 |
| **Small States: Top Three** | | | | Ernakulam (Kerala) | 94.9 | Pathanamthitta (Kerala) | 100 |
| Delhi | 78.2 | Goa | 76.1 | Thiruvananthapuram (Kerala) | 94.8 | Thiruvananthapuram (Kerala) | |
| Goa | 74.0 | Delhi | 67.0 | Mahe (Puducherry) | 94.3 | Thrissur (Kerala) | 100 |
| Himachal Pradesh | 58.4 | Tripura | 63.8 | Kottayam (Kerala) | 93.8 | Karikal (Puducherry) | 100 |
| **Union Territories: Top Three** | | | | Coimbatore (TN) | 89.7 | Mahe (Puducherry) | 100 |
| Puducherry | 82.2 | Puducherry | 89.4 | Kodagu (Karnataka) | 88.9 | Coimbatore (TN) | 100 |
| Chandigarh | 80.7 | Chandigarh | 75.4 | Hyderabad (AP) | 84.6 | Kodagu (Karnataka) | 99.5 |
| Lakshadweep | 65.7 | Lakshadweep | 65.7 | | | | |

*(Table 1.2 Continued)*

*(Table 1.2 Continued)*

| 2012 | | 2013 | | 2012 | | 2013 | |
|---|---|---|---|---|---|---|---|
| **State** | **Score** | **State** | **Score** | **District** | **Score** | **District** | **Score** |
| **Large States: Bottom Three** | | | | **Districts: Bottom 10** | | | |
| Bihar | 25.5 | Bihar | 30.2 | | | | |
| Jharkhand | 32.1 | Rajasthan | 39.4 | Kurung Kumey (Arunachal Pradesh) | 5.6 | Kurung Kumey (Arunachal Pradesh) | 5.3 |
| Rajasthan | 34.8 | Jharkhand | 39.4 | Mon (Nagaland) | 7.7 | South Garo Hills (Meghalaya) | 8.4 |
| **Small States: Bottom Three** | | | | South Garo Hills (Meghalaya) | 8.2 | Mon (Nagaland) | 8.9 |
| Manipur | 17.8 | Manipur | 21.6 | Imphal East (Manipur) | 8.8 | Kiphire (Nagaland) | 11.0 |
| Nagaland | 26.1 | Nagaland | 28.9 | Ukhrul (Manipur) | 9.3 | Tamenglong (Manipur) | 11.0 |
| Arunachal Pradesh | 28.4 | Arunachal Pradesh | 30.5 | Tamenglong (Manipur) | 9.7 | Ukhrul (Manipur) | 12.6 |
| **Union Territories: Bottom Three** | | | | Kiphire (Nagaland) | 10.3 | Imphal East (Manipur) | 13.7 |
| Dadra and Nagar Haveli | 40.3 | Dadra and Nagar Haveli | 43.7 | Thoubal (Manipur) | 10.6 | Bishnupur (Manipur) | 14.4 |
| Daman and Diu | 40.5 | Daman and Diu | 43.2 | Bishnupur (Manipur) | 11.3 | Longleng (Nagaland) | 15.0 |
| Andaman and Nicobar Islands | 50.9 | Andaman and Nicobar Islands | 54.6 | East Kameng (Arunachal Pradesh) | 12.6 | East Kameng (Arunachal Pradesh) | 15.1 |

*Source:* CRISIL Inclusix Volumes 2 and 3 (2014, 2015).

**Table 1.3** **Formal sector touchpoints across regions as of March 2014**

| Region | Post offices | Commercial banks | RRBs | UCBs | MFIs | Total formal | SHGs | Total touchpoints |
|---|---|---|---|---|---|---|---|---|
| North | 21,896 | 19,382 | 2,618 | 382 | 383 | 44,661 | 360,893 | 405,554 |
| North-east | 6,928 | 2,408 | 721 | 47 | 313 | 10,417 | 334,254 | 344,671 |
| East | 29,395 | 15,319 | 4,057 | 158 | 2,660 | 51,589 | 1,525,178 | 1,576,767 |
| Central | 31,864 | 18,275 | 5,821 | 479 | 1,624 | 58,063 | 817,722 | 875,785 |
| West | 21,837 | 17,379 | 1,294 | 6,448 | 1,079 | 48,037 | 954,681 | 1,002,718 |
| South | 42,962 | 29,663 | 4,028 | 2,012 | 3,460 | 82,125 | 3,719,925 | 3,802,050 |
| Total | 154,882 | 102,426 | 18,539 | 9,526 | 9,519 | 294,892 | 7,712,653 | 8,007,545 |

*Source:* Author's computations.

Most of the SHGs do not offer scale. However, what is important is to understand the way the network is penetrated and how it could be leveraged for undertaking meaningful financial inclusion.

The story about the regional spread does not significantly change with the southern region having almost 50% of the formal sector touchpoints. If the SHGs were to be added, this skew would be sharper, indicating that while the nation has achieved formidable spread of branches and penetration, this is not evenly spread out across the country. Therefore, a strategy that focusses on the regional penetration is urgently needed. While the new-generation players such as MFIs are marking their presence in the eastern and the north-eastern regions, their impact is not significant in comparison to the residual exclusion. Figures 1.6 and 1.7 speak for themselves.

## DIGITISATION AND INCLUSION

The Brookings financial and digital inclusion project report (Figure 1.8) ranks India in the ninth position in a 21-country study undertaken to measure the commitment, the regulatory architecture and

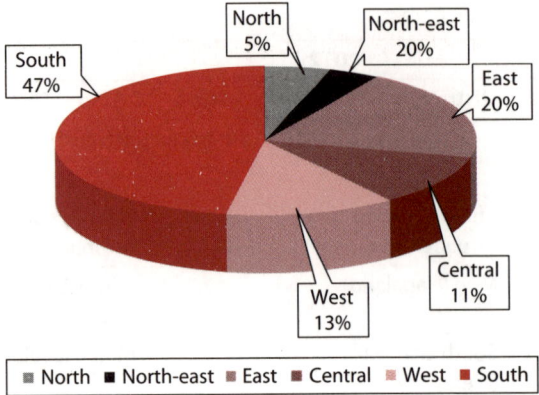

**Figure 1.6** Regional pie of formal sector touchpoints

the infrastructure in using digital technology specifically for financial inclusion (Villasenor et al., 2015). As can be seen there is a commitment by the Reserve Bank of India (RBI) to the Alliance for Financial Inclusion, and as per the report there is potential in carrying the technology-led financial inclusion agenda forward based on the aspects discussed earlier. The low score India obtains is on adoption, and this would be overcome with the new players—particularly the telecom companies

that would be operating as PBs in adopting the technology and leveraging the tremendous infrastructure and mobile capacity that the country has.

As the challenge of technology is being faced squarely, the 11 players who have been issued in-principle approval for setting up PBs would significantly contribute to the disruptive innovation in this space. Six of the licensees have been involved in the payments space and they would aggressively deploy technology for both opening of small accounts and remittances.

## REGULATION

One of the major issues in the rapid spread of financial services and its penetration amongst the poor and the excluded has been the fact that financial services—be it loans, remittances, social security products or savings—are all very highly regulated. The argument for regulation is obvious. If the customer is poor and vulnerable, then it becomes the obligation of the state to ensure that there are adequate customer protection frameworks. However, tight regulation also stymies innovation and growth. Any review of the financial inclusion space should therefore watch out for the changes in the regulatory space, as the regulatory

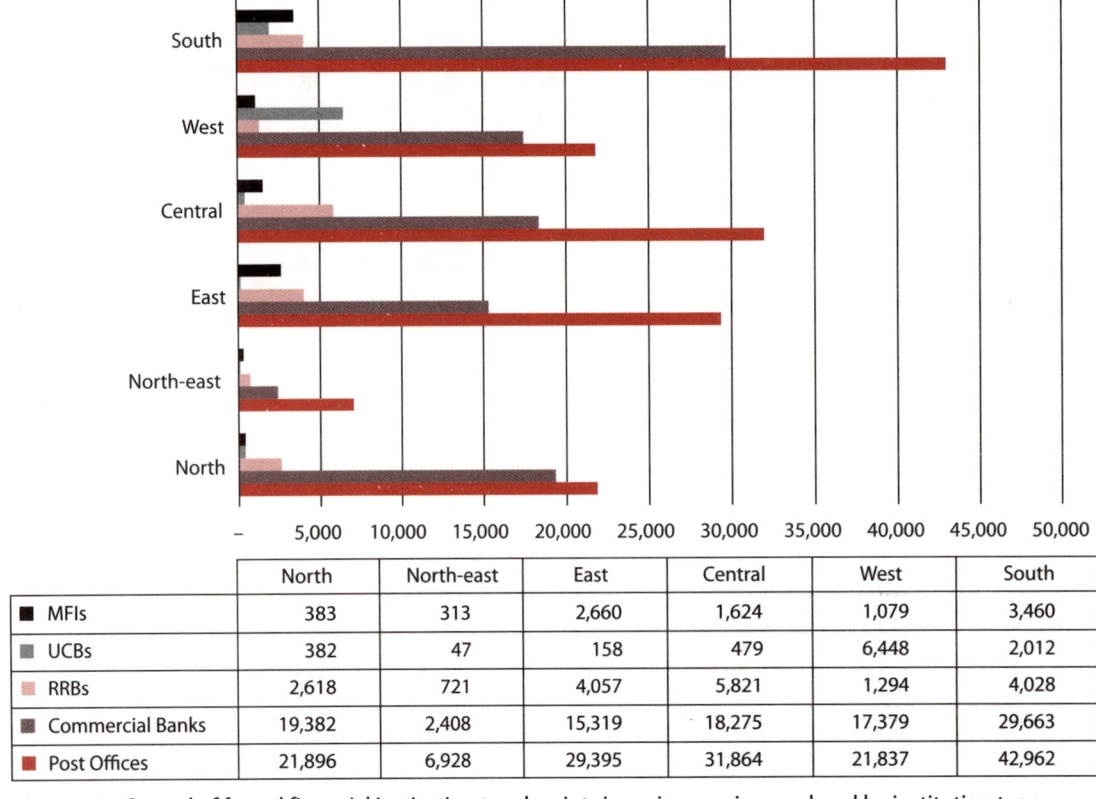

|  | North | North-east | East | Central | West | South |
|---|---|---|---|---|---|---|
| ■ MFIs | 383 | 313 | 2,660 | 1,624 | 1,079 | 3,460 |
| ■ UCBs | 382 | 47 | 158 | 479 | 6,448 | 2,012 |
| ■ RRBs | 2,618 | 721 | 4,057 | 5,821 | 1,294 | 4,028 |
| ■ Commercial Banks | 19,382 | 2,408 | 15,319 | 18,275 | 17,379 | 29,663 |
| ■ Post Offices | 21,896 | 6,928 | 29,395 | 31,864 | 21,837 | 42,962 |

**Figure 1.7** Spread of formal financial institution touchpoints in various regions ordered by institution type

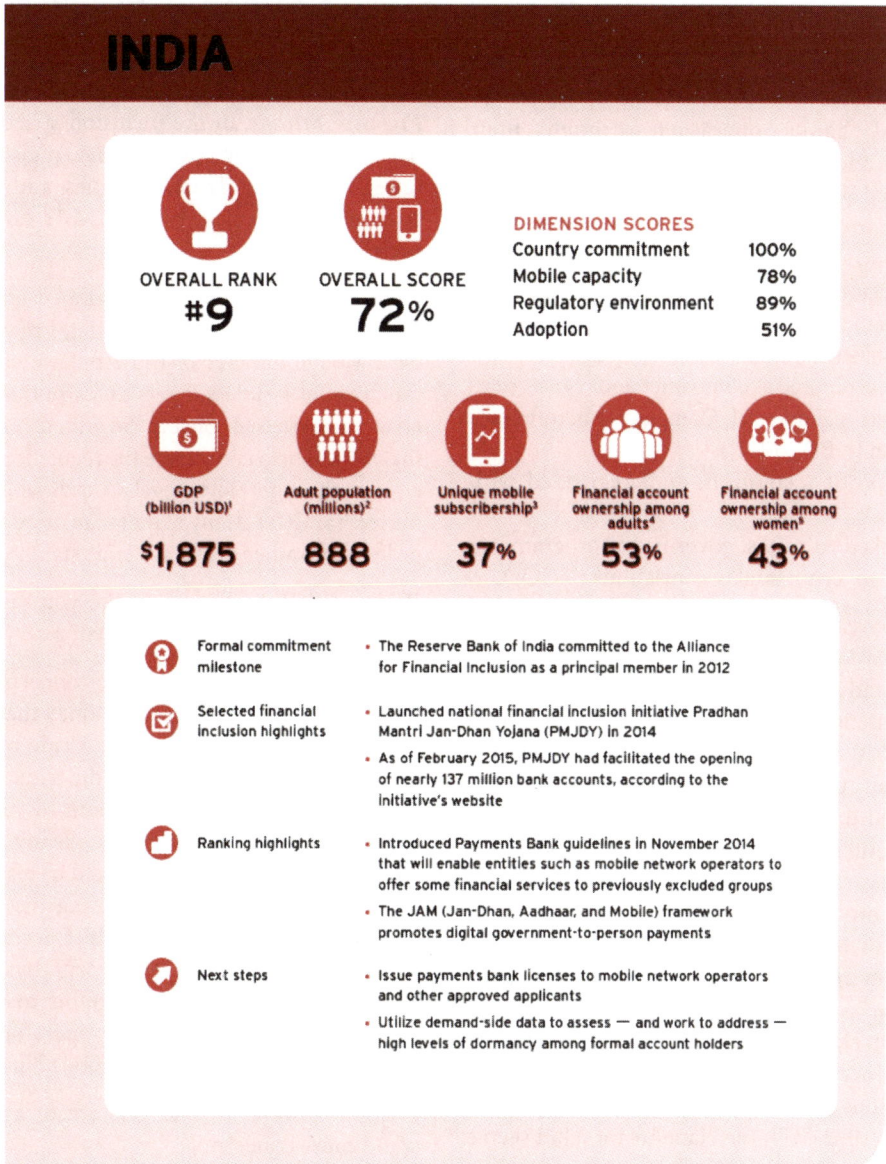

**Figure 1.8** Brookings financial and digital inclusion report: highlights

*Source:* Villasenor et al. (2015).

*Notes*: 1. See 2013 World Bank World Development Indicators data used for this indicator, available at http://data.worldbank.org/datacatalog/world-development-indicators.

2. Indicator calculated using 2013 World Bank World Development Indicators data, available at http://data.worldbank.org/data-catalog/world-development-indicators.

3. According to the GSMA, a unique mobile subscriber is considered a 'single individual that has subscribed to a mobile service and that person can hold multiple mobile connections (i.e., SIM cards).' See https://gsmaintelligence.com/research/2014/05/measuring-mobile-penetration/430/. Data is up to date as of the first quarter of 2015. See the GSMA Intelligence database, available (with subscription) at https://gsmaintelligence.com/.

4. According to the World Bank, this indicator 'denotes the percentage of respondents who report having an account (by themselves or together with someone else) at a bank or another type of financial institution; having a debit card in their own name; receiving wages, government transfers, or payments for agricultural products into an account or through a mobile phone at a financial institution in the past 12 months; paying utility bills or school fees from an account at a financial institution in the past 12 months; receiving wages or government transfers into a card in the past 12 months; or personally using a mobile phone to pay bills or to send or receive money through a GSM Association (GSMA) Mobile Money for the Unbanked (MMU) service in the past 12 months (% age 15+).' See 2014 World Bank Global Financial Inclusion Database data, available at http://datatopics.worldbank.org/financialinclusion/.

5. See 2014 World Bank Global Financial Inclusion Database data, available at http://datatopics.worldbank.org/financialinclusion/.

space is providing the canvas and framework for growth and innovation. The financial inclusion space is occupied by five types of players as of now:

1. Universal banks operating through their branches and the varied outreach models
2. Specialised banks focusing on certain regions or types of customers (banking function of the postal network, urban cooperative banks, local area banks, regional rural banks, district cooperative central banks); and addition of PBs and small finance banks (SFBs) in the coming days
3. MFIs (incorporated as companies and registered as Non-Banking Financial Company–Microfinance Institution [NBFC-MFI])
4. Not for profit institutions (not registered with the RBI)
5. SHGs linked to banks, government programmes and non-governmental organisations (NGOs).

Of the above, the activity of microfinance has been carried out by MFIs as well as NGOs. While there has been a demand from the microfinance sector to bring these organisations under regulation, it had not happened till 2010. The RBI treated MFIs that were companies as any other Non-Banking Finance Company (NBFC), and the NGOs were left out of the regulatory ambit. Attempts were made twice to pass an MFI bill which provided a regulatory framework for the sector. The broad objective of the regulation was to make way for MFIs to collect thrift from members; insulate them from oppressive local laws and regulate them on the basis of activity rather than the form of organisation. However, the bill was never passed.

With RBI accepting the Malegam Committee recommendations and creating a separate category of NBFCs as NBFC-MFI, the clamour for a bill seems to have subsided, though this classification does not address any of the three aspirations listed above. Even NBFC-MFIs registered under the RBI are subject to the Andhra Pradesh law that makes it almost impossible for MFIs to operate in that state and the newly formed Telangana state. Neither does this address the other two concerns. However, the fact that the new norms of NBFC-MFI address some of the concerns of the political class (as in the case of Andhra Pradesh in 2010)—that of usurious interest rates, profiteering at the cost of the poor, coercive recovery practices, etc.—the political risk may have subsided. With the RBI announcing the guidelines for SFBs which makes NBFC-MFIs eligible to apply for a licence, a window of hope emerges for MFIs to get into the thrift and deposit-taking activity. That leaves the only issue of NGOs operating in this area and not being under the regulatory ambit.

---

**Box 1.1 Governor Rajan on regulating the unregulated**

*Professor Sriram:* In the inclusion space we also have a lot of unregulated entities, registered but unregulated, like Trust, Societies and possibly section 8 companies. What is RBI's outlook on such entities?

*Dr Rajan:* As far the unincorporated entities go, including your local money lender, I mean we do have a huge number of those but we cannot do much about it unless it gets to a size that it starts creating a systemic concern. So our current view is that we will help coordinate the regulation of these entities through State Level Coordination Committees (SLCCs). Many of them are more a law and order issue rather than a systemic stability issue.

*Professor Sriram:* Therefore, are you saying that RBI should not be too concerned?

*Dr Rajan:* No, no, we should be concerned about them. When somebody loses money they are going to say that I was taken for a ride by this financial institution, where were the regulators? We have had enough adverse mentions by various judicial and investigative agencies. Clearly, even if it is not our baby the public will hold us responsible. So what we are doing is activating these SLCCs in every state which has the Chief Secretary, the Criminal Investigation Department, the Director General of Police, etc. come together to exchange information about who these operators are or where there is a possibility of public harm.

*Professor Sriram:* … and also are of a size that could cause concern.

*Dr Rajan:* Yes, the size will cause concern. For the tiny guys we are trying to say that if you take deposits, or what are deemed deposits, without having the regulatory permission, then it will essentially be a cognisable offense. So before you default on a deposit, even the act of taking it without licence should be seen as a cognisable offense. Otherwise you have these guys who are running Ponzi schemes and until they disappear they are fine, they are legal. So I think we need to make unlicensed deposit taking an offense. So those are two areas where we are pushing harder.

---

The announcement of Micro Units Development and Refinance Agency (MUDRA) bank has rekindled the aspiration for a benevolent activity-based regulation. It is being suggested that the elements of the MFI bill be inserted into the MUDRA bill when it is placed in the parliament, thereby giving the bank not only the function of refinancing and market development, but also the function of regulation. The jury on this is not out yet.

The announcement of MUDRA has opened up hope for the space that could be called the missing middle—credit with loan sizes of upto ₹1 million which is beyond the limit specified by MFIs and the limit for small borrowal accounts of banks.

This was a year that needed much celebration for the cause of inclusive finance. This is not because the regulatory space changed significantly, but more as a demonstration of what could be achieved in the existing regulatory architecture. The fact that the RBI has been talking about opening up the banking space to provide on-tap licences would keep the interests and aspirations open. The fact that the RBI invited applications for new differentiated banks created enthusiasm and eventually 21 new players were licensed to carry out specialised banking activities. Both the new innovations may not result in deep penetration and widespread inclusion by themselves. After all, all these institutions together are required to make an initial investment of ₹1 billion each and will take time to set up their networks, systems and back-end architecture, and roll out their business. Some of the players will also bring in significantly more investments than the stipulated minimum. But in a market that is almost like a bottomless pit with such a vast geography and population, this measure is small and insignificant by itself. However, the importance of these new initiatives cannot be dismissed by their size. What they bring to the table is disruption and innovation. They threaten existing business models and existing mindsets. They will show the way for the possibilities of roll-out because they operate under greater constraints than mainstream banks. These disruptive practices would then turn out to be methodologies for the mainstream bankers to adopt, adapt and roll out. That is where the scale and impact will happen.

The last initiative of the RBI in this space was the setting up of local area banks (LABs). Clearly the strategy did not work either at the level of innovation or at the level of disruption. The fact that there were many restrictions on the type of activities that they could undertake is well documented (Sriram and Krishna, 2014). There was no clamour for more LAB licences; except one LAB, the performance of the other LABs was not stellar and the innovation was a failure. When the draft guidelines for SFBs were issued, they appeared more like an incremental design change in LABs. The final guidelines for licensing SFBs provided them with a national footprint and took the regional restriction away. This would mean that the RBI has opted for a functional (small accounts) focus rather than on restricted geographical penetration. The enthusiasm with which the later guidelines were welcomed clearly shows where the interest was. While from a policy perspective, it might be important to have the geographical imperative—as can be seen from the type of regional imbalances—if the strategy is not viable enough for players to come in, then the impact of such innovation would be as insignificant as the LABs. Therefore, the experimentation of the new institutional initiatives holds out promise.

## POLICY PUSH

This was also a year where there was a major push from the government on getting people to the bank through the PMJDY and the associated insurance schemes. While such initiatives were undertaken in the past, it was never pursued on a mission mode. The results on the opening of incremental bank accounts were seen and this is discussed in detail in a later chapter.

The focus on the poor and the excluded continued through the review of the priority sector lending (PSL) requirements. While there were innovations suggested in the process of review, the reaffirmation of the commitment to inclusion was seen by a sub-target carved out for micro enterprises and for small and marginal farmers. The MUDRA initiative (discussed earlier) provides an institutional architecture to independently further the agenda, connect the dots and fill the gaps in provision of financial services.

## APPROACH AND ORGANISATION OF THE REPORT

This report is a departure from the past. It defines financial inclusion broadly on the institutional space, and focusses narrowly on the two main elements of inclusion—savings and credit. While it is important to recognise the role of social security measures such as insurance and pensions, for the present the report has not considered those spaces. Going forward, with more and more integration of the banking and the social security sectors, with functional definitions breaking down and specialised institutions coming in to carry forward the agenda of inclusion, the report will be more inclusive.

In keeping with the spirit of getting more insights into the inclusion market, two focussed chapters—one on the postal system and another on urban co-operative banks (UCBs)—have been brought in.

The report tries to use the latest available data; however, the banking data put out by the RBI come into the public domain only in December and therefore most of the analyses pertaining to the banks as well as the post offices are as of March 2014. The PMJDY data were up-to-date and the cut-off of March 2015 was generally used, though to make some points, later data are also referred to. The data for SHGs were made available by NABARD and represent March 2015. Same is the case with the microfinance data put out by Microfinance Institutions Network (MFIN). The Global Findex numbers are on the basis of a survey done in 2013, but the results were out in 2015. The CRISIL Inclusix data and scores are based on March 2013 data. This is a caveat to be mentioned upfront as there is a danger in putting these numbers together for timeline comparison purposes and there could be some mismatches.

The report moves from the banking system, reviewing the commercial banks, the Regional Rural Banks (RRBs) and the UCBs, followed by the postal system. The report then examines the MFI sector and the SHGs and reviews the new initiatives taken during the year. It also reviews the important issue of regional imbalances—cutting across all forms of organisational interventions and devotes a chapter on the physical infrastructure, technology and payment systems.

## REFERENCES

CRISIL (2015). *CRISIL Inclusix Volume III*. Mumbai: CRISIL Limited.

Demirguc-Kunt, Asli, Leora Klapper, Dorothe Singer and Peter Van Oudheusden. (2015). *The Global Findex Database 2014: Measuring Financial Inclusion around the World*. Policy Research Working Paper 7255. World Bank. Washington DC.

Sriram, M.S. and Krishna, Aparna (2015). Review of Local Area Banks and Policy Implications for Narrow Banks in India. *Economic and Political Weekly*, Vol. L, 11, pp. 52–60, 14 March 2015.

Villasenor, John D., West, Darrel M. and Lewis, Robin J. (2015). *The 2015 Brookings Financial and Digital Inclusion Project Report: Measuring Progress on Financial Access and Usage*. Washington DC: Center for Technology Innovations at Brookings.

# A review of the banking system

The banking system has been playing a significant role in the larger task of financial inclusion over the years. The agenda of financial inclusion has been made a part of the commercial banking architecture through several measures. It started with the nationalisation of large banks way back in 1969. After nationalisation, the government has taken several measures to push the agenda of the poor and the excluded through the banking system, including having a requirement to open rural branches, offering a certain fixed percentage for defined priority areas and also setting up new and specialised banking structures such as the Regional Rural Banks (RRBs). In the past few years the RBI has laid a great emphasis on not only the banks taking up the inclusion agenda aggressively, but also looking at the larger eco system. This chapter reviews the contribution of the banking system to the agenda of inclusion.

## BRANCH NETWORK

On the banking side, the expansion of branches continued. From a total of 117,280 outlets that were reported in March 2014, the number increased to 125,863 by March 2015 and continued to add another 1,480 branches in the next quarter. The latest numbers of branches are given in Table 2.1.

The banking network has been growing, and the rural and semi-urban branch network has largely kept pace with the growth in the branches of the urban branches. For a long time, the branch licencing was tightly controlled by RBI and there was a requirement that to get a licence to open a branch in a metropolitan area, the banks had to open four branches in unbanked centres. However, this rule was done away with, for a while, before reintroducing a new quota. Now the banks are free to open branches without the prior permission of RBI as long as they continue to open 25% of the new branches

in rural and unbanked locations. The growth of outlets according to their location is given in Figure 2.1. It can be seen from the figure that the rural and semi-urban branch network is growing faster than the other segments, even though the requirement is now to open only 25% of the incremental branches

**Table 2.1** Branches of scheduled commercial banks

| Branches of scheduled commercial banks | June 2015 | March 2015 |
|---|---|---|
| All scheduled commercial banks | 146 | 148 |
| of which, RRBs | 56 | 56 |
| No. of reporting offices | Jun-2015 | Mar-2015 |
| Rural | 48,531 | 48,033 |
| Semi-urban | 33,929 | 33,523 |
| Urban | 23,803 | 23,522 |
| Metropolitan | 21,080 | 20,785 |
| Total | 127,343 | 125,863 |

*Source:* Commercial Banks at a glance. RBI from http://dbie.rbi.org.in/OpenDocument/opendoc/openDocument.jsp, accessed on 31 August 2015.

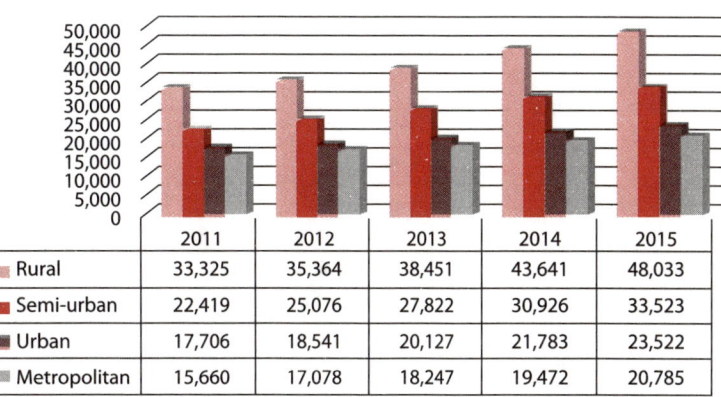

| | 2011 | 2012 | 2013 | 2014 | 2015 |
|---|---|---|---|---|---|
| Rural | 33,325 | 35,364 | 38,451 | 43,641 | 48,033 |
| Semi-urban | 22,419 | 25,076 | 27,822 | 30,926 | 33,523 |
| Urban | 17,706 | 18,541 | 20,127 | 21,783 | 23,522 |
| Metropolitan | 15,660 | 17,078 | 18,247 | 19,472 | 20,785 |

**Figure 2.1** Bank branch network 2011–15

*Source:* RBI Database at http://dbie.rbi.org.in/OpenDocument/opendoc/openDocument.jsp, accessed on 31 August 2015.

**Table 2.2** Number of unique rural and semi-urban locations that are served by banks

| Year | Rural | | | | | | Semi-urban | | | | | |
|---|---|---|---|---|---|---|---|---|---|---|---|---|
| | 2010 | 2011 | 2012 | 2013 | 2014 | 2015 | 2010 | 2011 | 2012 | 2013 | 2014 | 2015 |
| North | 4,371 | 4,451 | 4,685 | 5,111 | 5,830 | 6,466 | 616 | 616 | 624 | 635 | 646 | 655 |
| N. East | 1,079 | 1,089 | 1,099 | 1,127 | 1,197 | 1,270 | 144 | 146 | 146 | 150 | 154 | 154 |
| East | 6,734 | 6,814 | 6,983 | 7,186 | 7,671 | 8,190 | 920 | 930 | 940 | 956 | 989 | 1,082 |
| Central | 6,930 | 6,996 | 7,259 | 7,753 | 8,716 | 9,374 | 1,023 | 1,020 | 1,047 | 1,070 | 1,094 | 1,107 |
| West | 3,393 | 3,445 | 3,566 | 3,828 | 4,383 | 4,713 | 794 | 789 | 792 | 800 | 812 | 822 |
| South | 5,940 | 5,986 | 6,337 | 6,803 | 7,598 | 8,267 | 2,429 | 2,445 | 2,497 | 2,534 | 2,591 | 2,655 |
| Total | 28,447 | 28,781 | 29,929 | 31,808 | 35,395 | 38,280 | 5,926 | 5,946 | 6,046 | 6,145 | 6,286 | 6,475 |

*Source:* RBI Database at http://dbie.rbi.org.in/OpenDocument/opendoc/openDocument.jsp, accessed on 31 August 2015.

in unbanked locations. While the growth of branches in rural areas had fallen much below the rates of the urban and metropolitan branches in the early part of this decade, the growth of rural branches was faster in the last two years.

Just the growth of bank branches does not reveal the penetration of the Indian banking system, unless the number of unique rural and semi-urban locations that are covered is examined. It is quite possible that several banks open their branches in the same location where another bank already has a branch. While this analysis does not serve any purpose in urban and metro locations, where it is expected that multiple branches of the same bank may be present, it may be interesting to look at this data in rural and semi-urban locations (Table 2.2).

As can be seen from Figure 2.2, the growth of unique locations is lagging far behind the rate of growth of the rural and semi-urban banks per se.

While the regulation requires the banks to have a footprint in rural and semi-urban locations, a good number of these locations are those where there is already a bank branch in service. Going forward it is important to track this number because this would give the actual number of villages where the bank has a presence. As of March 2015, it can be seen that the rural branch presence is in about 38,000 villages as against a total number 48,000 rural branches. However, what is also important to note is that the number of unique rural locations has gone up by about 10,000 in the past five years. Much of the growth can be attributed to the thrust given by the RBI in having the banks draw up board approved financial inclusion plans as well as specific targets to have touchpoints in villages that had a population of more than 2,000.

## BEYOND THE BRANCH NETWORK

The approach of the state towards financial inclusion has been captured in the Finance Minister's budget speech where he alluded that the strategy would be on the three-way axis of Jan-Dhan, Aadhaar and Mobile (JAM). In the past the policy thrust was provided by the government in the design and publicity of the *Swabhimaan* initiative. But the action has happened traditionally by the RBI nudging the banks through policy push that led to the roll-out of institutional infrastructure. The broad policy approach has been in adopting the mission mode in institutional push through a two-pronged strategy:

1. Ensure that more bank branches are opened in rural and unbanked areas through a requirement that 25% of the incremental branches are located in centres that have population of up to 9,999;
2. Ensure that each habitation having a population of more than 2,000 is covered with a banking

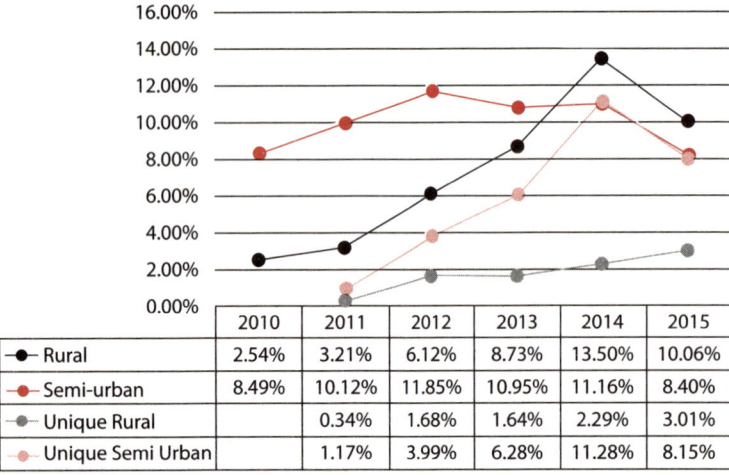

| | 2010 | 2011 | 2012 | 2013 | 2014 | 2015 |
|---|---|---|---|---|---|---|
| Rural | 2.54% | 3.21% | 6.12% | 8.73% | 13.50% | 10.06% |
| Semi-urban | 8.49% | 10.12% | 11.85% | 10.95% | 11.16% | 8.40% |
| Unique Rural | | 0.34% | 1.68% | 1.64% | 2.29% | 3.01% |
| Unique Semi Urban | | 1.17% | 3.99% | 6.28% | 11.28% | 8.15% |

**Figure 2.2** Growth rate of bank branches in rural and semi-urban areas

*Source:* RBI Database at http://dbie.rbi.org.in/OpenDocument/opendoc/openDocument.jsp, accessed on 31 August 2015.

touchpoint (branch, ultra-small branch [USB], business correspondent [BC], customer service point [CSP])

As a result of this strategy, significant progress was achieved. While the rural branches grew by a third in five years, there was nearly a 15-fold increase in the touchpoints in the villages, thereby creating an infrastructure that could pull the customers to the bank. The progress between March 2010 and March 2014 is given in Table 2.3. When the Prime Minister announced the ambitious PMJDY on the 15th of August 2014 the base architecture in terms of physical network and agents was laid out. The emphasis of the PMJDY was significantly different from the past—because it moved the targets from infrastructure creation to the customer—from pushing the institutions towards the customers, to pulling the customers towards the existing infrastructure.

A look at Table 2.3 and an analysis of the numbers in Table 2.4 show that the physical outreach of branches and BCs has led to a growth in the number of BSBD accounts but has not resulted in a dramatic multiplier. In particular to note is the number of customers that a BC was serving and the average amounts of savings parked in these accounts, particularly the accounts handled by the BCs. Similarly the number of accounts availing of overdraft facility is minimal and with low balances.

In addition to the bank branches, a network of 504,142 branchless outlets (including automated teller machines [ATMs], POS points, BCs, ultra-small branches [USBs], customer service points [CSPs]) in rural areas and 96,847 BC outlets in urban

**Table 2.3** **Financial inclusion: summary of progress (including RRBs)**

| Particulars | Year ended March 2010 | Year ended March 2013 | Year ended March 2014 | Year ended March 2015 |
|---|---|---|---|---|
| Banking outlets in villages—Branches | 33,378 | 40,837 | 46,126 | 49,571 |
| Banking outlets in villages—Branchless mode[1] | 34,316 | 227,617 | 337,678 | 504,142 |
| Banking outlets in villages—Total | 67,694 | 268,454 | 383,804 | 553,713 |
| Urban locations covered through BCs | 447 | 27,143 | 60,730 | 96,847 |
| Basic savings bank deposit a/c through branches (no. in million) | 60.2 | 100.8 | 126.0 | 210.3 |
| Basic savings bank deposit a/c through branches (amount in ₹ billion) | 44.3 | 164.7 | 273.3 | 365.0 |
| Basic savings bank deposit a/c through BCs (no. in million) | 13.3 | 81.3 | 116.9 | 187.8 |
| Basic savings bank deposit a/c through BCs (amount in ₹ billion) | 10.7 | 18.2 | 39.0 | 74.6 |
| Basic savings bank deposit a/c through total (no. in million) | 73.5 | 182.1 | 243 | 398.1 |
| Basic savings bank deposit a/c through total (amount in ₹ billion) | 55.0 | 182.9 | 312.3 | 439.5 |
| Overdraft facility availed in BSBDAs (no. in million) | 0.2 | 4.0 | 5.9 | 7.6 |
| Overdraft facility availed in BSBDAs (amount in ₹ billion) | 0.1 | 1.6 | 16.0 | 19.9 |
| KCCs (no. in million) | 24.3 | 33.8 | 39.9 | 42.5 |
| KCCs (amount in ₹ billion) | 1,240 | 2,623 | 3,684 | 4,382 |
| GCCs (no. in million) | 1.4 | 3.6 | 7.4 | 9.2 |
| GCCs (amount in ₹ billion) | 35 | 76 | 1,096 | 1,302 |
| ICT a/cs BC transaction during the year (no. in million) | 26.5 | 250.5 | 328.6 | 477.0 |
| ICT a/cs BC transaction during the year (amount in ₹ billion) | 6.9 | 233.9 | 524.4 | 859.8 |

*Source:* Annual Report of 2014, 2015. Mumbai: RBI.

[1] The branchless mode outlets include BCs, ATMs, POS points, USBs, mobile vans and any other mechanism that provides a touchpoint for the customer of the bank.

**Table 2.4** **Financial inclusion progress: numbers unpeeled**

| Particulars | Year ended March 2010 | Year ended March 2013 | Year ended March 2014 | Year ended March 2015 |
|---|---|---|---|---|
| Number of BSBD a/cs per branch | 1,803 | 2,468 | 2,731 | 4,236 |
| Average balance per BSBD a/c (₹) | 735 | 1,633 | 2,169 | 1,738 |
| Number of BSBD a/cs per BC | 387 | 357 | 346 | 370 |
| Average balance per BSBD a/c (₹) (BC) | 805 | 224 | 334 | 397 |
| Percentage of BSBD a/cs availing overdraft facility | 0.27% | 2.20% | 2.43% | 1.90% |
| Average overdraft balance in BSBD a/cs | 500 | 400 | 2,711 | 2,618 |

*Source:* Computations by the author based on Table 2.3.

areas were in operation as of March 2015. While this aggressive spread of last mile presence appears impressive, the data on the average transactions and average balances do not inspire confidence. There have been studies to look at how effective the agent network is and how many of the agents listed in the above numbers are dormant. What is evident from the numbers is that the supply side push has been massive, and this needs to be backed up by transactions that are meaningful.

Apart from the physical presence of outlets with human interface, an impressive 180,000 ATMs have been deployed, of which nearly half were on-site ATMs and were considered an integral part of the branch, while the other half were counted in the branchless touchpoints discussed above. Credit and debit cards of the banks can be swiped for commercial transactions in 1.13 million point of sale (POS) locations. In addition to the above, a total of 570 million debit cards and 21.5 million credit cards have been issued by the banks thereby allowing the customers the choice of transacting at a time of their choice. A look at the transaction data indicates that both in terms of number of transactions and the amount transacted, the customers are overwhelmingly preferring transactions at the ATMs to withdraw cash at the first instance, than to use the POS option. Obviously the preference seems to be more bank-driven than the ubiquitous use of technology.

It is very evident that the banking sector has adopted a radically different approach in dealing with the agenda of inclusion from 2010 onwards. While there is an impressive growth of bank branches, there is also an equally impressive growth of touchpoints beyond the bank branch both in rural and urban locations. All these touchpoints are leveraging technology. The investment in the inclusion infrastructure is impressive and the banking system is ready for a quantum jump on the other parameters of financial inclusion.

While the above analysis uses the data of BSBD accounts, it does not represent the complete picture as far as inclusion is concerned. These tables represent only certain types of borrowing—borrowing against and existing account and against a limit on the Kisan Credit Card (KCC) or a similar instrument. However, the definition of a small borrowal account as per the RBI is an account that has a sanction limit of ₹200,000. The limits set for an MFI loan to the customer is the maximum of ₹100,000 as per the NBFC-MFI master circular (RBI, 2014). If the data on these parameters are to be examined for the past five years, it is clear that the banks are not gaining significant volumes in the small accounts, while numbers of accounts are being opened on a mission mode and outlets are being provided to the customers.

While the RBI defines small borrowal accounts as any loan account that has a sanctioned limit of up to ₹200,000, the data are available on a smaller slab of ₹25,000 which was the cut-off for a small borrowal account prior to 1999. If that data is examined, it is clear that all the efforts of financial inclusion happening over the years have not affected the offtake of small credit directly from the banks. It is clear from Table 2.5 that the absolute number of accounts that had a sanction limit of less than ₹25,000 has actually fallen from 45 million accounts in 2010 to around 32 million in 2014. The amount sanctioned has also fallen in absolute terms.

An additional aspect to remember is that these accounts do not strictly represent the accounts of the 'poor', because the data have been classified according to the size of the account. However, if the data are sliced further, it will be evident that about 80% of the accounts would have gone to individuals. A large part of this portfolio (about 55% of the total number of small borrowal accounts and amounts) represents direct lending to agriculture (see Table 2.6).

**Table 2.5  Details of credit to small borrowal accounts over the years**

| Year ending March 31 → | 2010 | 2011 | 2012 | 2013 | 2014 |
|---|---|---|---|---|---|
| **Loan amount less than ₹25,000** | | | | | |
| Number of accounts (million) | 45.18 | 43.32 | 44.05 | 30.88 | 32.57 |
| Percentage to total accounts | 38% | 36% | 34% | 24.1% | 23.50% |
| Limit sanctioned (million) | 575,750 | 566,710 | 701,440 | 428,593 | 436,318 |
| Percentage to total amounts | 1.18% | 0.73% | 0.91% | 0.5% | 0.50% |
| Amount outstanding (million) | 435,890 | 473,990 | 762,160 | 736,827 | 436,318 |
| Percentage to total outstanding | 1.30% | 1.16% | 1.59% | 1.3% | 0.60% |
| **Loan amount ₹25,000–200,000** | | | | | |
| Number of accounts (million) | 57.45 | 58.83 | 65.06 | 71.43 | 76.66 |
| Percentage to total accounts | 48% | 49% | 50% | 56% | 55.20% |
| Limit sanctioned (million) | 4,440,760 | 4,574,070 | 5,056,960 | 5,734,745 | 6,170,673 |
| Percentage to total amounts | 5.93% | 5.93% | 6.58% | 6.90% | 6.50% |
| Amount outstanding (million) | 3,171,560 | 3,364,890 | 3,804,050 | 4,411,501 | 4,895,252 |
| Percentage to total outstanding | 8.26% | 8.26% | 7.92% | 8.00% | 7.80% |
| **Total up to ₹200,000** | | | | | |
| Number of accounts (million) | 102.63 | 102.15 | 109.11 | 102.31 | 109.23 |
| Percentage to total accounts | 87% | 85% | 83% | 80% | 79% |
| Limit sanctioned (million) | 5,016,510 | 5,140,780 | 5,758,400 | 6,163,337 | 6,606,991 |
| Percentage to total amounts | 7.11% | 6.66% | 7.49% | 7.40% | 7.00% |
| Amount outstanding (million) | 3,607,450 | 3,838,880 | 4,566,210 | 5,148,328 | 5,331,569 |
| Percentage to total outstanding | 9.56% | 9.42% | 9.51% | 9.30% | 8.40% |

*Source:* Banking Statistical Returns for the years 2011, 2012, 2013, 2014 and 2015. Mumbai: RBI.
*Note:* The gender-wise break-up of the accounts and the amounts indicate that more than 75% of the loan accounts and amounts have been made to men.

**Table 2.6  Purpose-wise break-up of small borrowal accounts as of 31 March 2014**

| | Accounts (million) | % of total | Sanction (₹ Tn) | % of total | Outstanding (₹ Tn) | % of total |
|---|---|---|---|---|---|---|
| Agriculture | 59.69 | 55% | 3.67 | 56% | 3.47 | 66% |
| Direct | 56.09 | 51% | 3.46 | 52% | 3.27 | 62% |
| Indirect | 3.60 | 3% | 0.22 | 3% | 0.20 | 4% |
| Industry | 1.53 | 1% | 0.09 | 1% | 0.07 | 1% |
| Transport operators | 1.08 | 1% | 0.08 | 1% | 0.05 | 1% |
| Professional and other services | 2.10 | 2% | 0.13 | 2% | 0.10 | 2% |
| Personal loans | 35.19 | 32% | 2.23 | 34% | 1.26 | 24% |
| Housing | 1.66 | 2% | 0.15 | 2% | 0.10 | 2% |
| Consumer durables | 0.60 | 1% | 0.04 | 1% | 0.03 | 1% |
| Other personal loans | 32.93 | 30% | 2.04 | 31% | 1.13 | 21% |
| Trade | 4.88 | 4% | 0.27 | 4% | 0.21 | 4% |
| Wholesale trade | 0.17 | 0% | 0.01 | 0% | 0.01 | 0% |
| Retail trade | 4.71 | 4% | 0.26 | 4% | 0.20 | 4% |
| Finance | 0.34 | 0% | 0.02 | 0% | 0.02 | 0% |
| All others | 4.42 | 4% | 0.11 | 2% | 0.09 | 2% |
| Total | 109.23 | 100% | 6.61 | 100% | 5.27 | 100% |

*Source:* Banking Statistical Returns 2014. Mumbai: RBI (2015).

**Table 2.7  Small (<₹25,000) term deposits from customers over the years**

| Year ending March 31 → | 2010 | 2011 | 2012 | 2013 | 2014 |
|---|---|---|---|---|---|
| Number of accounts (million) | 53.28 | 52.62 | 53.85 | 55.70 | 66.80 |
| % of total number of accounts | 37.10% | 35.80% | 32.80% | 30.90% | 33.30% |
| Growth | | −1.27% | 2.30% | 3.32% | 16.61% |
| Amount (₹ billion) | 1,405.21 | 1,691.67 | 1,375.19 | 1,387.30 | 1,130.10 |
| % of total deposits collected | 5.10% | 5.20% | 3.60% | 3.10% | 2.20% |
| Growth | | 16.93% | −23.01% | 0.87% | −22.76% |

*Source:* Banking Statistical Returns, 2011, 2012, 2013, 2014 and 2015. Mumbai: RBI.

Given that the loan books of the banks are growing, the fall in proportions to the total lending is even more drastic. While the number of accounts that have an approval of up to ₹200,000 has increased, the two categories taken together have shown a marginal increase from 102 million accounts to 109 million accounts over the past five years. This represents a constant decline in terms of proportion over all the five years both in terms of the number of accounts and the amounts disbursed. Therefore, all the exuberance on the outreach and the increased accounts and roll-out of technology does not seem to have resulted in tangible business for the banks in a meaningful manner.

The performance on the small deposits is no significantly better than the progress on loans. While RBI does not define 'small deposit accounts', for the purpose of analysis, term deposits less than ₹25,000 have been considered. If Table 2.7 is examined, it is evident that while the number of accounts has grown marginally in the earlier years, but significantly in 2013–14, the amount of deposits collected has indeed fallen. Therefore, it can be safely said that the entire activity of financial inclusion of account opening and providing for outlets is not necessarily getting reflected in the main activity of the bank of collecting deposits and providing loans.

## PRIORITY SECTOR LENDING

The PSL programme which directs banks to make financial services available to the vulnerable sections of the society is not peculiar to India. Box 2.1 has the details of the directed lending

| Box 2.1 Summary of directed lending programmes in the international setting | | |
|---|---|---|
| US | Small businesses, students/education, low income groups in rural areas/for creation of electricity, waste disposal facilities, low income groups, elderly and handicapped/housing (*involves credit guarantee in lending to some of these sectors*) | US government departments (either independently, or in collaboration with private investment companies) |
| EU (Denmark and Ireland) | Micro enterprises, Small and Medium Enterprises (*involves sectoral targets, credit guarantee*) | Private banking institutions |
| Brazil | Industry including SME sector/long-term investment credit, rural housing, agriculture, micro credit (*involves credit guarantee, interest subsidy and sectoral targets for some of these sectors*) | Public banking institutions (either directly or through local commercial banks) |
| People's Republic of China | Agriculture, micro and small enterprises (*involves sectoral growth targets, credit guarantee, interest rate subsidy*) | Public banking institutions |
| Pakistan | Agriculture, exports (*involves indicative targets and interest rate subsidy*) | Public and private banking institutions |
| Russian Federation | Agriculture and agro-based industries, rural infrastructure (*involves interest subsidies*) | Public banking institutions |

| Philippines | Agriculture (*involves credit guarantee*) | Public and private banking institutions/cooperatives |
| India | Agriculture, micro and small enterprises, education, housing, socio-economically weaker sections (*involves aggregate targets and sectoral targets for some sectors, credit guarantees and interest subsidy for some sectors*) | Public and private banking institutions |

*Source:* Report of the Internal Working Group to Revisit Existing Priority Sector Lending Guidelines. Mumbai: RBI. March 2015.

programmes of several other developed and developing countries.

While the new thrust of both the RBI and the government appears to be to get people to open savings accounts and bring them to the banks, the larger agenda of inclusion has also been traditionally addressed through directing the banks to earmark credit to the vulnerable sections of the society. While the current approach is much more specific to the client, the directed credit approach is much more sectoral in nature.

The current requirement is that 40% of every bank's adjusted net bank credit (ANBC) should be deployed under priority sector. While the entire basket of priority sector activities may not be addressing the inclusion agenda, there are parts in the priority sector that can be naturally seen as a part of carrying forward the inclusion agenda. Targets for agriculture (where there are a large number of small and marginal farmers operating) as well as the targets assigned for weaker sections (see Box 2.2) are of importance in the inclusion agenda, while the other targets for housing, education, export credit and for solar energy could be left aside.

While the overall targets for PSL are generally being met by the banks, in the last five years, the

---

**Box 2.2 Definition of weaker sections under the priority sector lending norms**

**Category**

(a) Small and marginal farmers

(b) Artisans, village and cottage industries where individual credit limits do not exceed ₹50,000

(c) Beneficiaries of Swarnjayanti Gram Swarozgar Yojana (SGSY), now National Rural Livelihoods Mission (NRLM)

(d) Scheduled Castes and Scheduled Tribes

(e) Beneficiaries of Differential Rate of Interest (DRI) scheme;

(f) Beneficiaries under Swarna Jayanti Shahari Rozgar Yojana (SJSRY), now National Urban Livelihood Mission (NULM)

(g) Beneficiaries under the Scheme for Rehabilitation of Manual Scavengers (SRMSs)

(h) Loans to self-help groups

(i) Loans to distressed farmers indebted to non-institutional lenders

(j) Loans to distressed persons other than farmers not exceeding ₹50,000 per borrower to prepay their debt to non-institutional lenders

(k) Loans to individual women beneficiaries upto ₹50,000 per borrower

(l) Loans sanctioned under (a) to (k) above to persons from minority communities as may be notified by Government of India from time to time. In states where one of the minority communities notified is, in fact, in majority, item (l) will cover only the other notified minorities. These states/union territories are Jammu & Kashmir, Punjab, Meghalaya, Mizoram, Nagaland and Lakshadweep.

*Source:* Report of the Internal Working Group to Revisit Existing Priority Sector Lending Guidelines. Mumbai: RBI. March 2015.

banks have fallen short of their targets 2012 and 2013. While the private sector banks have been consistently outperforming the public sector banks in the past five years on the overall achievement of PSL requirements, they have been falling short in the sub-target for agriculture and are far below the assigned target for weaker section loans (both of which are to be considered as a part of the inclusion agenda). The achievements on agriculture by the private and the public sector banks are depicted in Figure 2.3.

It is also clear that the banks are far from achieving the targets on the weaker section advances. The achievements under the broader definition of small borrowal accounts have been discussed above. The weaker section advances by the definition could at best be a subset of the small borrowal accounts (Figure 2.4). This is an area that clearly shows that the banking system has not achieved even the mandatory requirements as prescribed by the policy.

From the discussion above, it is clear that the banking system, in spite of all the initiatives taken by the state as well as the RBI, has not been able to make a major breakthrough. While during the same period under discussion there is evidence that both the Self-Help Group Bank Linkage Programme (SHGBLP) and the private sector microfinance initiatives have made significant breakthroughs and have grown at a rapid pace, the banks have not shown the same agility. While it is true that the banking system has been funding the SHGBLP and the MFIs in a big way, they have not been able to get into this market in a scale required of them, in spite of policy push, directives, technology and expansion of infrastructure. With the next round of push coming in with DBTs and the PMJDY accounts, it is to be seen whether these accounts would, like microfinance, be a pass through for the banking system or whether this would spur the banking system to look at disruptive innovations that bring the banks to the forefront on the inclusion agenda.

During the year, the RBI set up an Internal Working Group to Revisit the Existing Priority Sector Lending Guidelines which submitted its report (RBI, 2015, p. 6). The group recommended earmarking 7.5% of the ANBC for micro enterprises. The group also recommended that 8% of the ANBC be earmarked for credit to small and marginal farmers and this also has been notified (see Box 2.3 for salient recommendations). The recommendations on agricultural credit are a fundamental shift in the approach. In the past, the RBI has had sub-targets for direct lending to agriculture, with what was defined as direct lending loosely

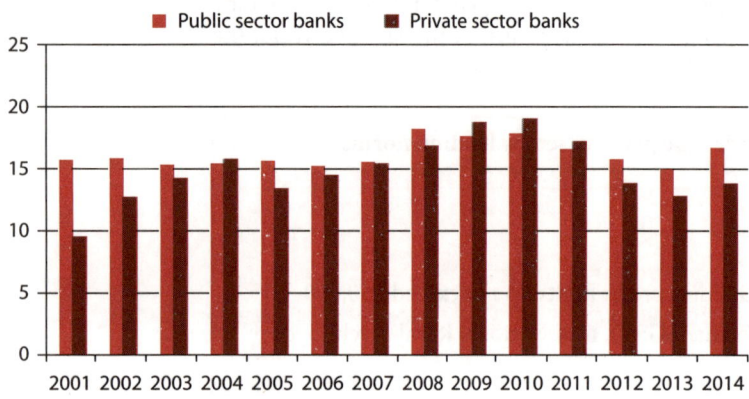

**Figure 2.3** Lending to agriculture as a percentage of ANBC over the years

*Source:* Report of the Internal Working Group to Revisit Existing Priority Sector Lending Guidelines. Mumbai: RBI. March 2015.

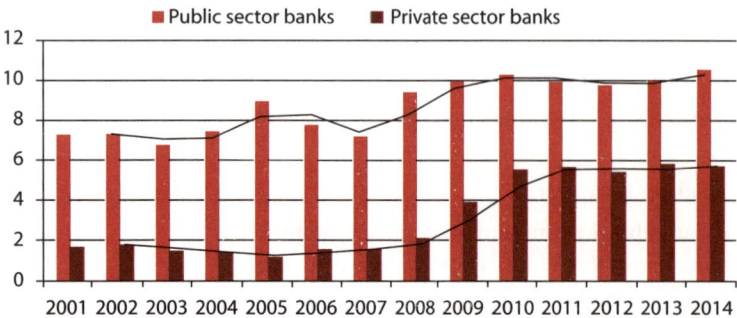

**Figure 2.4** Loans to weaker sections as a percentage of the ANBC

*Source:* Report of the Internal Working Group to Revisit Existing Priority Sector Lending Guidelines. Mumbai: RBI. March 2015.

---

**Box 2.3 Priority sector lending—a fresh look: recommendations of the internal working group**

The salient features of the revised PSL guidelines are:

- Separate targets of 8% for small and marginal farmers (within the agriculture target of 18%) and 7.5% for micro industries have been prescribed to be achieved in a phased manner by 2017. These targets will be made applicable to foreign banks with 20 branches and above post 2018 after a review in 2017.
- Priority sector widened to include medium enterprises, social infrastructure and renewable energy.

- Monitoring of PSL compliance on a 'quarterly' average basis at the end of the respective year from 2016 to 2017.
- Priority Sector Lending Certificates (PSLCs) will be an eligible tradable instrument for achieving priority sector targets. The buyer (a deficient bank) will pay a 'price/fee' to the seller bank (a bank which has over-achieved its PSL requirements) for purchasing a specified amount of PSL obligation applicable for a particular date.

*Source:* Annual Report of the RBI, 2015. Mumbai: RBI.

defined. As a result, over the years it was felt that the amounts may be misclassified, given that even metropolitan branches were showing substantial disbursement of agricultural loans. The new recommendation of targeting a certain percentage to small and marginal farmers will not only make it difficult for the bankers to achieve, but also force them to get more and more individual small and marginal farmers on board.

Given the fact that the banks have been struggling to achieve the agriculture target in general, these targets, for small and marginal farmers and micro enterprises, will prove extremely difficult, unless the banks look at alternative mechanisms of achieving these targets.

There are two distinct possibilities of how the more stringent PSL targets may be achieved. It is possible that the specialised MFIs will garner some part of the portfolio due to their agility, geographical specialisation and cost effective operations. This might open up more deals on securitisation and bring in an active market. According to RBI, 'the securitisation market which reached a high of ₹637.30 Billion by March 2008 dwindled down to ₹288 Billion by March 2014' (Gandhi, 2015). There was also an impression that the MFIs could have a large role due to the PSL obligations. This would be buying the portfolio from institutions that are differently regulated.

Added to this, the new SFBs with large portfolio of small loans might resort to diversifying their balance sheet through securitisation and 'SEBI is further examining the prospects of setting up a trading and reporting platform where all securitisation transactions will be reported and a central data repository will be available to the securitisation market participants' (Gandhi, 2015). Thus, there is bound to be action on this front in the years to come.

The internal working group of RBI (RBI, 2015), among other recommendations, suggested the introduction of a new instrument—the PSLC. It is also possible that the new SFBs might just trade out their portfolio with the larger banks through the PSLCs. It is important to note that these certificates cannot be traded outside of the banking system. The interesting design feature of the PSLC as suggested by the internal working group is that unlike a securitisation deal where the portfolio moves out of the balance sheet, in case of PSLC the portfolio remains with the originator (and therefore all attendant risk and capital requirements that go with it) and only the rights/obligations are traded. While the discussion on the PSLCs has been on for a while, this was probably for the first time that the internal group of RBI took an explicit stand on the matter. In the light of the new institutional interventions discussed below, this initiative if implemented would provide a new impetus for reaching out to the sectors that need credit through specialised and niche institutions, without necessarily compromising on the overall target for the banking sector.

---

**Box 2.4 Governor Rajan on priority sector lending and agriculture**

*Professor Sriram:* Would you like to talk about the PSL norms and the changes that are on the anvil?

*Dr Rajan:* Yes, we are increasing the small and marginal farmer support and the micro support. Our approach was, let us figure out who really needs access, because we have mixed up access and priority and national importance together. In some cases we don't know where it ends up. So these are the customers who desperately need access. Let us push here. For the rest, these are broadly national priorities, we'll put it broadly and you can choose between one and the other. Agriculture target is still 18% but 7% (going up to 8%) to small and marginal farmers is the harder target. Those are people who truly need credit. Once we achieve the marginal farmer and the micro enterprise category, the rest are probably going to be relatively easy to achieve. And therefore, it won't become that binding, but these two essentially become binding.

*Professor Sriram:* That brings me to the agriculture portfolio. It's a wicked problem in a typical public policy sense. When you are talking of trading of PSL notes, the report recommends trading of obligations without moving the portfolio and restricts this to banks. So there is no regulatory arbitrage. Does it make sense for us to think of actually encouraging a regulatory arbitrage? Say, NBFCs lend at a higher interest rate for agriculture and the banks achieve their targets by purchasing this portfolio. If that is possible then possibly there will be a specialised institution marked which actually caters to the needs, but banks also achieve their targets, in a lazy way.

*Dr Rajan:* The problem with that is it makes it too easy and the banks themselves will back off lending to the priority sector. The NBFCs that have been doing this lending will come into the market and sell. You will not get incremental lending to the priority sector, and maybe even a decline. Basically NBFCs will crowd out the banks and sell priority sector loans to them. So unless we impose targets on the NBFCs also, it will not serve the purpose.

*Professor Sriram:* With the recommendations of the internal working group on tradability of PSL obligations, do you think it may morph into a larger trading platform across structures in future or you want to keep it limited to the banking system?

*Dr Rajan:* As of now banks. But let's see how it goes.

*Professor Sriram:* Is there no other way, with which we can do anything about this subvention and make lending to agriculture inherently attractive?

*Dr Rajan:* No. Subvention doesn't necessarily imply that you have to lend at 9%. That's not so much the subvention than the fixed price. The subvention actually tries to make lending a little more attractive. We have said to the government that they should eliminate fixed price. Otherwise what happens is that you get an excessive focus on gold loans. We have this policy of saying do 'A' but you cannot either charge the appropriate interest rate or take collateral. In that case banks are basically saying 'Why should I do "A"?'

*Professor Sriram:* That's right. Then they'll do the minimalist thing required.

*Dr Rajan:* Or find somebody who looks like 'A' but is not really 'A'. I have pledged my gold, I get a gold loan. And that counts as agriculture.

*Professor Sriram:* But the banks still don't get the return and that's the problem. Even if they look at the total adjusted cost of funds, agriculture has to become a loss-making portfolio because of the interest rate cap.

*Dr Rajan:* It does not have to be that way. But we do worry about cases where the same guy who borrows from the bank goes back and re-deposits, because he is charged effectively 4% and earns 8% on fixed deposits.

**APPENDIX 2.1**

| Important indicators | June 1969 | March 2010 | March 2011 | March 2012 | March 2013 | March 2014 |
|---|---|---|---|---|---|---|
| **Progress of commercial banking at a glance** | | | | | | |
| Number of commercial banks | 89 | 169 | 169 | 173 | 155 | 151 |
| Scheduled commercial banks | 73 | 165 | 165 | 169 | 151 | 146 |
| Of which: regional rural banks | – | 82 | 82 | 82 | 64 | 57 |
| Non-scheduled commercial banks | 16 | 4 | 4 | 4 | 4 | 5 |
| Number of offices of sched-uledcommercial banks in India^ | 8,262 | 85,393 | 90,263 | 98,330 | 105,437 | 117,280 |
| (a) Rural | 1,833 | 32,624 | 33,683 | 36,356 | 39,195 | 45,177 |
| (b) Semi-urban | 3,342 | 20,740 | 22,843 | 25,797 | 28,165 | 31,442 |
| (c) Urban | 1,584 | 17,003 | 17,490 | 18,781 | 19,902 | 21,448 |
| (d) Metropolitan | 1,503 | 15,026 | 16,247 | 17,396 | 18,175 | 19,213 |
| Population per office (in thousands) | 64.0 | 13.8 | 13.4 | 12.3 | 11.9 | 10.8 |
| Deposits of scheduled commercial banks in India (₹ billion) | 46.46 | 44,928.26 | 52,079.69 | 59,090.82 | 69,342.80 | 79,134.43 |
| of which: (a) Demand | 21.04 | 6,456.10 | 6,417.05 | 6,253.30 | 7,671.61 | 8,272.11 |
| (b) Time | 25.42 | 38,472.16 | 45,662.64 | 52,837.52 | 61,671.19 | 70,862.32 |
| Credit of scheduled commercial banks in India (₹ billion) | 36 | 32,447.88 | 39,420.82 | 46,118.52 | 53,931.58 | 61,390.45 |
| Deposits of scheduled commercial banks per office (₹ million) | 5.6 | 526.1 | 577.0 | 600.9 | 657.7 | 674.7 |
| Credit of scheduled commercial banks per office (₹ million) | 4.4 | 380.0 | 436.7 | 469.0 | 511.5 | 523.5 |
| Per capita deposits of scheduled commercial banks (₹) | 88 | 38,062 | 43,034 | 48,732 | 55,445 | 62,252 |
| Per capita credit of scheduled commercial banks (₹) | 68 | 27,489 | 32,574 | 38,033 | 43,123 | 48,294 |
| Deposits of scheduled commercial banks as percentage of national income (NNP at factor cost, at current prices) | 15.5 | 86.6 | 82.3 | 81.1 | 84.0 | 86.3 |
| Scheduled commercial banks' advances to priority sector (₹ billion) | 5.04 | 11,384.06 | 13,373.33 | 14,909.15 | 18,179.70 | 21,549.17 |
| Share of priority sector advances intotal credit of scheduledcommercial banks (per cent) | 14.0 | 35.1 | 33.9 | 32.3 | 33.7 | 35.1 |
| Share of priority sector advances intotal non-food credit of sched-uledcommercial banks (per cent) | 15.0 | 35.6 | 34.5 | 32.9 | 34.3 | 35.7 |
| Credit deposit ratio | 77.5 | 72.2 | 75.7 | 78.0 | 77.8 | 77.6 |
| Investment deposit ratio | 29.3 | 30.8 | 28.8 | 29.4 | 28.8 | 28.3 |
| Cash deposit ratio | 8.2 | 6.8 | 6.7 | 6.1 | 5.6 | 5.4 |

^ Excludes administrative offices

*Source:* Basic Statistical Returns of Commercial Banks in India Volume 43. Mumbai, RBI (2015).

**APPENDIX 2.2**

**Percentage distribution of term deposits of scheduled commercial banks according to the size of deposits and broad ownership category March 2014 (%)**

| Size of deposits (in ₹ million) | Individuals | | Others | | Total | |
|---|---|---|---|---|---|---|
| | No. of accounts | Amount | No. of accounts | Amount | No. of accounts | Amount |
| Less than 0.025 | 33.3 | 2.2 | 37.5 | 1.1 | 33.7 | 1.7 |
| 0.025 and above but less than 0.1 | 37.2 | 14.2 | 30.0 | 7.0 | 36.5 | 11.0 |
| 0.1 and above but less than 1.5 | 28.8 | 52.5 | 28.0 | 22.8 | 28.7 | 39.1 |
| 1.5 and above but less than 10.0 | 0.7 | 12.6 | 3.4 | 16.1 | 1.0 | 14.2 |
| 10.0 and above | 0.1 | 18.5 | 1.2 | 52.8 | 0.2 | 34.0 |
| TOTAL | 100.0 | 100.0 | 100.0 | 100.0 | 100.0 | 100.0 |

*Source:* Basic Statistical Returns of Commercial Banks in India Volume 43. Mumbai, RBI (2015).

**APPENDIX 2.3**

**Percentage distribution of outstanding credit to small borrowal accounts of scheduled commercial banks according to broad category of borrowers March 2014 (%)**

| | Individual | | | | | | | |
|---|---|---|---|---|---|---|---|---|
| | Male | | Female | | Others | | Total | |
| Population group | No. of accounts | Amount outstanding | No. of accounts | Amount outstanding | No. of accounts | Amount outstanding | No. of accounts | Amount outstanding |
| Rural | 77.9 | 78.7 | 19.2 | 18.5 | 2.8 | 2.7 | 100.0 | 100.0 |
| Semi-urban | 72.1 | 73.1 | 25.0 | 24.1 | 2.9 | 2.8 | 100.0 | 100.0 |
| Urban | 72.5 | 71.3 | 23.7 | 23.7 | 3.8 | 5.1 | 100.0 | 100.0 |
| Metropolitan | 81.8 | 78.4 | 16.8 | 17.2 | 1.4 | 4.5 | 100.0 | 100.0 |
| All-India | 76.5 | 75.7 | 20.9 | 21.0 | 2.7 | 3.2 | 100.0 | 100.0 |

*Source:* Basic Statistical Returns of Commercial Banks in India Volume 43. Mumbai, RBI (2015).

**APPENDIX 2.4**

**Population group-wise outstanding credit of small borrowal accounts of scheduled commercial banks according to occupation March 2014 (amount in ₹ million)**

| | Rural | | | Semi-urban | | |
|---|---|---|---|---|---|---|
| Occupation | No. of accounts | Credit limit | Amount outstanding | No. of accounts | Credit limit | Amount outstanding |
| I. Agriculture | 33,144,749 | 1,903,956.8 | 1,790,299.6 | 20,850,606 | 1,372,655.0 | 1,320,592.8 |
| 1. Direct finance | 31,407,879 | 1,811,564.3 | 1,703,976.7 | 19,592,784 | 1,292,467.9 | 1,247,095.9 |
| 2. Indirect finance | 1,736,870 | 92,392.6 | 86,322.9 | 1,257,822 | 80,187.2 | 73,496.9 |
| II. Industry | 622,599 | 30,514.1 | 23,695.0 | 380,856 | 23,189.5 | 17,940.6 |
| III. Transport operators | 105,217 | 10,998.0 | 7,847.5 | 157,156 | 15,943.6 | 12,601.3 |
| IV. Professional and other services | 740,629 | 39,939.3 | 31,860.4 | 584,180 | 35,764.1 | 28,382.3 |
| V. Personal loans | 3,982,419 | 277,234.5 | 218,180.8 | 6,040,465 | 453,314.6 | 355,810.1 |
| 1. Loans for housing | 429,823 | 34,697.6 | 24,658.3 | 487,110 | 43,768.9 | 29,051.1 |
| 2. Loans for purchase of consumer durables | 182,808 | 12,945.4 | 9,182.1 | 165,303 | 13,494.8 | 9,753.4 |
| 3. Rest of the personal loans | 3,369,788 | 229,591.5 | 184,340.5 | 5,388,052 | 396,050.9 | 317,005.7 |

*(Continued)*

*(Continued)*

**Population group-wise outstanding credit of small borrowal accounts of scheduled commercial banks according to occupation March 2014 (amount in ₹ million)**

| Occupation | Rural | | | Semi-urban | | |
|---|---|---|---|---|---|---|
| | No. of accounts | Credit limit | Amount outstanding | No. of accounts | Credit limit | Amount outstanding |
| VI. Trade | 2,030,051 | 101,660.8 | 80,598.6 | 1,542,171 | 88,656.8 | 69,364.6 |
| 1. Wholesale trade | 50,347 | 2,862.8 | 2,355.6 | 52,124 | 3,064.5 | 2,472.4 |
| 2. Retail trade | 1,979,704 | 98,798.1 | 78,243.0 | 1,490,047 | 85,592.3 | 66,892.2 |
| VII. Finance | 166,052 | 10,515.9 | 8,024.7 | 105,365 | 6,647.7 | 5,010.7 |
| VIII. All others | 988,865 | 41,848.0 | 30,469.7 | 838,657 | 27,807.6 | 22,490.2 |
| Total BANK Credit | 41,780,581 | 2,416,667.4 | 2,190,976.3 | 30,499,456 | 2,023,978.8 | 1,832,192.6 |

| Occupation | Urban/metropolitan | | | All-India | | |
|---|---|---|---|---|---|---|
| | No. of accounts | Credit limit | Amount outstanding | No. of accounts | Credit limit | Amount outstanding |
| I. Agriculture | 5,692,519 | 395,480.8 | 354,682.1 | 59,687,874 | 3,672,092.7 | 3,465,574.5 |
| 1. Direct finance | 5,091,338 | 351,138.8 | 319,273.1 | 56,092,001 | 3,455,171.0 | 3,270,345.7 |
| 2. Indirect finance | 601,181 | 44,341.9 | 35,409.0 | 3,595,873 | 216,921.7 | 195,228.9 |
| II. Industry | 528,732 | 33,403.3 | 32,240.6 | 1,532,187 | 87,106.9 | 73,876.2 |
| III. Transport operators | 818,067 | 54,855.5 | 33,021.3 | 1,080,440 | 81,797.1 | 53,470.1 |
| IV. Professional and other services | 775,255 | 50,982.7 | 37,872.1 | 2,100,064 | 126,686.1 | 98,114.8 |
| V. Personal loans | 25,166,372 | 1,503,793.5 | 686,615.4 | 35,189,256 | 2,234,342.6 | 1,260,606.3 |
| 1. Loans for housing | 739,458 | 72,434.0 | 47,044.3 | 1,656,391 | 150,900.4 | 100,753.6 |
| 2. Loans for purchase of consumer durables | 252,466 | 16,804.0 | 10,648.0 | 600,577 | 43,244.3 | 29,583.5 |
| 3. Rest of the personal loans | 24,174,448 | 1,414,555.5 | 628,923.0 | 32,932,288 | 2,040,197.9 | 1,130,269.2 |
| VI. Trade | 1,303,734 | 79,487.0 | 60,425.6 | 4,875,956 | 269,804.6 | 210,388.8 |
| 1. Wholesale trade | 64,660 | 4,360.4 | 6,511.4 | 167,131 | 10,287.6 | 11,339.3 |
| 2. Retail trade | 1,239,074 | 75,126.6 | 53,914.2 | 4,708,825 | 259,517.0 | 199,049.5 |
| VII. Finance | 67,417 | 5,856.3 | 4,268.2 | 338,834 | 23,019.9 | 17,303.6 |
| VIII. All others | 2,593,264 | 42,485.9 | 34,616.8 | 4,420,786 | 112,141.4 | 87,576.6 |
| Total bank credit | 36,945,360 | 2,166,345.0 | 1,243,742.1 | 109,225,397 | 6,606,991.2 | 5,266,911.0 |

*Source:* Basic Statistical Returns of Commercial Banks in India Volume 43. Mumbai, RBI (2015).

# REFERENCES

Gandhi, R. (2015) Securitisation in India: Ambling Down or Revving Up? *Reserve Bank of India Bulletin.* August, Vol. LXIX, 8, pp. 15–22.

RBI (2014). *Master Circular 'Non Banking Finance Company—Microfinance Institutions' (NBFCMFIs)*

*Directions.* Department of Non Banking Supervision, Reserve Bank of India. Mumbai: RBI.

RBI (2015). *Report of the Internal Working Group (IWG) to Revisit the Existing Priority Sector Lending Guidelines.* Mumbai: Reserve Bank of India, Paragraph 5. p. 6.

# Regional rural banks and local area banks

The first step taken by the government to push the larger agenda of inclusion was to aggressively adopt the 'state partnership with cooperatives' as recommended by the All India Rural Credit Survey Committee Report (RBI, 1954). The next step was the nationalisation of commercial banks in two rounds—first in 1969 and next in 1980. In 1975, the government also took the bold step of setting up regional rural banks (RRBs), which would have the professionalism of a bank, with a local flavour. While the first of the RRBs were established in 1975 starting with six RRBs and 17 branches, by March 1990, the number of RRBs had spread across the country with 196 of these institutions and having around 14,000 branches.

The most significant event for the RRBs during the year 2015 was the amendment to the RRB Act, thereby paving the way for the RRBs to potentially attract investments from agencies and/or individuals other than the three promoters—the central government, the state government and the sponsor bank. These amendments also provided a framework for better governance by opening up the board positions to other shareholders as well. With consolidation and with the reforms in the law, it can be expected that this space could be watched for further developments in terms of growth in the coming years.

The RRBs had started the phase of stabilisation after the consolidation and merger of banks that happened in the past years. While at the end of 2013, there were 64 RRBs, as a result of further consolidation the number was reduced to 57. With the beginning of the phase of consolidation, there has been a faster spread of RRBs in terms of new branches (see Table 3.1). While in the 15 years from 1990 the number of branches grew by less than 1,000, the last five years has seen an expansion of near about 3,000

---

**Box 3.1 Amendments to the RRB Act, 1976**

During the year 2015, the RRB Act, 1976 was amended. The significant amendments that were carried out were:

1. The authorised capital of the RRBs was enhanced from ₹50 million to ₹2 billion.
2. The amendment also opened scope for a fourth investor (apart from the Central Government, the state government and the sponsor bank) to take a stake in the RRBs, with the proviso that the combined stake of the central government and the sponsor bank will not be less than 50% and that the state government will be consulted if the relative shareholding of the state government goes below 15%.
3. The managerial and financial assistance from sponsor banks could continue by mutual consent, and
4. Provisions for shareholders (other than those nominated by the central government, state government and the sponsor bank) to elect directors and fixed term period for directors appointed by the central government.

With these amendments the possibility of private investments coming into RRBs has opened.

---

branches. However, the overall growth of branches over almost two decades has been only about 26%. The others (public sector, private sector, new private sector, foreign banks and the State Bank group) together have more than doubled their branches in the same period.

During the past five years, the RRB branch network grew by nearly 20%. While a disproportionate growth in percentage terms came from opening

**Table 3.1    RRB branch network over the years (according to region)**

| Region | 1996 | 2010 | 2011 | 2012 | 2013 | 2014 | Growth from 1996 |
|---|---|---|---|---|---|---|---|
| North | 1,980 | 2,093 | 2,171 | 2,312 | 2,469 | 2,618 | 32% |
| North-east | 667 | 675 | 693 | 696 | 696 | 721 | 8% |
| East | 3,610 | 3,708 | 3,742 | 3,796 | 3,836 | 4,057 | 12% |
| Central | 4,670 | 4,783 | 4,912 | 5,127 | 5,440 | 5,821 | 25% |
| West | 1,022 | 1,021 | 1,052 | 1,142 | 1,192 | 1,294 | 27% |
| South | 2,723 | 3,268 | 3,328 | 3,556 | 3,849 | 4,028 | 48% |
| Total | 14,672 | 15,548 | 15,898 | 16,629 | 17,482 | 18,539 | 26% |

*Source:* Basic statistical returns of scheduled commercial banks in India. Mumbai: RBI, various years.

metropolitan branches—this should be seen in the perspective of added business lines as well as the fact that the growth was on a small base. However, even on the other parameters, we see that the urban, semi-urban branch network is growing faster than the rural branch network (see Table 3.2). This skew follows the change in the branch licencing policy of RBI which was relaxed for RRBs—subject to their meeting conditions on capital adequacy, financial health and solvency. The relaxation provided the RRBs the opportunity to open branches in any location that has population less up to 99,999 as per the latest census without the prior permission of the

RBI as long as 25% of the branches were in locations that had population of up to 9,999. The relaxation has helped in the RRBs to start moving towards larger locations where the business parameters could be better.

RRBs have had a chequered history with many of them suffering losses and eroding their capital base. There have been several committees that looked into the performance of the RRBs and the net result of all the initiatives has been both capital infusion and significant scale of consolidation (Table 3.3).

First the RRBs belonging to the same sponsor bank in a given state were encouraged to merge and

**Table 3.2    RRB branch network over the years (according to location)**

| Location | 2010 | 2011 | 2012 | 2013 | 2014 | Growth: RRB branch network | Share of RRBs in the banking network (2014) |
|---|---|---|---|---|---|---|---|
| Rural | 11,629 | 11,778 | 12,263 | 12,850 | 13,609 | 17.02% | 30.47% |
| Semi-urban | 2,916 | 3,026 | 3,192 | 3,362 | 3,569 | 22.39% | 11.27% |
| Urban | 887 | 960 | 1,009 | 1,080 | 1,153 | 29.98% | 4.93% |
| Metro | 116 | 134 | 165 | 190 | 208 | 79.31% | 0.98% |
| Total | 15,548 | 15,898 | 16,629 | 17,482 | 18,539 | 19.23% | 15.32% |

*Source:* Basic statistical returns of scheduled commercial banks in India. Mumbai: RBI, various years.

**Table 3.3    Recapitalisation of RRBs: various phases**

| Phase | Number of RRBs recapitalised | Amount of recap (₹ billion) |
|---|---|---|
| Till January 2000 (six phases) | 187 (158 fully, 29 partially) | 21.88 |
| 2007–08 | 27 | 17.96 |
| 2012 | 27 (16 fully capitalised, 11 partially capitalised) | 10.00 |
| 2013* | 10 (new, of which 8 fully capitalised and 2 partially) all the 11 that were partially capitalised were fully capitalised in 2013 | 12.00 |
| 2014 | 2 (completion of the capitalisation process) | |

* Total 40 RRBs were identified for recapitalisation. Period for completion of the entire process had been extended up to March 2014 with a total outlay of ₹ 22 billion.
*Source:* Trend and progress of banking India, Various Years. Mumbai: Reserve Bank of India.

in the second phase RRBs across sponsor banks within a state were encouraged to merge. By March 2015 there were 56 RRBs. The assets of the RRBs grew by 16% in 2013–14 with a significant increase in net interest income on the total assets increasing from 3.15% to 3.3%. With this consolidation and profitable performance, and infusion of capital, it appears that the RRBs are all set for the next phase of growth in the coming years. While the requirement of priority sector advances was reduced to 40% of the net bank credit in 1997, it was restored back to 60% in 2003–04, with a proviso that 15% of the total advances (as against a target of 10% for the other banks) be given to weaker sections. These two targets, with a reduced basket of other purposes (micro and small enterprises, microfinance, education loans, and housing credit) are applicable to RRBs.

The RRBs now can access money markets, borrow and lend funds within RRBs, be agents of insurance products (without risk participation); issue debit and credit cards and also manage currency chests. The RRBs are also allowed to deal with foreign currency deposits and could get licences as authorised dealers for foreign exchange.

---

**Box 3.2 Governor Rajan on RRBs**

*Professor Sriram:* Though RRBs did equalise this (regional) balance a little bit, possibly at the cost of the viability of some of the RRBs themselves, but if you look at the 1960s' data when it was predominately south and west, north has caught up over these decades and largely when I was looking at the data, the deeper penetration of rural branches has been much more of RRBs than commercial banks.

*Dr Rajan:* This is why we are trying to foster these new institutions. Locally managed institutions have a great incentive to give local loans. We have to ensure that they are viable and are not unstable because of their local dependency. That's why, we are willing to see a variety of them, and also maybe look at strengthening the urban cooperatives as well as the RRBs, including changes in their mode of governance. But the other thing is that we also have to look at the financial infrastructure that supports these. Today we have credit information bureaus; can they penetrate more fully in the rural area? Can Aadhaar be used every time a loan is made so that everybody knows the extent of indebtedness? Today, somebody who

wants a loan needs to get a no-objection certificate from everybody else.

*Professor Sriram:* This has always intrigued me, both on the LABs and the SFBs, you've always had a higher Capital to Risk-weighted Assets Ratio (CRAR) at 15%. But you know the issue is that the problem is on the assets side, because of either geographical concentration or functional concentration. With a high CRAR that risk doesn't go away. So how does a higher CRAR help, apart from the fact that it keeps the depositors a little safer? It does not attract capital because the Return on Equity (ROE) will not be great unless you have leveraged enough.

*Dr Rajan:* Presumably if you are taking on more risk, you'll have to charge a premium. This notion that somehow you're going to charge the riskier guys lower interest rates and still serve them rates doesn't make a good argument.

*Professor Sriram:* Is there any other way in which the assets side itself can be diversified by allowing them to do a lot more treasury and things like that?

*Dr Rajan:* You can do securitisation of loans. The only problem is you need to have adequate skin in the game to collect because you cannot securitise loans and then not be around to collect.

*Professor Sriram:* With Basel III kicking in do you think all the banks including RRBs, SFBs and cooperative banks be covered under the norms? How does that pan out?

*Dr Rajan:* Eventually some version of Basel will be there. I think apart from capital ratios, we have to have some notion of liquidity for all these entities, but the counter-cyclical capital buffers, this that, we'll have to see how to apply them across the board. But let us see.

*Professor Sriram:* Do you think RRBs should further consolidate?

*Dr Rajan:* I think there is a process by which this is taking place. There is some talk of one RRB per state rather than two.

*Professor Sriram:* That's right. That is what the ministry was pushing a couple of years ago.

*Dr Rajan:* Yes, I would say we need to maintain the local character of these institutions, rather than make them so big that policies are made in Delhi or in Mumbai, and not locally. I think when we get to that point we have created too big an RRB.

## BEYOND THE BRANCH NETWORK

As of March 2013 all the RRBs were completely computerised and on an interoperable core banking solution (CBS) platform. This enabled the banks to not only set up Automatic Teller Machines (ATMs) but also issue debit and credit cards. However, of the 57 banks only about 19 banks had started rolling out ATMs. Even more important is that 3 of the 19 banks had 79% of the ATMs (see Table 3.4). The progress report put out by the department of financial services (DFS), Government of India (GoI), on the progress of PMJDY indicates that the RRBs together had issued 17.82 million RuPay debit cards. While it is possible for the customers of the RRBs to operate their cards in the merchant establishments and in the ATMs of other banks including the white label ATMs, this data indicates that there is far more to be done by RRBs in roll out of technology-enabled touchpoints, given that the RRBs have more than 40% share of branches in the rural and semi-urban areas, there is much more to be done in terms of roll out of technology-enabled touchpoints for the clients.

## BUSINESS

From 1996, when a large number of RRBs were reporting losses to now has been a long journey but it appears that the RRBs are in a phase of stabilisation and growth. The government has infused capital as per the recommendations of the K.C. Chakrabarty committee to ensure that the RRBs attained a CRAR of 9%. With the consolidation and the new initiatives, infusion of capital and the expansion of branches it appears that RRBs have turned towards a greater vibrancy and profitability.

Table 3.5 shows that the general improvement in the overall financial performance of RRBs from the time the consolidation started, to culminate in 2014 (and 2015) where all the RRBs were in profit.

What is more interesting to note is that unlike the commercial banks, RRBs have a very high Current Accounts Savings Accounts (CASA) deposit base which helps them to keep the cost of funds in check. The CASA ratio for RRBs have been near about 60%, while the ratio for the other banks in 2014 has been ranging between 30% for public sector banks and about 40% for the private sector banks, with the

**Table 3.4** **ATM network of RRBs**

| Bank name | Metro and urban | Semi-urban | Rural | Total |
|---|---|---|---|---|
| 1.   Allahabad UP Gramin Bank | 11 | 26 | 65 | 102 |
| 2.   Andhra Pragathi Grameena Vikas Bank | 2 | 1 | 0 | 3 |
| 3.   Baroda Gujarat Gramin Bank | 0 | 2 | 6 | 8 |
| 4.   Baroda Rajasthan Kshetriya Gramin Bank | 5 | 2 | 1 | 8 |
| 5.   Baroda Uttar Prdaesh Gramin Bank | 2 | 1 | 0 | 3 |
| 6.   Chaitanya Godavari Grameena Bank | 0 | 0 | 13 | 13 |
| 7.   Dena Gujarat Gramin Bank | 2 | 1 | 5 | 8 |
| 8.   Karnataka Vikash Gramin Bank | 10 | 7 | 4 | 21 |
| 9.   Kashi Gomati Samyut Gramin Bank | 11 | 7 | 23 | 41 |
| 10.  Kaveri Grameena Bank | 1 | 0 | 0 | 1 |
| 11.  Kerala Gramin Bank | 12 | 162 | 28 | 202 |
| 12.  Maharashtra Gramin Bank | 11 | 0 | 0 | 11 |
| 13.  Malwa Gramin Bank | 1 | 1 | 0 | 2 |
| 14.  Odisha Gramya Bank | 0 | 0 | 1 | 1 |
| 15.  Pragathi Krishna Gramin Bank | 35 | 55 | 120 | 210 |
| 16.  Prathama Gramin Bank | 3 | 10 | 0 | 4 |
| 17.  Rajasthan Marudhara Gramin Bank | 3 | 1 | 1 | 5 |
| 18.  Sutlej Gramin Bank | 1 | 1 | 4 | 6 |
| 19.  Telangana Grameena Bank | 0 | 2 | 0 | 2 |
| **Total** | **119** | **270** | **271** | **651** |

*Source:* National Payments Corporation of India.

**Table 3.5** **Performance of RRBs over the years of consolidation (figures for 31 March of each year)**

| | 2006 | 2007 | 2008 | 2009 | 2010 | 2011 | 2012 | 2013 | 2014 |
|---|---|---|---|---|---|---|---|---|---|
| No. of RRBs | 133 | 96 | 90 | 86 | 82 | 82 | 82 | 64 | 57 |
| No. of branches | 14,489 | 14,563 | 14,790 | 15,524 | 15,475 | 16,024 | 16,914 | 17,867 | 19,082 |
| Net profit (₹ billion) | 6.17 | 6.25 | 10.27 | 13.35 | 18.84 | 17.85 | 18.86 | 22.73 | 26.94 |
| Profit/loss making RRBs | 111/22 | 81/15 | 82/8 | 80/6 | 79/3 | 75/7 | 79/3 | 63/1 | 57/0 |
| Deposits (₹ billion) | 713.29 | 831.44 | 990.93 | 1,201.89 | 1,450.35 | 1,662.32 | 1,863.36 | 2,053.56 | 2,332.72 |
| Loans and Advances (₹ billion) | 385.20 | 473.26 | 575.68 | 656.09 | 791.57 | 947.15 | 1,130.35 | 1,358.62 | 1,588.81 |
| CD ratio (%) | 55.7 | 58.3 | 59.5 | 56.4 | 57.6 | 59.51 | 63.3 | 64.82 | 66.56 |
| Share of CASA in deposits (%) | 59.14 | 61.21 | 59.63 | 58.35 | 57.90 | 60.35 | 58.51 | 57 | 56.88 |
| Share of PSA (%) | 81 | 82.2 | 82.9 | 83.4 | 82.2 | 83.5 | 80 | 86 | |
| Share of agri. Adv. to total (%) | 54.2 | 56.6 | 56.3 | 55.1 | 54.8 | 55.7 | 53 | 63 | |
| Gross NPA (%) | 7.3 | 6.55 | 6.1 | 4.2 | 3.72 | 3.75 | 5.03 | 6.08 | 6.09 |
| Net NPA (%) | | 3.46 | 3.36 | 1.81 | 1.62 | 2.05 | 2.98 | 3.59 | 3.52 |

*Source:* Trend and progress of banking India, Various Years. Mumbai: Reserve Bank of India, Financial Statements of RRBs, Mumbai: NABARD.

best ratio clocked by the State Bank group at 42.2%. This gives RRBs a significant advantage. However, the other figures in Table 3.5 seem to offset the advantage that the RRBs have got—the Credit-Deposit ratio has been around 65% (and improving significantly in the past two years) but still lower than the average of the banking sector at 79% for 2014.

## FINANCIAL INCLUSION

The performance on the inclusion parameters shows an interesting trend in case of RRBs. As the consolidation process was underway and the RRBs started reporting profits and moved towards a greater stability, the outreach parameters in terms of more branches and also reaching out to the customers through BC outlets were better. The RRBs opened around 2,500 new branches with a large number in unbanked locations under the financial inclusion targets assigned by the RBI. As of March

2012, the RRBs had nearly 19,000 BC outlets and it was growing (Pant-Joshi, 2013). However, as seen in Chapter 2 on the review of banks, the performance of banks on opening BSBD Accounts, branches and BC outlets has not added much to the content of the basic function of the bank—that is on the business of providing loans and collecting term deposits.

## Credit

Table 3.6 has details of loans made by RRBs in the loan categories of less than ₹25,000 and in the category of ₹25,000 to ₹200,000 (defined as small borrowal accounts). The numbers show that both the absolute number of accounts and the amount disbursed under the category of amounts up to ₹25,000 has decreased. In case of the intermediary category of up to ₹200,000, the amounts and the number of accounts have increased showing the shift towards larger loans. While there is a marginal

**Table 3.6** **Details of credit to small borrowal accounts over the years**

| Year ending March 31 → | 2010 | 2011 | 2012 | 2013 | 2014 |
|---|---|---|---|---|---|
| **Loan amount less than ₹25,000** | | | | | |
| Number of accounts (million) | 9.42 | 9.88 | 9.33 | 7.77 | 6.89 |
| Percentage to total accounts | 50.54% | 49.28% | 44.99% | 38.32% | 32.07% |
| Limit Sanctioned (₹ billion) | 155.43 | 164.20 | 167.43 | 115.31 | 115.24 |
| Percentage to total amounts | 15.24% | 13.85% | 10.80% | 5.27% | 4.98% |
| Amount outstanding (₹ billion) | 127.65 | 151.26 | 162.22 | 142.52 | 108.92 |
| Percentage to total outstanding | 15.42% | 15.42% | 13.94% | 10.49% | 6.86% |

*(Continued)*

*(Continued)*

| Year ending March 31 → | 2010 | 2011 | 2012 | 2013 | 2014 |
|---|---|---|---|---|---|
| **Loan amount ₹25,000 to ₹200,000** | | | | | |
| Number of accounts (million) | 8.59 | 9.34 | 10.29 | 10.95 | 12.60 |
| Percentage to total accounts | 46.15% | 46.55% | 49.63% | 53.98% | 59% |
| Limit sanctioned (₹ billion) | 590.26 | 662.80 | 720.90 | 794.58 | 915.14 |
| Percentage to total amounts | 57.90% | 55.91% | 46.50% | 36.30% | 40% |
| Amount outstanding (₹ billion) | 479.31 | 547.24 | 612.33 | 696.36 | 812.91 |
| Percentage to total outstanding | 57.91% | 55.77% | 52.61% | 51.26% | 51% |
| **Total up to ₹200,000** | | | | | |
| Number of accounts (million) | 18.01 | 19.22 | 19.62 | 18.72 | 19.49 |
| Percentage to total accounts with RRBs | 96.70% | 95.82% | 94.62% | 92.30% | 91% |
| Limit sanctioned | 745.66 | 827.01 | 888.33 | 909.89 | 1030.37 |
| Percentage to total amounts | 73.14% | 69.76% | 57.29% | 41.56% | 44.52% |
| Amount outstanding (₹ million) | 606.96 | 698.50 | 774.56 | 838.89 | 921.84 |
| Percentage to total outstanding with RRBs | 73.34% | 71.19% | 66.55% | 61.75% | 58.02% |

*Source:* Basic Statistical Returns of Scheduled Commercial Banks in India for the years 2011, 2012, 2013, 2014 and 2015. Mumbai: Reserve Bank of India.
*Note:* The gender-wise break-up of the accounts and the amounts indicate that more than 75% of the loan accounts and amounts have been made to men.

growth in the overall number of loans and loan amounts below ₹200,000 the proportion of the number of accounts against the loan book as well as the amount lent under this category as a proportion has shown a drastic fall.

As the RRBs consolidate, their growth is seen from the larger accounts and not from the smaller accounts. From an inclusion perspective, what is redeeming is that while the commercial banks have less than 10% of their portfolio in small borrowal accounts, the RRBs have had at least 50% of the amounts outstanding in these accounts. The trends indicate that this is only a passing phase and the RRBs would try and close the gap with the commercial banks in years to come.

An examination of the purpose-wise break-up of the portfolio of the RRBs shows that a large portion of the portfolio goes to agriculture and within that for direct finance to agriculture (Table 3.7). This is not only the number for the year 2014, but as demonstrated in Table 3.5, historically RRBs have been lending more than 60% of their portfolio for agriculture and a large chunk of that portfolio comes from direct lending to agriculture.

The break-up of the portfolio of the RRBs has some implications and some opportunities and going forward, it would be interesting to watch how this will play out. Even with the RBI restoring the requirements of PSL norms for RRBs to 60% of net bank credit, RRBs seem to achieve the target not only from agriculture, but also from the next significant part—personal loans which would include weaker section advances with focus on housing and education. Historically RRBs have been advancing more than 80% of their advances to priority sector. It is therefore surprising that there is no mention of any significant securitisation deals happening from this sector of these advances. The lack of securitisation deals might indicate two aspects.

(a) That the RRBs did not have wide opportunities in the non-priority sector credit market (indicated by their low CD ratio) and therefore there was no incentive to sell the portfolio for gaining liquidity, particularly if the additional liquidity did not have lucrative opportunities of deployment.

(b) That the RRBs were too many and spread across various locations and the players did not find the deal sizes to be of interest. To deal with 196 small entities is one matter and to deal with a consolidated entity almost representing a significant market share in one state—through the consolidated 57 entities—is quite another.

Therefore, going forward, it is possible that with the consolidation of RRBs an active securitisation market will open up for their portfolio. In addition, if the recommendation of the internal working group of RBI on PSLCs is notified, then there

**Table 3.7  Purpose-wise break-up of credit accounts of RRBs as of 31 March 2014**

| Purpose | No. of accounts | Relative % to total | Credit limit (₹ billion) | Relative % to total | Amount outstanding (₹ billion) | Relative % to total |
|---|---|---|---|---|---|---|
| I. Agriculture | **15.33** | **71%** | **1,531.71** | **66%** | **1,052.25** | **66%** |
| 1. Direct finance | 14.78 | 69% | 1,494.57 | 65% | 1,019.01 | 64% |
| 2. Indirect finance | 0.55 | 3% | 37.14 | 2% | 33.24 | 2% |
| II. Professional and other services | **0.54** | **3%** | **60.75** | **3%** | **46.04** | **3%** |
| III. Personal loans | **2.32** | **11%** | **314.74** | **14%** | **251.71** | **16%** |
| 1. Housing | 0.34 | 2% | 100.82 | 4% | 81.18 | 5% |
| 2. Consumer durables | 0.15 | 1% | 18.17 | 1% | 13.31 | 1% |
| 3. Vehicles | 0.10 | 0% | 21.02 | 1% | 15.63 | 1% |
| 4. Education | 0.09 | 0% | 20.56 | 1% | 17.83 | 1% |
| 5. Others | 1.63 | 8% | 154.18 | 7% | 123.77 | 8% |
| IV. Trade | **1.39** | **6%** | **106.18** | **5%** | **86.72** | **5%** |
| 1. Retail trade | 1.37 | 6% | 102.95 | 4% | 84.05 | 5% |
| V. Finance | **0.21** | **1%** | **116.58** | **5%** | **21.22** | **1%** |
| Other miscellaneous purposes | **1.69** | **0.08** | **184.70** | **0.08** | **130.87** | **0.08** |
| Total bank credit | **21.48** | **100%** | **2,314.67** | **100%** | **1,588.82** | **100%** |

would be income streams that would accrue to the RRBs, even without the portfolio moving out of the balance sheet.

While the deployment of credit to agriculture should be seen with a great deal of satisfaction from a larger inclusion perspective, it is also important to note that this leads to a significant concentration risk in one activity, an activity subject to political processes of waivers. This is also a portfolio that continues to have interest rate caps and therefore might not be lucrative. Going forward, the RRBs might want to focus on this sector because of their inherent strength, but quickly churn the portfolio through securitisation deals and then

look for opportunities beyond the current concentrated portfolio. Their size, and consequently their leadership that comes from a more senior level of bankers, will afford such an opportunity.

## Deposits

The data on the break-up of deposits by size was not available for RRBs separately. However, the break-up was available according to the location of the branches (Table 3.8).

It is obvious that the significant portion of the deposits are coming from the rural and semi-urban locations, as represented by the spread of the branch network. While there is disproportionate amount of

**Table 3.8  Deposits of RRBs classified according to the location of the branches as of March 2014**

| Type of deposits → | | Current | | Savings | | Term | | Total | |
|---|---|---|---|---|---|---|---|---|---|
| Population group | No. of offices | No. of accounts (million) | Amount (₹ billion) | No. of accounts (million) | Amount (₹ billion) | No. of accounts (million) | Amount (₹ billion) | No. of accounts (million) | Amount (₹ billion) |
| Rural | 13,609 | 1,192.64 | 38.63 | 98,895.21 | 778.32 | 10,253.52 | 549.02 | 110,341.37 | 1,365.97 |
| Semi-urban | 3,569 | 571.03 | 24.09 | 27,582.64 | 297.47 | 3,811.04 | 269.22 | 31,964.71 | 590.77 |
| Urban | 1,153 | 173.42 | 20.04 | 5,499.14 | 111.89 | 1,563.63 | 194.94 | 7,236.19 | 326.88 |
| Metro | 208 | 23.34 | 2.19 | 791.37 | 16.51 | 205.86 | 30.40 | 1,020.56 | 49.10 |
| All India | 18,539 | 1,960.43 | 84.95 | 132,768.35 | 1,204.19 | 15,834.06 | 1,043.58 | 150,562.83 | 2,332.72 |

*Source:* Basic Statistical Returns of Scheduled Commercial Banks in India. Mumbai: RBI.

deposits in proportion to the branch network from urban and metro centres, it is fairly low on absolute terms. As discussed earlier, the most significant chunk of the deposits is coming from savings accounts, followed by term deposits and then current accounts.

The data on the nature of ownership of accounts also indicates that the RRBs cater more to individuals. About 12% of the accounts with RRBs and about 19% of the deposit amounts come from sources other than individuals (Table 3.9). This is against the numbers for the banking system, where about 9% of the accounts belong to institutions, but these institutions account for about 45.5% of the deposits of the banking sector. Therefore, it is appropriate to broadly conclude that the design of the RRBs has been to cater to the individuals, with smaller loan and deposit sizes, lower cost of funds due to CASA. The only two aspects that the RRBs need to consider are: a

**Table 3.9** Deposits of RRBs classified according to ownership as of March 2014

| Details | Accounts (in million) | % of total | Amount (₹ billion) | % of total |
|---|---|---|---|---|
| Male | 99 | 66% | 1,469 | 63% |
| Female | 34 | 23% | 424 | 18% |
| Institutions and others | 17 | 12% | 440 | 19% |
| Total | 151 | 100% | 2,333 | 100% |

greater deployment of credit (represented by a better CD ratio) and a lower level of non-performing assets (NPAs) that would keep the profitability on track. It would be interesting to see the progress of these institutions now that the next phase of consolidation is concluded.

---

**Box 3.3 KGFS: an alternative model of rural and local banking**

Another model that has been operating in the rural areas has been the Kshetriya Grameen Financial Services (KGFS) Model operated by IFMR Rural Channels. The model initially started in three districts and has now spread to six districts across the country, though largely focussed in Tamil Nadu. The first of the units was set up way back in 2008 and has demonstrated what a locally focussed, technology-enabled unit can do in a limited area of operation. The model of KGFS is keeping the customer at the centre and providing the customer a suite of financial services. This is unlike the type of verticals seen in the traditional banking structure. The concept of wealth management, applied to the high net worth individuals is being applied on the smaller and the poorer customers, with significant use of technology.

Each KGFS is operated almost as an independent entity, with accountability for the overall performance parameters on both the income statement, capital requirement and other prudential aspects (including transfer pricing for capital). Since it is seen almost as an independent entity, there is tremendous amount of localisation and customisation depending on the economy and the cultural practices of the area.

The products offered by IFMR rural channels are given in the table below.

| Loan products | Insurance | Savings/investment | Remittances |
|---|---|---|---|
| JLG | Personal Accident Insurance | National Pension Scheme (NPS Lite) | International |
| Jewel Loan | Term Life Insurance | Savings Bank A/c | Domestic* |
| Salary Loan | Livestock Insurance | Fixed Deposit and Recurring Deposit* | |
| Crop Loan | Shop and content insurance | Index Fund* | |
| Education Loan | Weather Insurance* | Gold Fund* | |
| Micro-Enterprise Loan | Health Insurance* | Liquid Fund* | |
| Emergency Loan | Crop Insurance* | | |
| Personal Loan | | | |
| Livestock Loan | | | |

*Products under pilot testing.

While KGFS itself is an NBFC (and not registered as an NBFC-MFI), it is able to offer a bank-like service to its customers because of all the partnerships it has with various agencies to operate as an agent. The implication of not registering itself as an NBFC-MFI would be that they would not be able to claim benefits of the priority sector advances on their lending which makes it easier to access bulk funds from the banks (bank borrowings in 2013–14 were only ₹1.1 million as against assets under management of ₹2.97 billion). The model benefits from the securitisation deals being undertaken by the sister institutions as well as has access to other sources of funds. A large part of the activity is also off-balance sheet and it allows KGFS to earn some commissions and fee-based income which was about 13% of the revenue. This model, however, is yet to prove its profitability on a sustained basis. Both in 2012–13 and in 2013–14 the total losses suffered by IFMR rural channels were higher than its revenues. The sustainability at scale is something that this model needs to demonstrate.

The integrated model of KGFS is undergoing a rigorous research investigation on the impacts it has created in its area. The early findings of the research are:

- In areas serviced by a branch, the incidence of outstanding formal borrowing is 40% higher and the number of formal loans has increased by roughly 20% per household.
- The fraction of households reporting any outstanding informal loans was 11% lower in areas serviced by KGFS and the average outstanding informal loan amount was one sixth lower.
- The arrival of KGFS resulted in both a substantial increase in outstanding formal loans and decline in borrowing from informal channels.

*Source:* Author's interviews with IFMR Rural Channels; Handout: KGFS Impact on Lending Patterns (2–14 February) and http://ruralchannels.ifmr.co.in/, accessed on 13 September 2015.

## LOCAL AREA BANKS

Is this a year in which the RBI would have initiated a process of winding down the category of LABs as one category of banks? Something that started 17 years ago appears to be nearing a cycle of completion and leading to reinvention. Is it curtains for LABs?—is a question we necessarily need to ask, with the RBI opening up the space for SFBs and allowing the LABs also to apply for a conversion. While two of the four LABs have applied for an SFB licence, only one of them has managed to get a licence to become an SFB. The SFBs encompass all the functions that the LABs were undertaking and offer more. Of the four LABs that existed, Capital LAB based out of Jalandhar (Punjab) can be classified as the most successful and profitable. It also commanded more than 70% of the business of the LABs. While during inception, the LABs were expected to operate in three contiguous districts, in 2014, the RBI permitted LABs to expand their operations on a selective basis by offering more districts to the banks based on their capital and performance.

With the change in the format of the Trend and Progress of Banking in India report put out by the RBI, the data of LABs were not available at a centralised location. All the LABs together had an asset growth of 20% in 2013–14 but their profitability declined by 21% (RBI, 2014).

### Capital LAB[1]

Of the four banks Capital LAB was the largest with a total business of ₹24.36 billion as of March 2015. (The figure for 2013–14 was ₹20.21 billion.) Capital LAB grew its business by 27% during the year 2013–14 and by 20% in 2014–15. It remained profitable with an interest spread of 4.02% and 3.87%, respectively, for the past two years. Its portfolio also remained healthy with the gross NPA of less than half a percent. The bank also operated with a capital adequacy ratio of over 15%.

### Coastal LAB[2]

The next largest bank was Coastal LAB. It had a total business of ₹3.37 billion as of March 2014 and grew to 4.95 billion by March 2015. Coastal LAB remained profitable with an interest spread of over 7.5%. Its portfolio also remained healthy with the gross NPA of less than a percent. The high interest spread was a function of its high level of capital. The bank operated with a capital adequacy ratio of

[1] Data for this section sourced from the website of Capital LAB at http://www.capitalbank.co.in/index.php/financial-results, accessed on 13 September 2015.

[2] Data for this section sourced from the website of Coastal LAB at http://www.coastalareabank.com/, accessed on 13 September 2015.

over 24%. While the total net worth of Coastal LAB was around ₹414 million, it did apply for an SFB licence. It is possible that the promoters were willing to pump in more capital to meet the requirement of ₹1 billion for setting up an SFB.

### KBS LAB[3]

The numbers for KBS LAB was only available as of 2013–14. The bank had a total business of ₹300 million, with a gross NPA of under 2% (it was 3% in 2012–13). KBS LAB had a CD ratio of more than 80%. Its capital adequacy was also very high at 25% again indicating that it had not leveraged its capital enough and thus not attracted deposits, while the bank seemed to have lending opportunities indicated by the high CD ratio. The bank was making consistent profits in the previous few years. The total net worth of KBS LAB was ₹280 million. This amount was far away from the capital requirement for applying for an SFB licence and possibly was the reason why KBS LAB did not apply for a licence.

### Subhadra LAB[4]

Subhadra was the smallest bank of the lot, just crossing a total business of ₹1 billion during the year 2014–15, operating with mere 10 branches. During the year it also had a high NPA of 2.79%, a high CD ratio of more than 100% indicating its inability to attract enough deposits and lending out of its capital. Subhadra also did not apply for an SFB licence. The possible reason for the LAB not to consider the SFB format could have been its lack of capital. While the capital requirements for LABs were ₹50 million when they started, Subhadra had a total net worth of ₹300 million as of March 2015. The capital requirements for the new SFB were stipulated at ₹1 billion which it possibly could not raise.

## CONCLUDING NOTES

It is clear from the data that RRBs have a significant role to play in the larger agenda of inclusion. With the culmination of consolidation that has happened over the past five years laying a strong basis, and with the capitalisation programme bringing in adequate capital and with the RRBs turning in consistent profits the next phase of growth and how this growth would continue to be inclusive would be interesting to watch. The fact that the legal provisions have been amended to bring in capital from outside is positive. This would be tested on the ground, and if the RRBs are successful in raising capital from other sources, that would be evidence to prove that they have come of age.

On innovations, the model of KGFS seems interesting, though the model is yet to break even and establish its viability unequivocally. It also appears that with the new applications for the SFBs the way forward for the LABs would be to eventually merge, wind down or morph into an SFB. The consolidation of the RRBs also points out to the general directionality that the policy environment is looking at larger institutions serving the cause of the poor.

[3] Data for this section sourced from the website of KBS LAB http://kbsbankindia.com/downloads/AUDITED_RESULTS_2013_14.pdf, accessed on 13 September 2015.

[4] Data for this section sourced from the website of Subhadra LAB at http://www.subhadrabank.com/, accessed on 13 September 2015.

## APPENDIX 3.1
## Deposits and credit (including credit of small borrowal accounts) of RRBs as of March 2014

| Region | No. of offices | Deposits (balance) | | Total credit (outstanding) | | Of which: credit to small borrowers (outstanding) | |
|---|---|---|---|---|---|---|---|
| | | No. of accounts (million) | Amount (₹ billion) | No. of accounts (million) | Amount (₹ billion) | No. of accounts (million) | Amount (₹ billion) |
| **North** | **2,618** | **14.0** | **321.7** | **1.6** | **220.5** | **1.2** | **88.6** |
| Haryana | 553 | 3.47 | 86.24 | 0.40 | 58.15 | 0.30 | 23.86 |
| Himachal Pradesh | 189 | 0.84 | 24.62 | 0.09 | 9.53 | 0.07 | 3.43 |
| Jammu & Kashmir | 288 | 1.19 | 28.98 | 0.12 | 12.39 | 0.09 | 5.03 |
| Punjab | 332 | 1.56 | 44.81 | 0.18 | 36.89 | 0.11 | 8.24 |
| Rajasthan | 1,256 | 6.93 | 137.02 | 0.85 | 103.50 | 0.66 | 48.05 |
| **North-east** | **721** | **8.3** | **133.0** | **0.9** | **65.2** | **0.8** | **30.6** |
| Arunachal Pradesh | 26 | 0.10 | 3.16 | 0.01 | 0.56 | 0.00 | 0.13 |
| Assam | 409 | 5.51 | 68.48 | 0.55 | 38.23 | 0.51 | 21.18 |
| Manipur | 22 | 0.18 | 1.45 | 0.01 | 0.56 | 0.01 | 0.30 |
| Meghalaya | 60 | 0.30 | 9.83 | 0.03 | 4.74 | 0.03 | 1.20 |
| Mizoram | 66 | 0.39 | 13.16 | 0.04 | 6.19 | 0.03 | 1.91 |
| Nagaland | 11 | 0.02 | 0.73 | 0.00 | 0.24 | 0.00 | 0.07 |
| Tripura | 127 | 1.83 | 36.23 | 0.24 | 14.65 | 0.21 | 5.85 |
| **East** | **4,057** | **30** | **472** | **5** | **249** | **4** | **157** |
| Bihar | 1,785 | 11.84 | 182.85 | 2.10 | 100.32 | 2.04 | 77.72 |
| Jharkhand | 428 | 2.38 | 41.31 | 0.45 | 16.41 | 0.43 | 10.67 |
| Odisha | 910 | 6.06 | 110.07 | 1.13 | 66.68 | 1.06 | 38.61 |
| West Bengal | 934 | 9.93 | 137.54 | 1.05 | 65.13 | 0.96 | 29.80 |
| **Central** | **5,821** | **56** | **720** | **6** | **400** | **5** | **234** |
| Chhattisgarh | 575 | 4.05 | 65.52 | 0.35 | 20.82 | 0.32 | 13.62 |
| Madhya Pradesh | 1,221 | 7.88 | 142.30 | 0.97 | 79.60 | 0.87 | 47.94 |
| Uttar Pradesh | 3,772 | 43.24 | 487.41 | 4.41 | 284.94 | 3.95 | 166.85 |
| Uttarakhand | 253 | 1.02 | 24.67 | 0.12 | 15.13 | 0.10 | 5.32 |
| **West** | **1,294** | **8** | **142** | **1** | **88** | **1** | **46** |
| Goa | | | – | – | – | – | – |
| Gujarat | 602 | 3.49 | 71.14 | 0.39 | 38.33 | 0.34 | 17.96 |
| Maharashtra | 692 | 4.37 | 71.17 | 0.59 | 49.36 | 0.54 | 28.18 |
| **South** | **4,028** | **34** | **544** | **7** | **566** | **7** | **366** |
| Andhra Pradesh | 1,562 | 15.24 | 204.45 | 3.23 | 237.11 | 2.96 | 156.99 |
| Karnataka | 1,510 | 11.60 | 214.89 | 1.92 | 181.59 | 1.74 | 98.55 |
| Kerala | 536 | 4.60 | 76.93 | 1.20 | 88.91 | 1.13 | 60.49 |
| Tamil Nadu | 389 | 2.38 | 44.99 | 0.99 | 55.85 | 0.96 | 47.07 |
| Lakshadweep | | 0.00 | – | – | – | – | – |
| Puducherry | 31 | 0.15 | 2.77 | 0.05 | 3.02 | 0.05 | 2.80 |
| All India | 18,539 | 151 | 2,333 | 21 | 1,589 | 19 | 922 |

*Source:* RBI Datawarehouse at http://dbie.rbi.org.in/

### APPENDIX 3.2
### Deposits of RRBs as of 31 March 2014

| Region/state/ union territory | No. of offices | Accounts in '000 | | | | (Amount in ₹ billion) | | | |
| | | Current | | Savings | | Term | | Total | |
| | | No. of accounts | Amount | No. of accounts | Amount | No. of accounts | Amount | No. of accounts | Amount |
|---|---|---|---|---|---|---|---|---|---|
| **North** | **2,618** | **302.27** | **7.07** | **12,066** | **160** | **1,627.49** | **154.31** | **13,995** | **322** |
| Haryana | 553 | 22.35 | 1.76 | 3,247 | 48 | 199.98 | 36.70 | 3,469 | 86 |
| Himachal | 189 | 9.21 | 0.36 | 633 | 9 | 201.18 | 15.44 | 844 | 25 |
| J&K | 288 | 26.62 | 1.23 | 951 | 14 | 216.75 | 13.48 | 1,194 | 29 |
| Punjab | 332 | 178.27 | 1.06 | 1,202 | 19 | 181.84 | 24.82 | 1,562 | 45 |
| Rajasthan | 1,256 | 65.82 | 2.67 | 6,032 | 70 | 827.74 | 63.87 | 6,926 | 137 |
| **North-east** | **721** | **207.77** | **11.64** | **7,466** | **75** | **648.66** | **46.19** | **8,322** | **133** |
| Arunachal | 26 | 1.88 | 0.51 | 83 | 1 | 11.43 | 1.20 | 96 | 3 |
| Assam | 409 | 137.88 | 4.97 | 4,950 | 41 | 424.73 | 22.90 | 5,513 | 68 |
| Manipur | 22 | 6.18 | 0.19 | 163 | 1 | 7.25 | 0.46 | 176 | 1 |
| Meghalaya | 60 | 6.32 | 0.32 | 266 | 6 | 23.05 | 3.58 | 296 | 10 |
| Mizoram | 66 | 2.46 | 3.00 | 380 | 6 | 11.68 | 3.78 | 394 | 13 |
| Nagaland | 11 | 0.22 | 0.12 | 14 | 0 | 1.64 | 0.27 | 16 | 1 |
| Tripura | 127 | 52.84 | 2.53 | 1,610 | 20 | 168.87 | 14.00 | 1,832 | 36 |
| **East** | **4,057** | **294.03** | **15.42** | **25,939** | **266** | **3,989.75** | **190.37** | **30,223** | **472** |
| Bihar | 1,785 | 141.16 | 9.15 | 10,436 | 115 | 1,266.48 | 58.24 | 11,844 | 183 |
| Jharkhand | 428 | 5.11 | 0.70 | 2,068 | 24 | 311.42 | 16.54 | 2,385 | 41 |
| Odisha | 910 | 73.53 | 1.93 | 4,984 | 57 | 1,005.73 | 51.05 | 6,063 | 110 |
| West Bengal | 934 | 74.23 | 3.64 | 8,450 | 69 | 1,406.12 | 64.55 | 9,931 | 138 |
| **Central** | **5,821** | **649.38** | **30.68** | **50,995** | **450** | **4,550.82** | **239.46** | **56,195** | **720** |
| Chhattisgarh | 575 | 61.38 | 3.19 | 3,690 | 45 | 294.95 | 17.72 | 4,047 | 66 |
| Madhya Pradesh | 1,221 | 100.08 | 5.66 | 6,852 | 68 | 930.89 | 68.16 | 7,883 | 142 |
| Uttar Pradesh | 3,772 | 478.93 | 20.90 | 39,630 | 324 | 3,133.06 | 142.38 | 43,242 | 487 |
| Uttarakhand | 253 | 8.99 | 0.92 | 822 | 13 | 191.93 | 11.21 | 1,023 | 25 |
| **West** | **1,294** | **79.36** | **3.39** | **6,978** | **71** | **801.10** | **68.15** | **7,858** | **142** |
| Gujarat | 602 | 43.02 | 1.73 | 2,934 | 27 | 510.53 | 42.00 | 3,488 | 71 |
| Maharashtra | 692 | 36.34 | 1.66 | 4,043 | 43 | 290.58 | 26.15 | 4,370 | 71 |
| **South** | **4,028** | **427.62** | **16.75** | **29,326** | **182** | **4,216.23** | **345.11** | **33,969** | **544** |
| Andhra Pradesh | 1,562 | 68.18 | 6.59 | 13,537 | 66 | 1,631.13 | 132.07 | 15,236 | 204 |
| Karnataka | 1,510 | 191.38 | 7.81 | 9,714 | 74 | 1,695.53 | 133.07 | 11,601 | 215 |
| Kerala | 536 | 137.15 | 2.05 | 3,930 | 26 | 534.83 | 48.60 | 4,602 | 77 |
| Tamil Nadu | 389 | 29.43 | 0.25 | 2,007 | 16 | 343.50 | 29.19 | 2,380 | 45 |
| Puducherry | 31 | 1.47 | 0.05 | 137 | 1 | 11.25 | 2.17 | 150 | 3 |
| All-India | 18,539 | 1,960.43 | 84.95 | 132,768 | 1,204 | 15,834.06 | 1,043.58 | 150,563 | 2,333 |

*Source:* RBI Datawarehouse at http://dbie.rbi.org.in/

## REFERENCES

Pant-Joshi, D. (2013). *Inagural Address: Conference of Principal Code Compliance Officers and Chairmen of RRBs.* Mumbai: RBI.

RBI (1954). *All India Rural Credit Survey Committee Report.* Mumbai: RBI.

———— (2014). *Financial Stability Report (Including the Trend and Progress of Banking in India).* Mumbai: RBI.

# A review of Pradhan Mantri Jan Dhan Yojana*

## CONTEXT

Why are people excluded from the banking system? Should the agenda of inclusion be looked from the pull side, as to why people do not open accounts, or from the push side as to why the financial institutions do not provide the banking facilities to the excluded? These are difficult questions for the state to grapple with, when it comes to the agenda of inclusion. The Global Findex report gives a glimpse of why people do not deal with formal banking institutions for parking their savings. The results (see Figure 4.1) should throw some light on the strategy to be adopted by the state.

## PMJDY: A NEW APPROACH TO FINANCIAL INCLUSION

The approach of the state towards greater financial inclusion followed two strategies: First, setting up of new institutions like RRBs and MUDRA; second, providing policy directions for existing institutions to actively participate in the inclusion agenda. The launch of the PMJDY was different in its approach as it took the issue of inclusion from a supply side—passive architecture building project to the next level—the saturation of the demand side by adopting both the 'push' and the 'pull' strategies. There is another significant change of approach which had started during the earlier phase which is being reinforced by the PMJDY. The past inclusion efforts were aimed at 'ameliorating the poor from the clutches of the oppressive money lender', thereby putting institutional credit at the

centrepiece of the efforts. That was the case with the setting up of cooperative credit societies following the All India Rural Credit Survey Committee Report, the Integrated Rural Development Programme (IRDP) and the Swarna Jayanti Gram Swarozgar Yojana (SGSY). It was only the SHGBLP that moved the primacy from credit to savings. The Swavalamban programme was one of the few

**Self-reported barriers to use of an account at a financial institution**
Adults without an account reporting barrier as a reason for not having one (%), 2014

**Figure 4.1** Barriers for financial inclusion

*Source:* Demirguc-Kunt, Asli, Leora Klapper, Dorothe Singer, and Peter Van Oudheusden. 2015. 'The Global Findex Database 2014: Measuring Financial Inclusion around the World.' Policy Research Working Paper 7255, World Bank, Washington, DC.

---

*The author is thankful to Shri Anurag Jain, Joint Secretary, PMO and earlier Joint Secretary in the Department of Financial Services (DFS), Ministry of Finance, for explaining the process of implementing the PMJDY during his stint at DFS. The author has also drawn from public sources and other conversations in working on this chapter. While the author is thankful for the inputs of Shri Jain, he takes sole responsibility for any shortcomings.

programmes that not only put the bank at the centre, but also talked about multiple financial services and had the starting point as savings. The PMJDY not only reinforces the aspect of savings, it also takes it beyond to the next stage of social security through insurance.

The policy thrust is evident from the focus that the union government is giving to the PMJDY—an ambitious scheme to ensure that every household in the country would have access to a bank account. This account would be bundled with an insurance cover, a debit card and an overdraft facility. In addition, the finance minister not only talked about the achievements of PMJDY, but termed that as a game-changing reform, bundled with Aadhaar and Mobile (Jaitley, 2015, pp. 2–3). The intent of the government in making this a cornerstone of its inclusion agenda was reiterated in the announcement made about Pradhan Mantri Jeevan Jyoti Bima Yojana that provides life cover, Pradhan Mantri Bima Suraksha Yojana that provides accidental insurance cover and the Atal Pension Yojana that provides pension cover to the excluded.

The launch of PMDJY on this ambitious scale was possible because of the strong foundation laid out on the banking architecture that was available. The banking architecture laid out till 2014 had taken the physical penetration of brick and mortar branches and touchpoints (through multiple initiatives) deep into the country side. This provided a base for a mission approach to move beyond the physical infrastructure to the customers and to get the customers to the formal banking outlet. This phase can be seen as a phase where demand side and supply side are shaking hands. Also, it was important to note that the implementation of the scheme hinged on two aspects: (a) attention to detail and (b) monitoring and mid-course correction. The documents put out by the government seem to indicate that both these aspects were taken care of. Table 4.1 lists the differences between Swabhimaan approach and PMJDY approach.

**Table 4.1  The differences between Swabhimaan approach and PMJDY approach**

| Swabhimaan approach | PMJDY approach |
|---|---|
| Villages with population greater than 2,000 covered; thus limited geographical coverage | Focus on household: Sub-service area (SSA) for coverage of the whole country |
| Only rural | Both rural and urban |
| Bank Mitr (Business Correspondent) was visiting on fixed days only | Fixed point Bank Mitr in each SSA comprising 1,000 to 1,500 households (3 to 4 villages on an average) to visit other villages in the SSA on fixed days |
| Offline accounts opening—Technology lock in with the vendor | Only online accounts in core banking solution (CBS) of the bank |
| Focus on account opening and large number of accounts remained dormant | Account opening to be integrated with DBT, credit, insurance and pension |
| Interoperability of accounts was not there | Interoperability through RuPay Debit Card, AEPS, etc. |
| No use of Mobile Banking | Mobile wallet and USSD-based mobile banking to be utilised |
| Cumbersome KYC formalities | Simplified KYC/eKYC in place as per RBI guidelines |
| No guidelines on the remuneration of the Bank Mitr; Banks went generally with Corporate BCs who used to be least expensive to them | Minimum remuneration of the Bank Mitr to be ₹5,000 (fixed + variable) |
| A recent RBI survey finds that 47% of the Bank Mitr are unreachable | Viability and sustainability of Bank Mitr is identified as a critical component |
| Monitoring left to banks | Financial inclusion campaign in Mission Mode with structured monitoring mechanism at Centre, state and district level |
| Financial literacy had no focus | The rural branches of banks to have a dedicated Financial Literacy Cell |
| No active involvement of states/districts | State level and district level monitoring committees to be set up |
| No brand visibility of the Programme and Bank Mitr | Brand visibility for the programme and Bank Mitr proposed |
| Providing credit facilities was not encouraged | Overdraft limit after satisfactory operations/credit history of 6 months |
| No grievance redressal mechanism | Grievance redressal at SLBC level in respective states |

*Source:* Pradhan Mantri Jan Dhan Yojana: A National Mission for Financial Inclusion. New Delhi: Department of Financial Services, Ministry of Finance, Government of India, 2014.

However, for the financial inclusion agenda to move further, it would be the next phase of the inclusion challenge that would be the most meaningful. That is to make the customers use the accounts that they have opened.

When the Prime Minister announced the launch of PMJDY in August 2014, and handed an accelerated target to reach every household by January 2015 (Phase I), it was clear that the banking system had to leverage on the investments made in the past. It was also clear that the methodology was mission mode and the target was saturation. But the banking architecture alone was not sufficient for this agenda to be taken forward and there were many bits and pieces of the jigsaw that had to be arranged. This year will go down as a year of implementation challenges and out of the box ideas in implementation of a large national agenda.

The PMJDY rested on six pillars and was to be rolled out in two phases. The six pillars were:

- Universal access to banking services
  - Each district to have a sub-service area (SSA) covering 1,000 to 1,500 households
  - Banking service to be available within a reasonable distance of about 5 kilometre radius
- Providing basic banking accounts, with overdraft facilities and a RuPay debit card
- Financial Literacy Programme
- Creation of a Credit Guarantee Fund
- Providing micro insurance
- Providing unorganised sector pension scheme

In the Phase I, it was expected that the first three pillars will be covered.

The basic banking services covered four essential services of deposit and withdrawal, remittances, balance enquiry and a getting a mini statement on demand.

## EXISTING INFRASTRUCTURE

On the 'push' side, the task was to look at leveraging the banking architecture. All the banks in India were already on an interoperable technology platform. Therefore, the challenge of the technology handshake was at the last mile between the bank and the customer touchpoint. The design adequately addressed the issue, by identifying that the BC scheme had several lacunae and these were to be addressed quickly. The most important changes that the PMJDY approach implemented was to:

- convert a roving BC into a fixed point BC;
- make BCs interoperable using the Aadhaar bridge;

- assure a minimum return to the BC;
- put the BC touchpoint directly in contact with the bank's core database on a real time basis;
- augment the infrastructure of the BC by providing a loan of ₹50,000 for equipment, ₹25,000 for working capital and ₹50,000 for purchase of a two wheeler;
- eliminate 'missing' BCs and recruit new individual BCs as per the guidelines; and
- leverage 126,000 common service centres spread across the country (of which only 12,284 were BCs of banks) to undertake banking activities as well, by enrolling the rest as BCs.

Making BCs interoperable also addressed the issue of BC viability by providing a mass customer base who could have been potentially splintered between multiple banks.

With the government deciding not only to continue the enrolments under the unique identification project, but also to strengthen and continue issuing Aadhaar numbers, one of the single largest constraints of providing an identity and an address proof for the excluded to come into the mainstream banking system was addressed. With the RBI making eKYC an acceptable way of identity verification, this activity could be done without any paper work and with very minimal costs. A total of 650 million residents were already covered under Aadhaar when the PMJDY started (GoI, 2014a). This number stands at 901 million as of the end of August 2015.

The telecom network penetration was another bonus that could potentially help the PMJDY. Of the 0.59 million villages across the country, except for about 50,000 villages all other villages were covered by telecom connectivity (GoI, 2014a). While the PMJDY could leverage the existing network, the plan identified the areas that needed strengthening and also following up with the national telecom service provider—Bharat Sanchar Nigam Limited (BSNL)—to cover the rest of the villages with tele services. A nationwide telecom network indicated 76% penetration with 886 million mobile connections with technology backbone available for undertaking banking transactions through the mobile platform. The infrastructure included Immediate Payment System (IMPS) for which standards and protocols were already in place.

Pilot schemes for transfer of benefits directly into the accounts of the beneficiaries were already underway. The transfer of subsidy on cooking gas (liquefied petroleum gas: LPG) directly into the accounts and mapping the accounts with the Aadhaar number was already rolled out in 291 districts from 1st June 2013 in six phases. However, the implementation of DBTs with modifications on review of the experience was relaunched in 54 districts in November 2014 and across the country in January 2015 (GoI, undated). While LPG connections and DBT scheme may not have resulted in pulling the customers to open more bank accounts—as it was expected that LPG customers did not necessarily represent the poorer and excluded segments of the society—the proof of concept of mapping bank accounts for a specific benefit transfer through the use of a unique identity number was possible and was working. This created the platform for the government to design PMJDY where the government identified 26 centrally sponsored schemes involving eight different ministries that could push cash into the accounts of the beneficiaries (GoI, 2014). This potentially would provide the transaction throughput for the PMJDY accounts.

### Push strategy

The 'push' side implementation also broke down the tasks into smaller bits, by taking an SSA saturation approach and holding a specific agency responsible for the achievement of targets. These were monitored on a weekly basis. Not only was the progress monitored on a weekly basis, but there were two tasks to be undertaken in order to achieve universal coverage. First, a survey of households would reveal what the universe was, and progress could be monitored through the coverage. Second, for the residual households that might not have been surveyed, the strategy adopted was a 'pull' strategy. This was to be achieved by declaring saturation and inviting people to challenge the claim in case of an exclusion due to error of omission. This was done through local media coverage. The government also set up call centres at the national and regional levels for handling grievances. The lead bank was given the task of setting up a call centre that would address the concerns of the customers in their local language.

### Pull strategy

On the 'pull' side were three elements that the programme design made people to throng the bank branches even as the bankers were organising enrolment camps. The 'pull' elements were pertaining to:

- massive media campaign that was launched by the government and the buzz it created across the country;
- offer of accidental death insurance on all the accounts that were opened under the scheme—a scheme that was riding on the RuPay card's inherent product design;
- offer of a potential overdraft facility; and
- making the application form simpler and reducing the size from six pages to a single page.

As a result of the efforts in the Phase I, the banking system had achieved some impressive numbers which are reflected in Table 4.2. What is important to note is that a significant proportion of the new accounts opened (67%) had zero balance. With this statistic, it can be said that the push strategy had taken the banks to the vicinity of the customers; the pull strategy had got the customers to do the first hand-shake but the third and most important piece of filling this hand-shake with transactions to keep the accounts live and meaningful was still unfinished.

A look at the numbers beyond the first phase shows that as against 125.5 million accounts opened between August 2014 and January 2015,

**Table 4.2  PMJDY performance in Phase I**

| Bank category | Rural (No. in million) | Urban (No. in million) | Total A/cs opened (million) | No. of RuPay cards (million) | Balance (Amt ₹ billion) | No. of A/cs with '0' balance (million) | Average balance per active A/c (₹) |
|---|---|---|---|---|---|---|---|
| Public sector banks | 53.3 | 45.1 | 98.4 | 91.2 | 81.74 | 65.5 | 2,484 |
| Percentage share | 71% | 89% | 78% | 82% | 78% | 78% | |
| RRBs | 18.5 | 3.3 | 21.8 | 15.0 | 15.99 | 15.9 | 2,733 |
| Percentage share | 25% | 7% | 17% | 14% | 15% | 19% | |
| Private banks | 3.2 | 2.0 | 5.2 | 4.6 | 7.25 | 3.0 | 3,237 |
| Percentage shares | 4% | 4% | 4% | 4% | 7% | 4% | |
| Grand Total | 75.0 | 50.5 | 125.5 | 110.8 | 104.99 | 84.5 | 2,561 |

*Source:* PMJDY performance report, Phase 1, http://pmjdy.gov.in/account-statistics-country.aspx, accessed on 20 August 2015.

**Table 4.3** PMDJY performance after Phase I (up to August 2015)

| Bank category | Rural (No. in million) | Urban (No. in million) | Total A/cs opened (million) | No. of RuPay cards (million) | Balance (Amt ₹ billion) | No. of A/cs with '0' balance (million) | Average balance per active A/c (₹) |
|---|---|---|---|---|---|---|---|
| Public sector banks | 75.3 | 61.9 | 137.2 | 126.2 | 175.57 | 62.1 | 2,612 |
| Percentage share | 71% | 89% | 78% | 81% | 78% | 77% | |
| RRBs | 26.8 | 4.6 | 31.4 | 23.2 | 37.48 | 15.0 | 2,271 |
| Percentage share | 25% | 7% | 17% | 15% | 17% | 19% | |
| Private banks | 4.2 | 2.8 | 7.0 | 6.2 | 10.89 | 3.2 | 2,943 |
| Percentage shares | 4% | 4% | 4% | 4% | 5% | 4% | |
| Grand total | 106.3 | 69.3 | 175.7 | 155.6 | 223.94 | 80.4 | 2,349 |

*Source:* PMJDY performance report, Phase 1, http://pmjdy.gov.in/account-statistics-country.aspx, accessed on 20 August 2015.

only 50.5 million incremental accounts were opened in the period up to August 2015, indicating that the campaign mode might have yielded results and the numbers were near saturation and the residual was small, slow and painful to include (Table 4.3). The August 2015 numbers showed that about 45% of the accounts were having zero balance indicating that the other accounts were having some balance. The average balance in the accounts having non-zero balances had fallen marginally, but was around ₹2,300.

## CHALLENGES WITH PHASE I

The mission mode in which the financial inclusion drive was carried out posed its own challenges. One of the challenges was related to the 'pull' communication. With the publicity pertaining to insurance as well as the overdraft facility, there were apprehensions that people were opening new accounts, while they already had an account in the bank, leading to duplication. The added fact was that the bank staff members were also working with a stiff target against a hard deadline. It was estimated that in the first 5 crore accounts that were opened 20% of the accounts were not exclusive accounts (Jain, 2015). The ministry resorted to a mid-course correction by issuing a circular on 15th September 2014 indicating that if customers are having existing accounts, they were eligible for a RuPay card as well as the associated benefits of the PMJDY account (GoI, 2014b). In addition to the issue of the circular, exclusion was being assessed by carrying out a household survey. This issue of capturing the details of pre-existing accounts was highlighted in the survey. By the time the enrolments went up to 130 million accounts, the non-exclusive accounts had gone up

to 15 million accounts in number, but significantly lower in proportion.

The foolproof way in which the above challenge could be met was by mapping the new PMJDY accounts with Aadhaar. The circular on the 29th of September 2014 made Aadhaar an essential piece of the PMJDY campaign (GoI, 2015). The circular made three significant points:

- Aadhaar numbers will be a part of every bank account opened under JDY.
- To the extent possible Aadhaar numbers will be used as eKYC for opening bank accounts.
- Wherever Aadhaar enrolment is lagging, UIDAI will coordinate with the banks to ensure that Aadhaar enrolment takes place at the time of opening the bank account itself.

It is evident that much of overcoming the challenges was dependent on making Aadhaar the centrepiece of the programme.

There were other challenges in the scheme as well. While there was an insurance product loaded on to the PMJDY, this was in fact a product that was available ex-ante, designed by the National Payments Corporation of India (NPCI). This insurance cover for disability/death due to an accident was available only to RuPay card holders subject to the condition that they had used the card at least once in a 45-day window. While the card itself would usually be valid for a period of 7 years from the month of issue, the insurance cover would not be available if the card was not used at least once in a 45-day window. This stipulation was essentially introduced in the RuPay card to popularise the use of these cards. With a large proportion of accounts having zero balance, it was quite likely that there would be no card-based transaction and therefore the insurance cover might not eventually be available to the customer. Since this scheme was an incentive for card usage, changing the window to a larger time frame would not help. The government therefore, through the budget speech of the finance minister in February 2015, introduced two insurance products (accident and life) which could be linked to the PMJDY account, with an auto debit of insurance premium, thereby ensuring that the account was active if the customer opted for these programmes and these accounts would have some balance accounts.

## PUSH AND PULL IN PHASE II

The four items for roll-out in Phase II is now being offered, though not at the same pace at which the Phase I was rolled out. The strategy for the new insurance and pension schemes was largely through extensive campaigning in the media and a pull towards the bank. By linking these schemes to the PMJDY account, the government has provided a single one-stop service. The enrolments on these schemes are picking up.

The most attractive aspect of the PMJDY was the assumption that everybody who has an account will be naturally eligible for an overdraft. This element had to be seen a bit carefully. The checks introduced by the scheme should help the customers to transact more. The government issued a circular that if the account is more than 6 months old, an overdraft facility could be issued to the customer under the following conditions:

- the account should be seeded to the Aadhaar number (thus ensuring that the same person would not borrow from multiple accounts);

- the amount of overdraft would be the lower of 50% of credit summations in an account or 6 monthly average balance maintained in the account, subject to a maximum of ₹5,000;
- the interest rate would be 2% above base rate;
- the duration would be for a maximum period of 36 months; and
- all benefits under the various DBT schemes would be transferred to this account, thereby providing for natural credits to reduce the overdraft balance.

The achievements in terms of numbers after the roll-out of Phase I and Phase II of the PMJDY are given in Table 4.4.

## DISCUSSION ON THE APPROACH, SHORTCOMINGS AND PATHWAYS FOR PMJDY

As indicated in the beginning of this chapter, the mission approach to open bank accounts has been a great idea and the design of the scheme of implementation has been detailed with adequate midcourse correction taken. The impacts of this would be felt only when these accounts become quickly meaningful for the beneficiaries. The numbers in Table 4.4 are an indication of the difficult path and a distant goal to be covered to make inclusion under PMJDY more meaningful. As the table indicates, while there is significant progress in the reduction of zero balance accounts, it is still a sizeable number. Given that the bedrock of the overdraft account has been linking the account to the Aadhaar number and less than 50% of the new accounts have been linked to Aadhaar, this is a long path to be

**Table 4.4  Summary statistics on the PMJDY as of 1 August 2015**

| | |
|---|---|
| Total number of PMJDY accounts opened | 175.6 million accounts |
| Total number of PMJDY accounts with zero balance | 80 million accounts |
| Number of accounts where RuPay card was issued | 155.6 million accounts |
| Number of accounts with Aadhaar seeding | 72.7 million accounts |
| Number of accounts provided with overdraft facility | 108,000 accounts |
| Beneficiaries under Pradhan Mantri Suraksha Beema Yojana (accident insurance) | 66.2 million customers |
| Beneficiaries under Pradhan Mantri Jeevan Jyoti Beema Yojana (life insurance) | 22.2 million customers |
| Beneficiaries under the Atal Pension Yojana (pension) | 588,000 customers |
| Claims settled under life insurance cover of ₹30,000 provided as an incentive to open PMJDY accounts between August 2014 and January 2015 | 742 (Nos.) |
| Claims settled under the accident insurance of ₹1 lakh associated with RuPay card | 208 (Nos.) |

*Source:* PMJDY Progress Report available at http://pmjdy.gov.in/ArchiveFile/2015/8/12.08.2015.pdf and Press Note dated 12 August 2015 available at http://pmjdy.gov.in/press_release.aspx both, accessed on 21 August 2015.

<table>
<tr><td>

**Box 4.1 Governor Rajan on PMJDY**

**Approach to financial inclusion: PMJDY**

*Professor Sriram:* We have both Reserve Bank of India (RBI) and the Government of India (GoI) being interested in this agenda in a big way and the objectives of both RBI and GoI are converging. However, while the objectives may be converging, are the paths really converging? If they are not, then how do we manage this? I ask this in the backdrop of the ambitious announcement that the GoI made about the PMJDY and the caution that RBI has tried to exercise on the scheme.

*Dr Rajan:* Historically, if we outline the paths of the government and the RBI, we implicitly believe that a push is needed and given a sufficient push, it can become self-sustaining. Now, over time we have discovered that it hasn't become self-sustaining. So, either the push hasn't been enough or that the notion that sufficient push will create self-sustainability itself is wrong. There is something else that needs to be done and we unfortunately have not found what it is thus far.

With PMJDY the government is giving yet another push and saying let's cover everybody to the extent possible. There is some virtue in this approach. This is because some programmes such as DBTs are intended to be linked to these accounts. These programmes can work well if everybody is covered. If something like Aadhaar is also universal and linked to these accounts, it also helps in measuring the extent of indebtedness. If the coverage is partial, it does not quite work. So, the thrust on universal accounts, Aadhaar and DBT are good.

</td></tr>
</table>

taken. Even when substantial numbers of accounts have been linked to Aadhaar, the overdraft facility has been extended only to about 0.15% of the potentially eligible (Aadhaar-linked) accounts. Most likely these are the accounts that did not otherwise qualify on the average balance or the cumulative credits criteria.

The accident insurance scheme which was initially bundled on the PMJDY accounts was basically bundled as an incentive on the usage of RuPay cards, and given the above statistics where almost half the accounts are having zero balance and the other half are having an average balance of ₹2,349, this added facility would have had marginal impact and it is evident in the number in Table 4.4 where for a total of 15.56 crore RuPay cards issued, the claims were only 208. The government seems to have made a quick mid-course correction on this. While it retained the feature on the RuPay card, it also simultaneously launched the insurance scheme that was unlinked to the card. Again from the statistics above, it can be seen that the accident and life insurance coverage has been availed by a much smaller number and the pension scheme has not picked up steam. The difference between opening of accounts on the mission mode where the investment to be made by the customer was a trip to the branch or to the touchpoint, with no cash outflow to choosing other elements of the six pillars where the customer has to consciously pay (even if a marginal amount) is evident. This would certainly slow down the process of coverage under Phase II.

UIDAI suggests that the mapping of Aadhaar with the bank account will help in seamlessly transferring the insurance compensation to the beneficiary if the nominee's account details are given.

Data is not available on the usage intensity of the RuPay cards to make an assessment. While the banks were advised to issue all the PMJDY-based RuPay cards on a specific Issuer Identification Number (IIN, the first four digits on the 16 digit card number), this has not happened in the field and therefore it is now not possible to track the performance of these cards on how frequently they have been used. Moreover, the NPCI can only track the number of transactions that happen on an interoperable environment and not when the transactions happen within the network of the issuing branch. In an interaction with the bankers conducted at Indian Banks Association, the RuPay cards were identified as the weakest link in the programme. The main issue was not technical—the issue was about delivering the RuPay cards, the personal identification number (PIN) mailer, and then activating the cards. One significant lacuna in the programme was that there was insufficient information sharing with the account holders on the potential of the RuPay card and how it could be used. Given that a significant number of branches that opened the PMJDY accounts were RRBs, they did not have adequate ATMs where even basic transactions such as balance inquiry, mini statement and withdrawal could be made. The ATM network and the ubiquitous presence of POS devices were the two missing blocks in encouraging the usage of opened accounts.

In addition, a large proportion of the accounts were opened with the help of BCs. While BCs were good for opening accounts, the Intermedia tracker (Intermedia, 2015) study has indicated that the BCs were not compensated enough on transactions, and the interoperability and the Aadhaar-enabled payment system (AEPS) bridge was not rolled out throughout the country uniformly—thus creating an infrastructural bottleneck. Therefore, it is obvious that the cards are not being effectively used. Unfortunately since IIN numbering was not strictly observed for PMJDY cards, it is also difficult to track the transactions. The only indicative statistic available for the cards issued by the bank and the insurance claims thereof.

While the approach document indicated that the postal network and the cooperative network will be integral to the roll-out of PMJDY, in implementation it can be seen that it has been only bank led. Even in case of cooperatives, the stipulation of the government was that the cooperatives have to be on a CBS platform and in a position to issue the RuPay card, which naturally puts a significant part of the cooperative network out of this scheme. Similarly the government only talked about using *grameen dak sewaks* (GDSs) where BCs were not effective, or not available.

A study by MicroSave (see Box 4.2) highlighted the major issues in the field at the transaction level. While this study was conducted just two months after the PMJDY was rolled out and some of the issues might have been sorted out, it is important for us to appreciate the complexity of the task involved.

---

**Box 4.2 Findings of the MicroSave Dipstick study on PMJDY**

**Key findings**

We highlight below key findings from the Wave 1 survey (note that Wave 1 was conducted just two months after the launch of PMJDY):

(a) 69% of Bank Mitrs were physically present at the stated location. An additional 11% were working locally, but from a different location than that stated in the lists provided by banks. Therefore, 80% of BMs could be considered 'available'. However, it is unclear what portion of the 11% are fixed point locations (with incorrect address details) and what portion are 'roaming' BMs. Note that all BMs established under PMJDY should be fixed point locations.

(b) Only 48% of BMs were 'transaction ready' when the BMs were visited. We define 'transaction ready' as a customer being able to walk in and conduct a transaction. The 52% of BMs who were not transaction ready cited several factors, including the recentness of their appointment as a BM, lack of a transaction device, technology issues (e.g. downtime) and BM dormancy (often due to inadequate remuneration). Interestingly, lack of liquidity was not cited as a significant issue by BMs, but this may emerge as a challenge once transaction volumes increase.

(c) As mentioned, 11% of BMs were untraceable—they were not found at the address mentioned in the official list, residents did not know about them, and their contact numbers were not reachable.

(d) 48% of BMs had signage of some sort displayed. The bank logo was visible at 22% of outlets and the PMJDY logo was visible at 13% of outlets.

(e) BMs who were present conducted an average of 195 transactions per month (or 6 transactions per day). As a benchmark, the typical (median) agent in Kenya conducts 46 transactions per day. This low level of transaction activity raises concerns about BMs' willingness to continue offering the service. Moreover, only 53% of BMs have received their commission on time.

(f) 86% of PMJDY account holders reported that this was their first bank account. While this number is very encouraging, we should recognise that PMJDY services (e.g. overdraft, insurance, etc.) are marketed to 'first time' account holders, so PMJDY account holders have a strong incentive to report that this is their first account.

(g) 45% of account holders have an Aadhaar number, of which 79% had linked their Aadhaar number with their PMJDY accounts (this linkage enables government departments to deliver government payments using the recipient's Aadhaar number).

(h) 18% of account holders had received their RuPay card.

**Conclusions**

This Wave 1 survey was conducted just over two months after PMJDY was launched. The results show that availability of Bank Mitrs has considerably improved the situation compared to the situation few months ago. Similarly, banks appear to be making a genuine effort to open accounts for previously unbanked households. Banks also appear to be working to resolve the remaining barriers to the PMJDY roll-out, including branding, transaction-readiness, and proper database management by local authorities and banks to identify unbanked households.

Assuming these teething issues are properly dealt with, PMJDY is well positioned for success. Some challenges will take longer to resolve, such as the delivery of RuPay cards, Aadhaar enrolment and account mapping, and the commercial viability of overdraft and insurance services. But there is clear evidence of significant progress towards expanding account access.

*Source:* MicroSave India Focus Note #114 accessed on 21 August 2015, from http://www.microsave.net/files/pdf/IFN_114_Assessment_of_Bank_Mitrs_under_PMJDY.pdf

## OTHER BENEFITS OF PMJDY

While it is evident from the preceding discussion that the roll-out of PMJDY was an exercise in detail and unprecedented in its focus towards the mission, it has had its shortcomings on the difficult part of filling in the transactions after the handshake. However, there has been one significant benefit from the programme. The inventory of RuPay cards before the launch of PMJDY was around 25 million cards. Currently the inventory of cards issued and as reported by the banks to NPCI stands at 187 million cards. It is quite likely that a portion of the 155.6 million cards reported as issued might not have been delivered and reported to NPCI. Even if that number were to be discounted, the initiative is accelerating the inventory of RuPay cards in the eco-system.

Very much the way the Swabhimaan programme had laid the foundation for PMJDY to take off—this initiative might lead to a large number of cashless transactions picking up once the POS network expands. However, it is important to ensure that the momentum is not lost in the process.

## CONCLUDING NOTES

To conclude, PMJDY is one of the most significant events that has happened in the financial inclusion space in the current year, and certainly deserves a complete chapter. While the programme has laid a strong foundation for inclusion, unless the DBT programme, and the usage of RuPay cards picks up steam, there is every danger that these well-intentioned accounts opened with such enthusiasm might remain inoperative. Therefore, there are miles to go and significant numbers are to be achieved in Phase II parameters if successes in Phase I were to be claimed.

## REFERENCES

Government of India (GoI) (2014a). *Pradhan Mantri Jan Dhan Yojana: A National Mission for Financial Inclusion.* New Delhi: GoI, Department of Financial Services, Ministry of Finance.

——— (2014b). *Circular to CMDs of All Public Sector Banks—Number 1/9/2-14-FI dated 15 September 2014.* New Delhi: GoI.

——— (2015). *Circular No. F.No.20/2/2010-FI (Vol. II) addressed to CMDs of Public Sector Banks.* New Delhi: Government of India.

——— (Undated). *Handbook on PAHAL (DBTL) Version 2.0.* New Delhi: Government of India, Ministry of Petroleum and Natural Gas.

Intermedia (2015). *India: Driving Digital Financial Inclusion, Wave 2.* Washington DC: Intermedia.

Jain, Anurag (2015). Personal Communication. New Delhi.

Jaitley, Arun (2015). *Budget 2015–16.* New Delhi: Ministry of Finance, Government of India.

# Technology and the last mile delivery architecture

The most important space to watch out in the inclusion story is the development of technology. Three major initiatives have brought in technology in a big way into the inclusion initiatives.

The first was the policy decision of the RBI to allow banks to appoint BCs—extension agents of the banks to deal with small ticket transactions and reach out to people in remote areas. On the one hand, the RBI allowed banks to appoint agents, and on the other mandated that the banks should have a point of presence in all inhabitations that have a population of more than 2,000. This meant that these agents had to be linked to the banks' accounts in some manner. While the past years have seen multiple models being tried out, the outreach model that will eventually stabilise and scale would be a model that can perform four basic functions of deposit, withdrawal, remittance and balance inquiry and be linked to the bank's database or CBS.

The problems of the last mile connectivity are not exclusively of the poor. These are infrastructural issues to be addressed in any case. The alternatives have been through the physical presence of BCs; through technology-enabled ATMs; or a hybrid presence of BCs hooked to the bank server through an AEPS bridge.

Even the much-talked about PMJDY is universal in its design and does not have a defined target. In that sense, when rural branches, and last mile technology-enabled banking touchpoint, are discussed they are not exclusively targeted at the poor. However, it is assumed that this architecture would greatly benefit the inclusion agenda. Therefore, the discussion of the issues in this chapter should be seen from the perspective of an architecture that also benefits the poor rather than looking at it as an exclusive agenda to foster financial inclusion.

The physical infrastructure for having technology-enabled touchpoints increased significantly in the past four years and concurrently the number of transactions on these platforms also increased. While the statistics on credit cards may not be so relevant to the inclusion numbers, the other infrastructure could be potentially used by all. Table 5.1 clearly indicates the phenomenal growth achieved in the past four years with doubling of both the infrastructure and the transactions. With the aggressive roll-out of PMJDY which would be largely of inclusive customers, this infrastructure has the potential of being used more effectively and more infrastructure rolled out.

## ATMs

The Intermedia FII Tracker survey which does a sample survey to find the financial inclusion indicators found that between the last survey of 2013 and the latest survey of 2014, the access to bank accounts through ATMs had moved up from 26% to 34% of the customers, while the proportion of customers approaching the bank branch had fallen from 98% to 96%. However, other forms of transactions with the bank were really negligible (Intermedia, 2015).

## AADHAAR

To make the above infrastructure work effectively, the next initiative was important. The second initiative was the policy decision of providing a biometric-based identity to every resident through the UIDAI by providing Aadhaar numbers. Unlike the other identity projects in the past, Aadhaar was collecting biometrics of the individuals at the time of registration, de-duplicating those with the data base and thereby providing a unique identity to each individual. Once this unique identity was captured,

**Table 5.1** Data on technology-enabled touchpoints and transactions over the years

| Detail | 2012 | 2013 | 2014 | 2015 | Growth |
|---|---|---|---|---|---|
| Infrastructure | | | | | |
| Onsite ATMs | 47,545 | 55,760 | 83,379 | 89,061 | 87% |
| Offsite ATMs | 48,141 | 58,254 | 76,676 | 92,337 | 92% |
| Online POS | 647,869 | 840,983 | 1,050,323 | 1,126,389 | 74% |
| Offline POS | 13,051 | 13,307 | 15,661 | 346 | −97% |
| Total touchpoints | 756,606 | 968,304 | 1,226,039 | 1,308,133 | 73% |
| Credit cards | | | | | |
| Outstanding credit cards | 17,653,818 | 19,538,329 | 19,181,567 | 21,110,653 | 20% |
| Transactions at ATMs | 202,106 | 225,770 | 296,548 | 437,278 | 116% |
| Transactions at POS | 28,744,710 | 35,616,482 | 46,105,415 | 56,906,942 | 98% |
| Amounts (₹ million) at ATM | 1,209 | 1,493 | 1,662 | 2,344 | 94% |
| Amounts (₹ million) at POS | 88,374 | 111,217 | 145,487 | 178,988 | 103% |
| Debit cards | | | | | |
| Outstanding debit cards | 278,282,839 | 331,196,720 | 394,421,738 | 553,451,553 | 99% |
| Transactions at ATMs | 471,031,623 | 482,004,645 | 571,497,661 | 624,205,135 | 33% |
| Transactions at POS | 30,668,922 | 45,376,619 | 56,981,333 | 76,105,726 | 148% |
| Amounts (₹ million) at ATM | 1,317,168 | 1,556,406 | 1,796,099 | 1,987,480 | 51% |
| Amounts (₹ million) at POS | 46,534 | 66,873 | 85,771 | 108,283 | 133% |

*Source:* RBI website at https://rbi.org.in/scripts/ATMView.aspx?atmid=49 for various years accessed on 19 September 2015, for the table above.
The overall ATM statistics are available at the National Payments Corporation of India website at http://www.npci.org.in/nfsatm.aspx, accessed on 19 September 2015.
*Notes:*
1. The above numbers pertain to the ATMs of 55 scheduled commercial banks in the following ownership category—foreign banks, public sector banks (including IDBI Bank) and old and new private sector banks. However, some foreign banks, Bharatiya Mahila Bank, RRBs and all the cooperative banks (both rural and urban) were left out. Totally there were 207,819 ATMs as of August 2015.
2. Of these, 647 ATMs belonged to RRBs and 10,133 were white label ATMs—independent stand-alone entities providing just the ATM service to the banking sector. The numbers of ATMs owned by RRBs and cooperative banks are discussed in the respective chapters.

then it could be mapped on to the bank account as well. In addition to providing the identity, Aadhaar also built a bridge for undertaking AEPS where customers could access their bank accounts through an independent agent in an interoperable environment. This platform would make it viable for a BC to service a larger number of customers and compete. As of August a total of 900 million numbers were issued (see Figure 5.1) and this forms a solid base for having technology-enabled banking.

The fact that Aadhaar has been approved as an eKYC document, the transaction costs of opening an account could drastically come down. While the traditional KYC would require copies of documents, in case of eKYC no copy of the document including the letter indicating the Aadhaar number

needs to be provided. This means that not only will the poor save costs of providing identity proof, but also the system cost of opening an account also comes down making it possible for banks to seamlessly open accounts. Unfortunately the benefit of technology of opening accounts through eKYC has not taken off as it should have. On the other hand, the customer transaction with the bank and the payment system could also happen without much exchange of currency if the mobile technology is embraced. The PMJDY could have leapfrogged into the mobile technology, which it did not do.

The third initiative that is coming from the policy side is to ensure that with the mapping of Aadhaar numbers to the bank accounts. All subsidies aimed

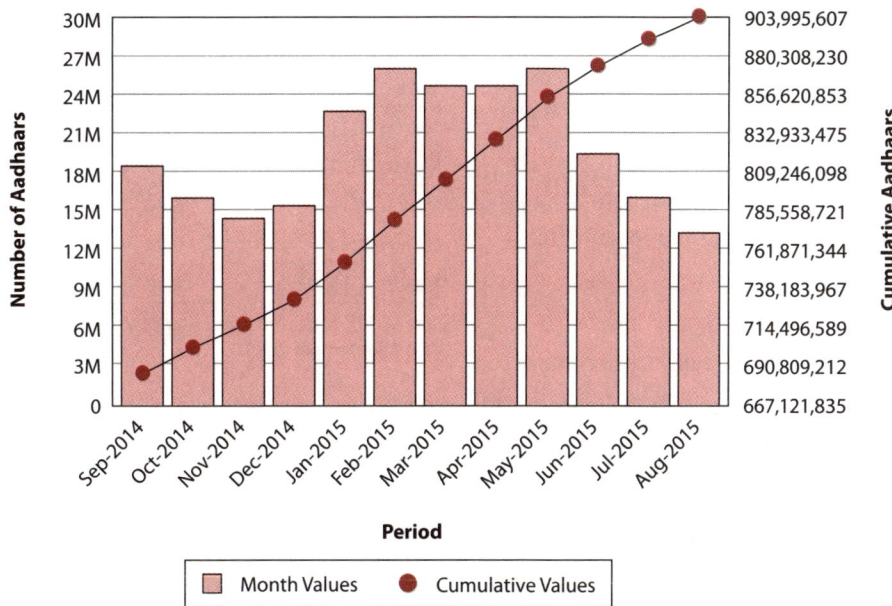

**Figure 5.1** Month-wise issue of unique ID numbers and cumulative progress
*Source:* UIDAI, 2015.

at individuals and other DBTs will happen straight to the beneficiaries' bank account. This would drive transaction traffic to the account. With technology it is possible to do a centralised transfer without any intermediary steps and the PAHAL scheme of transferring subsidy for cooking gas has demonstrated the power of technology.

The provision of biometric identity and linking the identity to banking suffered a setback due to a ruling by the Supreme Court of India. The case which questions the enrolment process on the basis of not having a legal sanction and adequate measures that protect the privacy of the citizens has been referred to a larger constitutional bench and in the interregnum the court has stayed the use of biometric numbers and linking them with payments in all cases except a few where the roll-out has been significant. The decision on this case is critical since many plans of the government are being linked to the Aadhaar. Mapping the bank accounts with the Aadhaar numbers is fundamental for the plans. The linking, it is believed, will also result in the data being uniquely identifiable and therefore would result in better credit decisions and a higher quality of input for policy making.

In the preceding analysis, the important point to note is that each transaction is being undertaken through the intervention of a touchpoint that is controlled by the banking system—whether it is the

**Box 5.1 Resistance to Aadhaar**

Apart from the genuine concerns raised by several rights activists about not having a regulatory framework that protects the citizen's privacy, there have been other sources of resistance in the financial inclusion space ever since Aadhaar was rolled out. First, while the RBI agreed to recognise Aadhaar as an identity document, it did not agree to recognise it as a document providing address proof. Second, there were also some doubts on who would accept the liability in case of an adverse event. Third, it was the mindset of the bankers that continued to use Aadhaar as a physical proof of identity rather than a virtual proof, thereby negating the cost advantages of virtual storage of identity document electronically as well as cutting the costs of making copies of physical documents.

Some of these issues have been sorted out. The RBI has recognised Aadhaar as a valid basis to open an account, including using Aadhaar number virtually without the need for a paper trail. The liability issue has been sorted out—with UIDAI accepting liability for all technology-related errors that might happen at its end and devolving the liability to the bank at the transaction level. The mindset of the bankers in using electronic proof of identity is to be worked on.

ATM centre, or the POS device. The next leapfrogging of technology-enabled banking would happen when the payments happen without the intervention of an intermediary bank-owned device such as the mobile phone. The architecture and the standards have been laid out, and going forward these transactions have the potential of expanding, making banking ubiquitous and inclusion meaningful.

## MOBILE BANKING

A look at the mobile banking statistics in comparison to the overall banking transactions shows that the last mile technology-enabled connectivity is yet to happen at scale (see Table 5.2). This was also reaffirmed by the Brookings report discussed in Chapter 1. However, the numbers over the past five years indicate rapid growth in the number of transactions—though the overall number of transactions is a miniscule part of the overall transactions or the technology-enabled transactions. However, this has the potential to grow fast (Table 5.3), particularly with new players coming and changing the rules of the game.

One of the important aspects that is needed for the mobile payments to spread fast is the transaction fees to be paid for the mobile companies. As Box 5.2 indicates, there are still issues on the charges

**Table 5.3** Data on transactions on the mobile

| Year | Volume (millions of transactions) | Value (₹ billion) |
|---|---|---|
| March 2011 | 1.05 | 0.84 |
| March 2012 | 3.12 | 2.32 |
| March 2013 | 6.40 | 9.91 |
| March 2014 | 10.74 | 34.07 |
| March 2015 | 19.76 | 169.14 |

*Source:* RBI https://rbi.org.in/scripts/NEFTView.aspx, accessed on 19 September 2015.

to be paid on the mobile banking platform. While the mobile telecom operators seem to be directly dealing with the banks on the mobile banking, it might be important to also deal with a bridge that brings in all the accounts on one platform through the National Unified USSD Platform (NUUP).

In addition to the above policy initiatives, the state of the technology and the interest in innovation are in place. As several players (telecom companies, technology companies and finance companies) are examining this space, there have been significant innovations in use of technology for movement of money. While 11 players have got an in-principle licence to set up PBs, four are clearly identifiable

**Table 5.2** Intermedia financial inclusion tracker survey

**Growth in bank account access has driven a range of key financial indicators over the past year**

| Indicators | 2013 | 2014 |
|---|---|---|
| % of adults (15+) that have a bank account | 47% | 55% |
| % of adults (15+) to have ever accessed a mobile money account | 0.3% | 0.3% |
| % of adults (15+) with active accounts* | 25% | 29% |
| % of adults (15+) below the poverty line with active accounts | 20% | 24% |
| % of males (15+) with active accounts | 32% | 36% |
| % of females (15+) with active accounts | 18% | 21% |
| % of rural males (15+) with active accounts | 26% | 30% |
| % of rural females (15+) with active accounts | 15% | 19% |
| % adults actively use accounts beyond basic wallet, P2P and bill pay | 9% | 9% |
| % of adults (15+) below the poverty line who actively use accounts beyond basic wallet, P2P and bill pay payments | 7% | 7% |
| % of males (15+) who actively use accounts beyond basic wallet, P2P and bill pay payments | 12% | 12% |
| % of females (15+) who actively use accounts beyond basic wallet, P2P and bill pay payments | 6% | 6% |
| % of rurals males (15+) who actively use accounts beyond basic wallet, P2P and bill pay payments | 10% | 10% |
| % of rural females (15+) who actively use accounts beyond basic wallet, P2P and bill pay payments | 5% | 6% |

* Active account holder is an individual who has a registered account and has used it in the last 90 days.
*Source:* InterMedia India FII Tracker surveys: Wave1 (N=45,024, 15+) October 2013-January 2014; Wave 2 (N=45,087 15+) September–December 2014.

**Box 5.2 National Payments Corporation of India and its role in inclusion**

The National Payments Corporation of India (NPCI) is playing a pivotal role in providing the interoperable infrastructure for the banking system. In addition to being the technology backbone, the corporation also issues RuPay cards that make the technology-enabled transactions possible. While the ATMs and the POS points are growing, they become viable only when people start using these extensively. To meet the challenge, the NPCI introduced the RuPay card that could be interoperably used at the ATM counters as well as the POS devices. With the PMJDY bundling the new accounts with RuPay, the inventory of RuPay has significantly increased and this increase could largely be considered as an achievement under the financial inclusion agenda.

In addition, the NPCI undertakes the following activities that foster the inclusion programme:

1. RuPay card to every Jan Dhan Account holder
2. DBT through Aadhaar Payments Bridge (more than 210 million Aadhaar numbers are mapped on to the NPCI mapper)
3. Micro ATM transactions at the BC level is cleared through AEPS of NPCI
4. eKYC gateway service, for opening bank accounts based on Aadhaar platform
5. Mobile banking through NUUP
6. Aadhaar seeding query service—particularly used in DBT programmes
7. Overdraft verification service
8. Linking all the RRBs and cooperative banks to national payment systems

Of the above, the most promising platform for financial inclusion is the mobile banking through NUUP. This is because any customer can do banking on a Global System for Mobile Communication (GSM) handset, without the need for a smart phone with Internet connectivity or a message under the Short Message Service (SMS). This uses the protocol *99# and directly connects to the banking menu, if the mobile number is mapped to the bank account. A customer can get access to the following services:

- *Non-financial:* Balance inquiry; mini statement; know the mobile money identifier (MMID) allotted to the customer; generate mobile personal identification number (MPIN) for undertaking financial transactions; change MPIN and generate one time password (OTP) for financial transactions
- *Financial:* Fund transfer using MMID with the mobile number of the beneficiary and fund transfer using IFSC code and account number
- *Value Added Services (VAS):* Query service on Aadhaar Mapper

However, apart from the government-owned telecom companies—Bharat Sanchar Nigam Limited (BSNL) and Mahanagar Telecom Nigam Limited (MTNL)—the other telecom companies have not shown interest in going through NPCI. Instead most of the mobile-based transactions are happening through the deals struck by the mobile telecom companies with the banks directly and through the applications that have been developed for smart phones. One of the most significant points of disagreements between NPCI and the telecom companies was about the charges per transaction, where NPCI had offered ₹0.25 per transaction—an amount not acceptable to the mobile companies. However, with the mobile companies themselves getting licences to set up payment banks, this technology might roll out in a big way in future. If it does, it makes banking ubiquitous and accessible to the last person having a mobile number-mapped bank account.

to groups having interests in the telecom space and one has a tie-up with a telecom company. There are others who have been in the payments space largely through operating prepaid instruments (PPIs) and understand the technology well. Therefore, these players will eventually redefine the payments space and touch-free banking might become a reality soon. This architecture would immensely benefit the poor and the excluded.

There are already 40 players authorised to issue PPIs and mobile wallets; five players who are in the card network; eight players who are in the cross border inbound money transfer business. All these players have made significant investments in moving money electronically. Of the 40 players authorised to issue PPIs, four are telecom companies and several of the players are acting as corporate BCs to banks. Entities related to six of the PPI licensees have been granted an in-principle approval for a PB licence. Given the change in the status, it is good to expect a fair amount of innovation that would eventually benefit the poor.

**Box 5.3 List of PPI licensees and white label ATM operators**

| | Prepaid payment instruments | | White label ATM operators |
|---|---|---|---|
| 1. | Aircel Smart Money Limited | 1. | AGS Transact Technologies Ltd. |
| 2. | Airtel M Commerce Services Limited* | 2. | BTI Payments Pvt. Ltd. |
| 3. | Atom Technologies Limited | 3. | Muthoot Finance Ltd. |
| 4. | Card Pro Solutions Private Limited | 4. | Prizm Payment Services Pvt. Ltd. |
| 5. | Citrus Payment Solutions Private Limited | 5. | RiddiSiddhi Bullions Limited |
| 6. | Delhi Integrated Multi-Modal Transit System Limited | 6. | SREI Infrastructure Finance Ltd. |
| 7. | Digisecure India Private Limited | 7. | Tata Communications Payment Solutions |
| 8. | Edenred (India) Private Limited | 8. | Vakrangee Limited |
| 9. | Eko India Financial Services Private Limited | | |
| 10. | Fino Paytech Ltd.* | | |
| 11. | FX Mart Pvt. Ltd. | | |
| 12. | GI Technology Private Limited | | |
| 13. | Idea Mobile Commerce Services Ltd.* | | |
| 14. | India Transact Services Limited | | |
| 15. | Itz Cash Card Ltd. | | |
| 16. | Kedia Infotech Ltd. | | |
| 17. | MMP Mobi Wallet Payment Systems Ltd. | | |
| 18. | Mpurse Services Pvt. Ltd. | | |
| 19. | Muthoot Vehicle & Asset Finance Ltd. | | |
| 20. | My Mobile Payments Limited | | |
| 21. | One97 Communications Ltd. | | |
| 22. | One Mobikwik Systems Pvt. Limited | | |
| 23. | Oxigen Services (India) Pvt. Ltd. | | |
| 24. | Paul Fincap Pvt. Ltd. | | |
| 25. | PayMate India Pvt. Limited | | |
| 26. | Pay Point India Network Private Limited | | |
| 27. | Premium eBusiness Ventures Private Limited | | |
| 28. | Pyro Telecommunications Ltd. | | |
| 29. | QwikCilver Solutions Pvt. Ltd. | | |
| 30. | Reliance Payment Solution Limited* | | |
| 31. | Smart Payment Solutions Pvt. Ltd. | | |
| 32. | Sodexo SVC India Pvt. Ltd. | | |
| 33. | Spice Digital Ltd. | | |
| 34. | Tech Mahindra Limited* | | |
| 35. | Transaction Analysts (India) Private Ltd. | | |
| 36. | UAE Exchange & Financial Services Ltd. | | |
| 37. | UTI Infrastructure Technology and Services Ltd. | | |
| 38. | Vodafone m-pesa Limited* | | |
| 39. | Y-Cash Software Solutions Private Limited | | |
| 40. | ZipCash Card Services Pvt. Ltd. | | |

*Firms that have got in-principle licence to set up PBs.
*Source:* RBI, 2015.

## AGENTS

Apart from the models that were examined above—all pertaining to technology-enabled touchpoints, without necessarily having a human interface—over the years the Indian banking system has increasingly used agents. The policy on employing agents has been inconsistent. The banks were trying to understand the new arrangement and rolled out different models. The government suggested some models keeping its agenda of DBTs in mind.

The Indian banking system has gone through various experiments in the agent network—a network that provides the last mile interface from the bank to the customer. In the first phase (2006) banks were allowed to hire only not-for-profit players as agents to reach out to the unreached. It was only in 2010 that the for-profit companies were allowed to function as agents of the bank—termed as BCs. In the meantime, the banks were also directly hiring some local individuals as BC agents, directly reporting to the bank without an intermediary organisation. Table 5.4 gives the alternate models that are in operation.

The agent network has never worked smoothly because of multiple problems. The incentive in the chain is loaded towards opening of accounts—particularly when accounts are opened on a mission

**Table 5.4  Agent network models**

| There are three major agent network models in India | | |
|---|---|---|
| **Banks directly manage agent networks** | **Specialised ANMs (BCNMs)\* manage agent networks** | **MNOs manage agent networks** |
| **Banks**<br>• Product ownership<br>• Agent network establishment and day to day management<br>• Agent remuneration<br>• Liquidity management<br>• Customer and agent support<br>• Monitoring and supervision | **Banks**<br>• Product ownership<br>• Remuneration to BCNMs<br>• Liquidity management<br>• Customer support<br>• Monitoring and supervision of BCNMs | **Banks**<br>• Product ownership<br>• Remuneration to MNOs<br>• Monitoring and supervision of MNOs |
| **Agents**<br>• Customer acquisition<br>• Transaction facilitation<br>• Last mile customer support | **Agents**<br>• Agent network establishment and day to day management<br>• Marketing and promotion<br>• Agent remuneration<br>• Liquidity management<br>• Customer and agent support<br>• Monitoring and supervision of agents | **MNOs**<br>• Working with banks to assist in product design<br>• Agent network establishment and day to day management<br>• Marketing and promotion<br>• Agent remuneration<br>• Liquidity management<br>• Customer and agent support<br>• Monitoring and supervision of agents |
| | **Agents**<br>• Customer acquisition<br>• Transaction facilitation<br>• Last mile customer support | **Agents**<br>• Customer acquisition<br>• Transaction facilitation<br>• Last mile customer support |

\*BCNM = Business Correspondent Network Manager.

*Source:* Agent network accelerator survey: India country report 2015. Helix Institute of Digital Finance.

mode. The agents get a certain fee but the compensation for the agent is not lucrative as their commission comes only from transactions, and a large number of transactions are needed to make the job of an agent lucrative. The second problem was of interoperability. An agent was expected to have an exclusive arrangement with a single bank. A recent study that analysed the agent network system indicted that agents that were exclusive (to a single institution) and dedicated (not having any other profession or source of income) tended to suffer most by low volumes of business and low remuneration (Mehrotra and George, 2015).

For the last mile to function effectively on simple transactions such as balance inquiry, withdrawal,

---

**Box 5.4 Governor Rajan on last mile delivery**

*Professor Sriram:* On the last mile delivery of financial services, the last big idea that we tried was BC and that has had mixed response and mixed results. Are there any other big ideas you have on this?

*Dr Rajan:* I think BC has to go together with connectivity and with mobile transfers. BC has to be perhaps cash in–cash out. But having agents who do other functions acting as a BC may also allow for recovery of cost.

*Professor Sriram:* That's the State Bank of India model, where they have put this CSP very near the branch in most of the places so they divert small ticket traffic to the CSP. It's safe in the sense that the exposure of the CSP is backed up by a fixed deposit. As the point is near the branch, anytime CSP runs out of limits they can go top it up. They have given limited access to CBS. It's a very interesting model but not many banks have picked it up.

*Dr Rajan:* Well some have, but I was thinking more in terms of he's doing another business, and the BC is on the side. So the other business which is not a banking business, like he's running a shop and he does BC also on the side.

*Professor Sriram:* Yes, these guys also do photocopying, selling insurance products and other small services.

*Dr Rajan:* In some states they are doing government business.

*Professor Sriram:* Yes, the Sahaj is doing that, wherein you share the sunk costs across.

---

*Dr Rajan:* Exactly! The fixed costs are shared, so that, I think, would work. We are trying to figure out what we can do with white label BCs. So allow them to do business for multiple banks. Now there the problem right now is which bank controls them. Let them have one bank which they do primary business with, but let the bank not make it disadvantageous to work with other banks.

---

deposit and remittances, the poor needed proximate access and it was assumed that the BCs would provide the answer. However, the tracker survey indicates the problems with the agents included the issue of exclusivity—which did not give enough business for the agent to stay invested in the relationship and activity; and the issue of dedication—the agent solely depending on this stream of income without any other avenue for employment. In general, the study found that the agents were better off when they were interoperable. The Aadhaar-Enabled Payment Bridge managed by the NPCI provides the interoperability facility in micro ATMs. However, the space is still fluid, till a set of control systems and operating protocols for interoperability are worked out. The other issue that the agent network analysis tracker study indicates is that there is no transaction traffic except in remittance corridors and that the government payments still form a miniscule part of the overall transactions, because of the very low commissions paid by the government.

From the preceding discussion, it is evident that the last mile connectivity with the client needs a significant innovation. As of now the technology backbone is in place, and this appears scalable. The two issues that need to be addressed are: providing a human interface with the technology so that the transactions become better for the customer and getting the economics of that channel right; changing the way people access banks over a longer time horizon. Both these will get a boost with the new PB licences and it would be very interesting to watch this space.

## REFERENCES

Intermedia (2015). *India: Driving Digital Financial Inclusion, Wave 2.* Washington DC: Intermedia.

Mehrotra, A. and George, D. (2015). *Agent Network Accelerator Survey: India Country Report 2015.* Nairobi: Helix Institute of Digital Finance.

# Urban cooperative banks

Urban cooperative banks (UCBs) are small and neighbourhood banks, and usually cater to a large section of population that are left out of the mainstream banking system. They are usually incorporated under the local Cooperative Societies Act, and accorded a banking licence by the RBI. Some of the banks have registered themselves under the Multi-state Cooperative Societies Act by virtue of having membership cutting across multiple states. Cooperatives are expected to function on the principles of mutuality and trust. This, by definition, assumes that they are neighbourhood institutions and small in nature. While across the world there have been very large cooperative banks, it is important to understand that these so-called large banks rest on the foundation of very large number of primary, independent and somewhat autonomous cooperative societies. This is indeed the case with the Indian rural cooperative system. However, in case of the urban cooperative sector, several of these neighbourhood institutions have grown to become large institutions operating across the country almost like a commercial bank.

The urban cooperative banking sector can be divided into three distinct segments. The urban cooperative thrift and credit societies form the base of this structure. While statistics for this sector is not readily available, these are expected to be small and run on the principle of mutuality. They are not expected to seek deposits from non-members and loaning is also amongst the members themselves. Going forward, it would be important to capture data about these institutions if the financial inclusion parameters were to be measured more holistically. The second segment consists of the cooperatives that have been accorded a licence by the RBI, but do not have a scheduled status. The third segment consists of the scheduled urban cooperative banks.

In general, it is believed that the urban cooperative banks have inherent design problems—the members who are borrowers also manage the governance system thereby creating a conflict of interest. These banks are regulated by the cooperative department of the respective state government (or the central government in case of multi-state cooperatives) for aspects of election, board, governance and matters of compliance with regard to incorporation, while they are governed by the RBI for their banking function, thereby creating a duality in regulation. While the RBI recognises their role in being an institution that fosters financial inclusion, it also recognises the risk it causes to the financial system because of weak governance and more frequent instances of failure.

The difference between the other commercial banks and the cooperative banks that are directly supervised by the RBI lies in the large numbers. While the public sector and private sector banks (both old and new) number less than 50, the foreign banks are less than 100 with a limited footprint and the regional rural banks after the consolidation have been reduced to 57 in number. On the other hand, the sheer numbers of UCBs have been large. As far back as in 1966, there were 1,100 in number (Table 6.1) (RBI, 2015), and licences were liberally issued to spread the presence of these local and neighbourhood institutions. By 2004, there were 1,926 UCBs accounting for about ₹1,020 billion deposits and ₹650 billion in loans. However, there was a crisis as a result of the failure of a large UCB in Gujarat and there were several collateral collapses in the UCB sector. This slowed down the licencing process. As a result of the crisis there were greater coordination

**Table 6.1  UCBs in the recent years**

| Year | No. of UCBs | Deposits (₹ billion) | Advances (₹ billion) |
|---|---|---|---|
| 2008 | 1,770 | 1,398.71 | 904.44 |
| 2009 | 1,721 | 1,570.42 | 962.34 |
| 2010 | 1,674 | 1,831.50 | 1,124.36 |
| 2011 | 1,645 | 2,118.80 | 1,364.98 |
| 2012 | 1,618 | 2,386.41 | 1,577.93 |
| 2013 | 1,606 | 2,768.30 | 1,810.31 |
| 2014 | 1,589 | 3,155.03 | 1,996.51 |

*Source:* RBI, 2015.

efforts between the regulators to ensure that the dual regulation did not create arbitrage opportunities, the RBI stopped issuing fresh licences and encouraged the sector to consolidate and stabilise.

As a result of the pause and consolidation, the UCBs now number 1,579 as of March 2015. As of March 2014, the UCBs as a category hold about

₹3,155 billion in deposits and have a loan outstanding of ₹1,996 billion. The region-wise spread of UCBs and their branch network is given in Table 6.2.

The spread of the branch network somewhat mirrors the growth of the commercial banking in India, in terms of all regions except the west and the southern region. In case of UCBs the spread of cooperative banking is far deeper both in terms of the number of banks and branches in the western region. The west represents half of the UCB and a two-third of the branch network.

## HOW INCLUSIVE ARE UCBs?

Sliced data on UCBs is not available in the data warehouse of RBI. However, a study undertaken on behest of the High Powered Committee on UCBs revealed the following data for both scheduled and non-scheduled UCBs (Tables 6.3 and 6.4). This shows that the non-scheduled UCBs are closer to the inclusive customers, with 93% of their accounts

**Table 6.2  Region-wise spread of UCBs as of March 2014**

| Region | No. of UCBs | No. of branches (including head office) | No. of extension counters | No. of ATMs | No. of districts with a UCB branch | No. of districts without a UCB branch | Deposits (₹ billion) | Advances (₹ billion) |
|---|---|---|---|---|---|---|---|---|
| North | 73 | 382 | 14 | 49 | 57 | 64 | 109.09 | 69.70 |
| North-east | 17 | 47 | 1 | – | 18 | 49 | 13.06 | 7.61 |
| East | 59 | 158 | 5 | 7 | 29 | 83 | 50.80 | 25.40 |
| Central | 137 | 479 | 23 | 61 | 93 | 73 | 114.92 | 61.68 |
| West | 746 | 6,448 | 132 | 2,880 | 65 | 8 | 2,332.82 | 1,467.10 |
| South | 557 | 2,012 | 61 | 178 | 99 | 4 | 534.33 | 365.02 |
| All-India | 1,589 | 9,526 | 236 | 3,175 | 361 | 281 | 3,155.03 | 1,996.51 |

*Source:* Statistical Tables Relating to Banks in India 2013–14. Accessed on 14 September 2015 from http://dbie.rbi.org.in/DBIE/dbie.rbi?site=publications#!3

**Table 6.3  Loan outstandings of scheduled UCBs as per loan size**

| Range of loan (₹ million) | No. of accounts | % of total no. of accounts | Amount (₹ billion) | % of total amounts |
|---|---|---|---|---|
| Up to 0.5 | 569,855 | 53.02 | 76.56 | 10.75 |
| 0.5–1.0 | 276,314 | 25.71 | 44.22 | 6.21 |
| 1.0–1.5 | 171,148 | 15.92 | 26.79 | 3.76 |
| 1.5–2.0 | 14,166 | 1.32 | 21.68 | 3.04 |
| 2.0–2.5 | 9,308 | 0.87 | 17.55 | 2.46 |
| 2.5–5.0 | 15,320 | 1.43 | 49.18 | 6.90 |
| 5.0–10.0 | 8,017 | 0.75 | 51.91 | 7.28 |
| 10.0–50.0 | 8,150 | 0.76 | 166.93 | 23.43 |
| Above 50.0 | 2,417 | 0.22 | 257.72 | 36.17 |
| Total | 1,074,695 | 100.00 | 712.54 | 100.00 |

*Source:* Report of the High Powered Committee on Urban Cooperative Banks, 2015. Mumbai: RBI.

**Table 6.4** Loan outstandings of non-scheduled UCBs as per loan size

| Range of loan (₹ million) | No. of accounts | % of total no. of accounts | Amount (₹ billion) | % of total amounts |
|---|---|---|---|---|
| Up to 0.5 | 5,768,074 | 93.56 | 535.88 | 47.46 |
| 0.5–1.0 | 248,762 | 4.03 | 136.08 | 12.05 |
| 1.0–1.5 | 56,167 | 0.91 | 63.29 | 5.60 |
| 1.5–2.0 | 27,679 | 0.45 | 43.43 | 3.84 |
| 2.0–2.5 | 18,072 | 0.29 | 38.00 | 3.36 |
| 2.5–5.0 | 27,670 | 0.45 | 89.16 | 7.90 |
| 5.0–10.0 | 11,722 | 0.19 | 73.93 | 6.55 |
| 10.0–50.0 | 6,814 | 0.11 | 120.79 | 10.70 |
| Above 50.0 | 436 | 0.01 | 28.65 | 2.54 |
| Total | 6,165,396 | 100.00 | 1,129.22 | 100.00 |

*Source:* Report of the High Powered Committee on Urban Cooperative Banks, 2015. Mumbai: RBI.

coming from loan sizes less than ₹0.5 million. In case of the scheduled UCBs, this proportion is much smaller at 53%.

If data were available on the small ticket loans, there is a high probability that these would match up to the numbers of the RRBs in terms of inclusivity. Therefore, the argument that UCBs are institutions that naturally achieve some of the inclusion numbers is a valid argument. They may not be dealing with the same segment of the customers as MFIs, but they would most likely be a friendly neighbourhood bank for the missing middle—small traders, micro-enterprises and small industries largely located in urban areas.

In terms of PSL, the numbers for the UCBs were as specified in Table 6.5.

From the data it is clear that the UCBs have been lending near about 49% of their portfolio to priority sector with almost 13% of the deployment to weaker sections. On both the counts the UCBs exceed the

**Table 6.5** Composition of credit to priority sectors by UCBs (as of end of March 2014)

| Sector | Composition of total priority sector credit | | *Of which*, composition of credit to weaker sections | |
|---|---|---|---|---|
| | Amount (₹ billion) | Percentage to total | Amount (₹ billion) | Percentage to total |
| 1. Agricultural credit | 58 | 2.9 | 24 | 1.2 |
| 1.1 Direct agricultural credit | 23 | 1.1 | 9 | 0.5 |
| 1.2 Indirect agricultural credit | 35 | 1.8 | 15 | 0.7 |
| 2. Micro and small enterprises | 461 | 23.1 | 78 | 3.9 |
| 2.1 Direct credit to micro and small enterprises | 398 | 19.9 | 62 | 3.1 |
| 2.2 Indirect credit to micro and small enterprises | 62 | 3.1 | 17 | 0.8 |
| 3. Micro Credit | 32 | 1.6 | 11 | 0.6 |
| 4. State-sponsored organisations for SC/ST | 2 | 0.1 | 1 | 0.1 |
| 5. Education loans | 17 | 0.9 | 7 | 0.3 |
| 6. Housing loans | 206 | 10.3 | 70 | 3.5 |
| 7. Others | 200 | 10 | 65 | 3.2 |
| All priority sectors | 976 | 48.9 | 257 | 12.9 |

*Source:* Statistical Statements Relating to Banks in India, 2014. Mumbai: RBI (2015). Accessed on 14 September 2015 and available at http://dbie.rbi.org.in/DBIE/dbie.rbi?site=publications#!3
*Notes:* 1. Percentages are with respect to total credit of UCBs.
2. Components m ʹ not add up to the total due to rounding off.

expectations. The area where they fall short significantly when compared to the other banks in the system is in agricultural lending. This is understandable given that they are all located largely in urban areas and designed to be urban banks. The lack of achievement in agricultural loans is made up by the lending to micro enterprises and the housing portfolio.

The financial performance of UCBs was satisfactory. The average return on assets of the banking system was 0.81 for the year 2013–14. The best returns were obtained by the private sector banks at 1.65% indicating the scope for improvement of the other players in the banking system including UCBs. Similarly the average return on equity of the banking sector was at 10.68%. In general, it can be seen that the non-scheduled UCBs have a better performance (Table 6.6).

While this could improve, it is important to note that only six of the 57 banks suffered losses during 2013–14. Given that the UCB sector has stabilised in the past few years, the RBI was looking at issuing new licences for UCBs. The thought process for opening up the licences started in 2011, when an Expert Committee headed by Mr Y.H. Malegam submitted a report recommending the norms for new UCBs given in Box 6.1.

However, based on the recommendations given in Box 6.1, no licences were issued in the past few years. With RBI articulating its position on the proposed banking structure (RBI, 2013), there were a new set of discussions on whether there should be new UCBs. Accordingly a new high-powered committee was set up by the RBI which advocates granting of licences, keeping in mind the issues in

**Table 6.6** Select financial indicators of UCBs (as on 31 March)

| | | | | | | (%) |
|---|---|---|---|---|---|---|
| **Financial indicators** | **Scheduled UCBs** | | **Non-scheduled UCBs** | | **All UCBs** | |
| | 2012–13 | 2013–14 | 2012–13 | 2013–14 | 2012–13 | 2013–14 |
| (1) | (2) | (3) | (4) | (5) | (6) | (7) |
| Return on assets | 0.78 | 0.72 | 0.73 | 1.00 | 0.75 | 0.87 |
| Return on equity | 8.60 | 9.25 | 6.22 | 8.90 | 7.19 | 9.03 |
| Net interest margin | 2.83 | 2.68 | 3.47 | 3.32 | 3.17 | 3.02 |

*Source:* Mumbai: Reserve Bank of India database at http://dbie.rbi.org.in/DBIE/dbie.rbi?site=publications#!3
*Note:* Data for 2013–14 are provisional.

| **Box 6.1 Recommendations of the Expert Committee on UCBs for grant of new licences (2011)** | |
|---|---|
| **Area of operation** | **Minimum capital required for licencing** |
| UCB operating in only one state in | |
| (i) North-eastern states | |
| (ii) In other states but confined to unbanked districts | ₹5 million |
| (iii) In other states but confined to 'C' and 'D' category population centres of banked districts | |
| UCB operating in only one state with 50% or more branches in 'C' and 'D' category population centres | ₹10 million |
| UCB operating in only one state but without requirement to have branches in 'C' and 'D' category population centres | ₹30 million |
| UCB which wishes to operate in more than one state after five years of successful operation | ₹50 million |

*Source:* Report of the Expert Committee on licencing new UCBs. RBI. 2011. Mumbai: Reserve Bank of India.

growth, governance, duality of control and the need for having niche and local banks. A summary of the recommendations of the committee is reproduced in Appendix 6.1.

## UCBs: THE WAY FORWARD

The most significant event in the UCB sector during the year was the submission of the report of the High Powered Committee headed by the Deputy Governor of the RBI Mr R. Gandhi. The report built upon the recommendations of the Malegam Committee (discussed earlier) and laid out a road map for the UCBs—suggesting that they could start as mutuals—as a cooperative society and as they grow could become banks, first as cooperative banks and later morph into commercial banks through the SFB route.

The committee suggested the following entry-point norms:

(a) To operate as a multi-state UCB—₹1 billion
(b) To operate beyond two districts and as a state-level UCB—₹500 million
(c) To operate as a district-level UCB (up to 2 districts)—₹250 million
(d) In case of conversion of cooperative credit societies in unbanked areas and in the north-east, suitable relaxations may be made by the RBI

It is to be noted with caution and concern that both the Malegam Committee (RBI, 2011) and the Gandhi Committee (RBI, 2015) have made recommendations that could have implications on the very fabric of the cooperative nature of the organisations. While both the committees look at the issue from a banking perspective, the more important point is to note that cooperatives are fundamentally different from banks. Cooperatives operate on the principle of mutuality and therefore the relationship of the members of the cooperative is not necessarily that of the investors. While in the commercial banking sector there would be Chinese walls drawn between the borrowers and the investors, this is not so in the case of cooperatives. In a way, having a cooperative 'bank' is a contradiction, because a bank by definition deals with the public at large and cooperatives in principle should only deal with the members. However, the set of members might want the status of a bank in order for the cooperative to connect to the larger financial system outside. But to propose that a cooperative bank could convert itself into a banking corporation is a thought that should be seen with caution.

---

### Box 6.2 Governor Rajan on cooperatives

*Professor Sriram:* You are moving towards converting cooperatives into mainstream banks. But the form of the organisation doesn't permit you to do that in one sense, because there is no residual claim on liquidation income as far as cooperatives are concerned. There is only residual claim on current income. With all these large banks, what route would you take?

*Dr Rajan:* There are two options for cooperatives that we regulate. They could morph into the kind of structure that the Malegam Committee has proposed, which gives us a little more regulatory confidence. The other is to transform into the joint stock bank. In the United States when it went through this, they did basically give the equity rights to the existing depositors. We'll have to worry about how the membership of the cooperative will get rights to the equity.

*Professor Sriram:* Particularly since these banks are largely controlled by borrowers rather than depositors.

*Dr Rajan:* Exactly!

*Professor Sriram:* So, that is a tougher problem and much more gradual issue.

*Dr Rajan:* We'll have to figure out how to do it. So we'll have to make sure that members are involved in the proportion they share the cost of subscription. Maybe the appropriate proportion would be one member, one equity share. And so that way we don't get an excess concentration of the surplus value in a few hands.

*Professor Sriram:* What do you do with the accumulated reserves and the surpluses?

*Dr Rajan:* So it would be divided up equally across the membership. That would also accord with the cooperative nature. However, all this needs to be thought through in discussions with stakeholders.

---

This development is to be seen in the larger context of licences being awarded to SFBs and PBs. While the road map of the RBI looks interesting from a regulatory perspective, it is important to underscore the fact that cooperatives and commercial banks are fundamentally different. While cooperatives function on the principles of mutuality and self-help, a bank by definition starts its life by dealing with public deposit. The cooperative structure is designed to be member-owned and member-oriented business and therefore a bank structure for cooperatives is in itself inappropriate at scale. Now with the road map for conversion of UCBs into SFBs, the RBI would be inviting a range of players that would treat cooperatives more like a special-purpose vehicle that would fetch them a banking licence in due course. If we were to retain the cooperative nature of the UCBs and keep them as instruments of financial inclusion, these recommendations may have to be fundamentally reconsidered. From the recommendations of the Gandhi Committee (see Appendix 6.1), it appears that the committee considers a cooperative society as an entry-point institution, and as the size increases, the committee seems to believe that they should be accorded a banking licence in the first instance and later should be converted into an SFB. It is one thing to say that we should have small banks and as they grow, they should get more and more facilities to do additional activities—which seems to be the logic of the argument of the Gandhi Committee, as against the actual recommendation that organisations set up as mutual move into an investor-oriented format. It is hoped this will be debated in a larger forum with stakeholders who understand the concept of cooperative presenting their views before the regulator. However, the ensuing years will see action on this front and there is a lot to watch out in this space.

### APPENDIX 6.1
#### Gandhi Committee summary recommendations and suggestions

**Business size and conversion of MS-UCBs into joint stock banks:** The Committee feels that a business size of ₹20,000 crore (₹200 billion) or more may be the threshold limit beyond which a UCB may be expected to convert to a commercial bank. This may necessitate some transition facilities also. The conversion need not be *de jure* compulsory and large UCBs can continue the way they operate currently in terms of balance sheet/asset size. However, it will be subject to the regulatory guidelines requiring that the types of businesses that they undertake remain within the limits of plain vanilla products and services and their growth will be at a much slower pace. Their expansion in terms of branches, area of operations and business lines may thus be carefully calibrated to restrict unrestrained growth. (paras 2.19, 3.20 and 3.21)

**Conversion of other UCBs into SFBs:** As per the Committee, smaller UCBs voluntarily willing to convert to SFBs can do so irrespective of the threshold limit provided they fulfil all the eligibility criteria and selection process prescribed by the RBI and further provided that the small finance bank's licensing window is open. (paras 3.22 and 3.23)

**Issue of fresh licences:** The Committee unanimously recommends that licences may be issued to financially sound and well-managed cooperative credit societies having a minimum track record of 5 years which satisfy the regulatory prescriptions set by the RBI as licensing conditions. With regard to the concern of providing banking access in unbanked areas, the Committee recommends that the RBI may put in place an appropriate set of incentives for existing banks to open branches there. (para 4.9)

**Board of Management in addition to Board of Directors:** The Committee recommends that the concept of Board of Management put forward by the Malegam Committee has to be one of the mandatory licensing conditions for issuing licences to new UCBs and in the expansion of existing UCBs. (para 4.12)

**Entry-point norms:** The Committee also feels that licences may be issued to well-managed cooperative credit societies which satisfy the following capital requirements:

(a) To operate as a multi-state UCB—₹100 crore (₹1 billion)
(b) To operate beyond two districts and as a state-level UCB—₹50 crore (₹500 million)
(c) To operate as a district-level UCB (up to two districts)—₹25 crore (₹250 million)
(d) In case of conversion of cooperative credit societies in unbanked areas and in the north-east, suitable relaxations may be made by the RBI. (para 4.14)

**Depositors as voting members:** It was concluded that depositors ought to have a say on the boards of UCBs. For this, a majority of the board's seats be reserved for depositors by making suitable provisions in the bye-laws. (para 4.15)

## SUGGESTIONS

The Committee, during deliberations on the specific terms of reference, also had occasion to discuss some issues that have relevance to the sector but did not pursue them in detail both because they were not specifically relevant to the aspects that the Committee was looking into and also because that would have delayed the conclusion of the report. The Committee therefore has not dealt with these in this report but feels it necessary to highlight them so that they can be taken forward in an appropriate manner and time as determined by the bank. These are:

(i) At present, no powers are available with the RBI for constituting boards of UCBs, removal of directors, supersession of Board of Directors (BoD), auditing of UCBs and winding up and liquidation of UCBs. However, such powers for commercial banks are vested with the RBI. There are certain sections in the BR, Act 1949 such as provisions of Section 10A (professional BoD), 10B (removal of a whole time chairman), 30 (Audit), 44 (winding-up of banks), 44A (amalgamation of banking companies) and 45(suspension of business) which were not replicated while amending Section 56 of the BR Act, 1949. These amendments can be incorporated in Section 56 of the Act for effective regulation and supervision of UCBs. In addition to these, the Committee identified and deliberated in detail on the problems and issues afflicting the sector including restricted ability of UCBs to raise capital resources and to handle risks, lack of RBI's powers for supervision and regulation of UCBs at par with commercial banks, lack of powers for compulsory/voluntary mergers, etc. apart from the basic fault lines in the structure of the urban cooperative banking sector. However, in view of the limited terms of reference and the given time frame of the Committee, the long-term solution to all the problems could not be covered under the recommendations.

(ii) Resolution mechanism: The resolution regime for UCBs exists in a rudimentary form in as much as it ensures pay-outs to small depositors by DICGC while large depositors' interests are not taken care of fully in the event of cancellation of the licence of a bank. As belated action accentuates problems of resolution, any prompt corrective action framework should require supervisory action at the initial stages. As time is of essence in any resolution framework, there is a need to review the existing supervisory action, revisiting existing guidelines on mergers, revision in instructions on restructuring negative net worth UCBs including revisiting instruments for augmenting capital for UCBs. Moving forward, it is necessary to start with the requirement that UCBs need to frame their recovery and resolution plans within the current legal framework when they are operating on sound lines. There is also a need to empower the RBI for implementing resolution techniques without involving other regulators such as RCS and CRCS. There should be a regulatory set-up to provide legal backing for the RBI to play a central role in the winding up of the banking business of UCBs without the intervention of the authorities under the cooperative societies' laws. The possibility of winding up of the banking business of UCBs by the RBI directly by appointing DICGC as the liquidator for liquidating the banking business of a UCB may also be explored.

(iii) Umbrella organisation: The concept of having an 'umbrella organisation' for UCBs in India has been mooted for a long time. In fact, the Malegam Committee deliberated on the issue in detail. Some of the members referred to the structure of Rabobank running successfully abroad. The Committee feels that a prerequisite for such a successful umbrella organisation is inherently sound and well-run member institutions. However, the question remains whether the Rabobank kind of model is possible under existing laws in India.

Thus, although such a structure has long been envisaged, certain legal hurdles are precluding its implementation.

The Committee recommends that given the importance of the issue, the RBI may expedite the decision on the structure of the urban cooperative banking system and appropriate umbrella organisation/s.

## APPENDIX 6.2
### Financial performance of UCBs (as on 31 March 2014)

(Amount in ₹ billion)

| Item | Scheduled UCBs | | Non-scheduled UCBs | | All UCBs | | |
|---|---|---|---|---|---|---|---|
| | 2012–13 | 2013–14 | 2012–13 | 2013–14 | 2012–13 | 2013–14 | % growth |
| Interest/discount received | 137.18 | 153.34 | 172.03 | 195.29 | 309.21 | 348.63 | 12.75 |
| Other income | 16.27 | 16.55 | 8.47 | 12.25 | 24.73 | 28.80 | 16.45 |
| Total income | 153.45 | 169.89 | 180.49 | 207.54 | 333.94 | 377.43 | 13.02 |
| Interest paid | 94.10 | 106.96 | 112.26 | 130.61 | 206.36 | 237.57 | 15.13 |
| Expenses on staff, directors and auditors | 16.01 | 17.10 | 23.34 | 26.03 | 39.35 | 43.13 | 9.59 |
| Other operating expenses | 16.38 | 17.79 | 17.45 | 19.59 | 33.83 | 37.39 | 10.52 |
| Total expenses | 126.49 | 141.85 | 153.05 | 176.24 | 279.54 | 318.08 | 13.79 |
| Operating profit | 26.95 | 28.04 | 27.45 | 31.31 | 54.40 | 59.34 | 9.09 |
| Provision against risks/contingencies | 9.12 | 10.88 | 7.61 | 6.23 | 16.73 | 17.11 | 2.27 |
| Net profit (+)/loss (–) before taxes | 17.84 | 17.15 | 19.83 | 25.08 | 37.67 | 42.24 | 12.12 |
| Provisions for taxes | 5.96 | 4.65 | 7.27 | 5.68 | 13.23 | 10.32 | −21.96 |
| Net profit (+)/loss (–) after taxes | 11.88 | 12.51 | 12.56 | 19.40 | 24.44 | 31.91 | 30.57 |

*Source:* RBI Data Warehouse at http://dbie.rbi.org.in/DBIE/dbie.rbi?site=publications#!3, accessed on 16 September 2015.
*Notes:* 1. Data for 2013–14 are provisional.
2. Components may not add up/subtract to the whole due to rounding off.
3. Percentage variation could be slightly different because absolute numbers have been rounded off to ₹ billion.
4. Value zero indicates nil or negligible.

## APPENDIX 6.3
### Liabilities and assets of UCBs

(Amount in ₹ billion)

| Item | Scheduled UCBs | | Non-scheduled UCBs | | All UCBs | | Scheduled UCBs | Non-scheduled CBs | All UCBs |
|---|---|---|---|---|---|---|---|---|---|
| | 2013 | 2014 | 2013 | 2014 | 2013 | 2014 | 2014 | 2014 | 2014 |
| Liabilities | | | | | | | | | |
| Capital | 25.04 | 27.99 | 55.43 | 61.37 | 80.47 | 89.36 | 11.77 | 10.72 | 11.05 |
| | (1.59) | (1.54) | (3.02) | (2.98) | (2.36) | (2.31) | | | |
| Reserves and surplus | 101.78 | 115.79 | 155.12 | 164.21 | 256.90 | 280.00 | 13.77 | 5.86 | 9.00 |
| | (6.45) | (6.37) | (8.44) | (7.99) | (7.52) | (7.23) | | | |
| Deposits | 1,261.90 | 1,456.04 | 1,506.41 | 1,698.99 | 2,768.30 | 3,155.03 | 15.38 | 12.78 | 13.97 |
| | (79.99) | (80.13) | (82.00) | (82.63) | (81.07) | (81.46) | | | |
| Borrowings | 18.78 | 21.27 | 8.09 | 4.83 | 26.87 | 26.10 | 13.27 | −40.27 | −2.85 |
| | (1.19) | (1.17) | (0.44) | (0.23) | (0.79) | (0.67) | | | |
| Other liabilities | 170.15 | 195.92 | 112.05 | 126.75 | 282.20 | 322.67 | 15.14 | 13.12 | 14.34 |
| | (10.79) | (10.78) | (6.10) | (6.16) | (8.26) | (8.33) | | | |
| Total liabilities | 1,577.65 | 1,817.02 | 1,837.09 | 2,056.15 | 3,414.74 | 3,873.17 | 15.17 | 11.92 | 13.42 |

*(Continued)*

(Continued)

(Amount in ₹ billion)

| Item | Scheduled UCBs | | Non-scheduled UCBs | | All UCBs | | Scheduled UCBs | Non-scheduled CBs | All UCBs |
|---|---|---|---|---|---|---|---|---|---|
| | 2013 | 2014 | 2013 | 2014 | 2013 | 2014 | 2014 | 2014 | 2014 |
| Assets | | | | | | | | | |
| Cash | 9.07 | 8.76 | 25.82 | 25.22 | 34.89 | 33.99 | −3.37 | −2.29 | −2.57 |
| | (0.57) | (0.48) | (1.41) | (1.23) | (1.02) | (0.88) | | | |
| Balances with banks | 65.17 | 86.70 | 139.07 | 165.45 | 204.24 | 252.14 | 33.03 | 18.96 | 23.45 |
| | (4.13) | (4.77) | (7.57) | (8.05) | (5.98) | (6.51) | | | |
| Call and short notice | 4.64 | 4.95 | 8.91 | 8.49 | 13.55 | 13.44 | 6.63 | −4.78 | −0.88 |
| | (0.29) | (0.27) | (0.49) | (0.41) | (0.40) | (0.35) | | | |
| Investments | 454.11 | 532.78 | 631.07 | 671.89 | 1,085.18 | 1,204.67 | 17.32 | 6.47 | 11.01 |
| | (28.78) | (29.32) | (34.35) | (32.68) | (31.78) | (31.10) | | | |
| Loans and advances | 840.18 | 939.21 | 970.13 | 1,057.29 | 1,810.31 | 1,996.51 | 11.79 | 8.98 | 10.29 |
| | (53.25) | (51.69) | (52.81) | (51.42) | (53.01) | (51.55) | | | |
| Other assets | 204.48 | 244.61 | 62.09 | 127.81 | 266.57 | 372.43 | 19.63 | 105.86 | 39.71 |
| | (12.96) | (13.46) | (3.38) | (6.22) | (7.81) | (9.62) | | | |
| Total assets | 1,577.65 | 1,817.02 | 1,837.09 | 2,056.15 | 3,414.74 | 3,873.17 | 15.17 | 11.92 | 13.42 |

*Source:* RBI Data Warehouse at http://dbie.rbi.org.in/DBIE/dbie.rbi?site=publications#!3, accessed on 16 September 2015.
*Notes:* 1. Data for 2014 are provisional.
2. Figures in brackets are percentages to total liabilities/assets.
3. Components may not add up to the whole due to rounding off.
4. Percentage variation could be slightly different because absolute numbers have been rounded off to ₹ billion.

### APPENDIX 6.4
### Distribution of UCBs by size of deposits and advances as on 31 March 2014

| | Distribution based on deposits | | | | | Distribution based on advances | | | |
|---|---|---|---|---|---|---|---|---|---|
| | No. of UCBs | | Deposits | | | No. of UCBs | | Advances | |
| Deposits | No. | % share to total | Amount | % share to total | Advances | No. | % share to total | Amount | % share to total |
| 1 | 2 | 3 | 4 | 5 | 6 | 7 | 8 | 9 | 10 |
| 0.00 ≤ D < 0.10 | 195 | 12.27 | 11.28 | 0.36 | 0.00 ≤ A < 0.10 | 363 | 22.84 | 19.62 | 0.98 |
| 0.10 ≤ D < 0.25 | 299 | 18.82 | 51.40 | 1.63 | 0.10 ≤ A < 0.25 | 399 | 25.11 | 67.18 | 3.37 |
| 0.25 ≤ D < 0.50 | 335 | 21.08 | 119.34 | 3.78 | 0.25 ≤ A < 0.50 | 279 | 17.56 | 99.74 | 5.01 |
| 0.50 ≤ D < 1.00 | 272 | 17.12 | 194.05 | 6.15 | 0.50 ≤ A < 1.00 | 230 | 14.47 | 163.34 | 8.20 |
| 1.00 ≤ D < 2.50 | 266 | 16.74 | 408.71 | 12.95 | 1.00 ≤ A < 2.50 | 180 | 11.33 | 284.46 | 14.28 |
| 2.50 ≤ D < 5.00 | 113 | 7.11 | 399.76 | 12.67 | 2.50 ≤ A < 5.00 | 71 | 4.47 | 241.50 | 12.12 |
| 5.00 ≤ D < 10.00 | 61 | 3.84 | 416.30 | 13.20 | 5.00 ≤ A < 10.00 | 37 | 2.33 | 246.68 | 12.38 |
| 10.00 ≤ D | 48 | 3.02 | 1,554.18 | 49.26 | 10.00 ≤ A | 30 | 1.89 | 873.97 | 43.86 |
| Total | 1,589 | 100.00 | 3,155.03 | 100.00 | Total | 1,589 | 100.00 | 1,996.51 | 100.19 |

*Source:* RBI Data Warehouse at http://dbie.rbi.org.in/DBIE/dbie.rbi?site=publications#!3, accessed on 16 September 2015.
*Notes:* 1. Data are provisional.
2. Components may not add up to the whole due to rounding off.

**APPENDIX 6.5**
**Rating-wise distribution of UCBs as on 31 March 2014**

(Amount in ₹ billion)

| Ratings | No. of UCBs | % share in total | Deposits | % share in total | Advances | % share in total |
|---|---|---|---|---|---|---|
| A | 392 | 24.67 | 1,462.99 | 46.37 | 946.34 | 47.40 |
| B | 805 | 50.66 | 1,283.78 | 40.69 | 807.59 | 40.45 |
| C | 311 | 19.57 | 337.90 | 10.71 | 207.24 | 10.38 |
| D | 81 | 5.10 | 70.67 | 2.24 | 35.34 | 1.77 |
| Total | 1,589 | 100.00 | 3,155.03 | 100.00 | 1,996.51 | 100.00 |

*Source:* RBI Data Warehouse at http://dbie.rbi.org.in/DBIE/dbie.rbi?site=publications#!3, accessed on 16 September 2015.
*Notes:* 1. Data are provisional.
2. Components may not add up to the whole due to rounding off.
3. Ratings are based on the inspection conducted during the financial years (FYs) 2012–13 to 2013–14.
4. Percentage variation could be slightly different because absolute numbers have been rounded off to ₹ billion.

## REFERENCES

RBI (2011). *Report of the Expert Committee on Licencing New Urban Cooperative Banks.* Mumbai: RBI.

——— (2013). *Discussion Paper on Banking Structure, the Way Forward.* Mumbai: RBI.

——— (2015). *Report of the High Powered Committee on Urban Cooperative Banks.* Mumbai: RBI.

# India Post and the inclusion agenda

## BACKGROUND

In general, the literature on financial inclusion usually pays a lip service to the postal department, by cursorily mentioning the number of postal outlets and highlighting the potential of India Post. However, during the past year, India Post has made a strong case to draw attention to the fact that they could be a formidable network in the inclusion agenda. While it was well known that India Post plays a significant role in small savings, small insurance and remittance services, the attention to their potential was drawn when India Post in a surprise move applied for a universal bank licence.

The RBI did not grant a licence for a universal bank. However, the case of India Post to carry out the larger agenda of financial inclusion remains strong. The Governor of the RBI said that 'at that time we did not proceed with the universal bank application because it had not been sent with government approval' (see, Interview with the author). Initially it appeared that a universal banking licence was still open. The RBI indicated that 'India Post could still get a licence with the regulator saying it may issue one to the institution with the largest presence across the country after discussions with the government' (*Economic Times*, 2014). The application of India Post was possibly not done in haste. Sufficient preparation for the foray into banking had already happened. At the ground level with computerisation of post offices had happened. The CBS platform was introduced into the postal outlets. They also commissioned consulting major EY to advise them on the new banking foray and build a road map on setting up of a new bank (and not converting the existing postal network into a bank), while leveraging on the vast postal network they already had (Unnikrishnan, 2013).

India Post followed up its bid for obtaining a universal bank by setting up a Task Force on Leveraging the Post Office Network under the chairmanship of former Cabinet Secretary T.S.R. Subramanian (the main recommendations pertaining to insurance banking and remittances and insurance are reproduced in Appendix 7.2). While the terms of reference of the task force was largely pertaining to the restructuring of the postal department in the light of larger changes in the economy and to redefine the role of India Post, there was also a bid to strengthen the case of India Post to obtain a licence for setting up a universal bank. The arguments for India Post to set up a universal bank rather than a PB are made in chapter 13 of the report which is titled 'The Post Bank of India' (Subramanian, 2014). The report also makes a significant point that the PMJDY would be much more effective if it was inclusive of the postal network, rather than having just the banking network as the main focus of financial inclusion.

Finally in August 2015, India Post was granted an in-principle licence to operate a PB rather than a universal bank.

While the postal department has obtained a licence for a PB, the presence of the India Post in the inclusion space is significant. There are three areas in which India Post is a significant player. India Post collects savings through seven products it offers through the postal network; it is a significant player in the micro insurance market through its Postal Life Insurance (PLI) and Rural Postal Life Insurance (RPLI) products; and it is a significant player in the remittances market through it money transfer products. This chapter discusses not only the role and contribution of India Post, but also the plans India Post has as an agenda for future.

---

**Box 7.1 Governor Rajan on post bank**

*Professor Sriram:* Can we talk about the post bank. I am not sure what happened but they had applied for a licence as a mainstream bank; the Finance Minister announced in the budget that they will be a PB. Any reasons why they were not considered for a universal bank?

*Dr Rajan:* At that time we did not proceed with the universal bank application because it had not been sent with government approval. With the PB application announced in the budget, we are examining the proposal for a PB.

*Professor Sriram:* Do you think it would have been a good idea to grant a universal bank licence?

*Dr Rajan:* I would say it would be appropriate for them to first start as a PB.

*Professor Sriram:* But they are already a PB in one sense.

*Dr Rajan:* Yes, well they say that. But it would be nice to segregate all that properly into a structure, have a clear accounting, have a sense of who is in the structure, who is not. There is a need for transparency about the banking operations. What kind of a relationship do they have with the postal department? That needs to be clarified substantially. Once that is clear, the separation is clear.

*Professor Sriram:* Postal department had a consultant's report which had a road map, basically saying that every post office will not have a bank branch but in 6–7 years every district headquarter will have a banking outlet.

*Dr Rajan:* See, our worry about credit to any untested organisation, especially if the organisation can in a span of a year or two generate ₹2 trillion in deposits, how will that be deployed? What kinds of loans will be made? Where is the credit evaluation capacity? We need to have a greater comfort with that.

*Professor Sriram:* One of the arguments made was that they don't have credit experience. That is an oxymoronic argument. But you are saying size is the argument ...

*Dr Rajan:* Exactly, but let us first get the bank management, cash management and the structure together. Once we have confidence that all those things are working well and there are no operational risks then we can start slowly seeing how we can move the post PB towards more. In a number of countries the postal bank is just cash in–cash out, no lending. It doesn't make loans. Some advocates are basically saying the postman knows the local area and can make loans. But the postman has no financial experience. He can only do KYC at best. He can't make the loans objectively, because his friends are there. So in what sense is he going to make loans and collect them?

---

## STRUCTURE OF THE POSTAL NETWORK FOR FINANCIAL INCLUSION

The postal department has multiple activities, and based on the recommendations of the Subramanian Committee (see Figure 7.1), it can be bucketed into five different strategic business units. Of these, apart from managing government business and e-commerce, the rest of the activities pertain to financial services.

### Structure proposed by the Subramanian Committee

The postal network currently offers savings, remittance services, third-party products and insurance services. The only aspect of financial inclusion that is missing in the current bouquet of services is credit. It also has a formidable network of offices spread across the country and the department has been strengthening this network. Currently there is a post office in 60% of the country's gram panchayats.

The uniqueness of the postal network is something that the banking network is now rediscovering. The postal network is administered in two distinct buckets as far as staffing and management is concerned. While the departmental post offices (DPOs) are fully staffed by full-time employees of the postal department, providing full services for at least eight hours in a day, the GDS post offices are managed by GDSs (numbering 259,604, a number higher than departmental employees) who work anywhere between three to five hours a day. These GDSs are similar to BCs of the banking system, but have been tested over time, a clear accountability has been established and are compensated according to their intensity of work. On an average these GDSs get a remuneration of around ₹6,000 per month with minimal benefits pertaining to family pension.

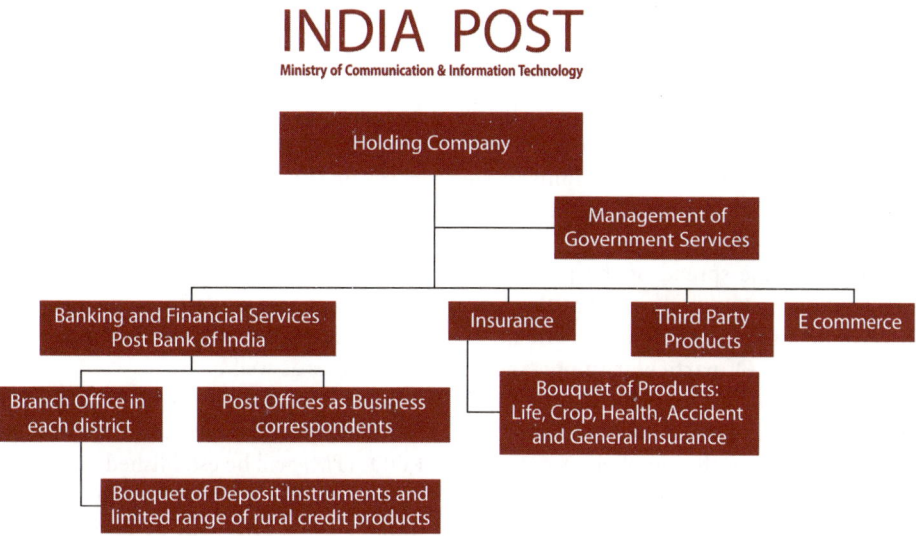

**Figure 7.1** The proposed corporate structure of India Post

## PHYSICAL OUTREACH OF THE POSTAL NETWORK

India Post has a formidable network of DPOs, sub-post offices and postal service points across the length and breadth of the country. Table 7.1 gives the details of the reach of the postal network broken down into regions.[1]

Of the network given in Table 7.1, 92,983 post offices were offering a full range of services and 146,910 offices were undertaking delivery services. What is important to note here is that the total number of postal outlets in urban centres was only 15,700 as compared to banking outlets where there were about 44,336 branches in urban and metropolitan centres, indicating that the post offices were serving more rural centres than the banks. The number of postal outlets in rural areas was around 139,182. As against this number, the rural and semi-urban branches numbering 81,527 were serving only 44,755 centres (villages/towns) (see Table 2.2 for details). On an average, a postal outlet served around 8,221 persons and in the rural outlet the penetration of the postal outlet was to

**Table 7.1** Number of postal outlets as of March 2014

| Region | Departmental post offices | | | Grameen Dak Sewak post offices | | | Total post offices | | |
|---|---|---|---|---|---|---|---|---|---|
| | Rural | Urban | Total | Rural | Urban | Total | Rural | Urban | Total |
| North | 1,675 | 2,071 | 3,746 | 17,977 | 173 | 18,150 | 19,652 | 2,244 | 21,896 |
| North-east | 575 | 383 | 958 | 5,753 | 217 | 5,970 | 6,328 | 600 | 6,928 |
| East | 2,265 | 2,195 | 4,460 | 24,680 | 255 | 24,935 | 26,945 | 2,450 | 29,395 |
| Central | 1,494 | 2,859 | 4,353 | 27,115 | 396 | 27,511 | 28,609 | 3,255 | 31,864 |
| West | 1,670 | 1,880 | 3,550 | 18,082 | 205 | 18,287 | 19,752 | 2,085 | 21,837 |
| South | 4,523 | 3,903 | 8,426 | 33,373 | 1,163 | 34,536 | 37,896 | 5,066 | 42,962 |
| Total All India | 12,202 | 13,291 | 25,493 | 126,980 | 2,409 | 129,389 | 139,182 | 15,700 | 154,882 |

*Source:* Government of India (2015) Annual Report 2014–15, New Delhi: Department of Posts, Ministry of Communications and Information Technology, Government of India.

[1] The data is organised into six regions (North, North-east, East, Central, West and South) and two classifications (rural and urban). This is done in order to have a comparison with the banking network which is also organised into six regions. In the chapter, where banking is discussed, banking statistics is consolidated into comparable classifications by merging rural and semi-urban into one basket and urban and metropolitan into another.

the extent of 6,193 persons per postal outlet. On an average, there was one postal outlet for every 21.22 square kilometres of area (GoI, 2015). The potential of the physical outreach of post offices, particularly in rural areas, need not be emphasised more and therefore if the department of posts is willing to undertake financial services, it should form an integral part of the inclusion agenda.

A comparison of the spread of the postal network with banking network shows that there are more postal outlets than banking outlets in all the regions except north. Of particular importance is the number of postal outlets in the north-east which is more than double the number of banking outlets. Even in the north where the number of outlets is marginally higher than the postal outlets, around 40% of the banking outlets are in urban centres, while only 10% of the postal outlets are in urban centres, with the remaining 90% of the outlets serving the rural areas.

It is also interesting to note that the GDSs were offering the last mile connectivity with the clients operated out of their own premises or the premises of the Gram Panchayat. The postal network thus had found a solution to operate its service by having a one-point arrangement with the GDS, without multiple lease contracts for premises. Of the DPOs that India Post had, about 1,669 were being operated from rent-free premises; while 4,047 were being operated out of premises owned by India Post. The department had rented out around 19,671 premises to carry out its operations (GoI, 2015).

India Post is making an investment of ₹49.09 billion for modernisation of its information technology (IT) architecture. This includes a significant outlay that will take care of the banking services as well. As a result of this initiative, all the departmental post offices in the country are fully computerised, and almost all the post offices in the country are interconnected through a wide area network. As of December 2014, around 1,436 post offices had also migrated to the CBS platform (GoI, 2015, p. 38). India Post operates on a 'hub and spoke' model, with all the postal outlets linked to the nearest DPO. So ultimately all transactions rest in the accounting system maintained by the head post office of the department. With the modernisation of the IT infrastructure, while all the DPOs are covered and linked on a wide area network (of the 28,847 offices, 26,597 offices are already linked on a wide area network as of March 2014), the outreach will continue through the GDS through a hand-held device which runs both on grid and on solar power. This device can link all the GDS postal outlets (numbering near about 130,000) and the villages under its coverage. Each hand-held device is capable of maintaining full details (including Aadhaar and other identity details) of up to 2,000 account holders. A pilot for this roll-out is being tested in Telangana.

The department ran two pilots one in Andhra Pradesh and another in Jharkhand to examine the feasibility of handling DBT to eligible citizens. This experiment was done through micro ATMs using the AEPS. The experiment will now be rolled out in other states as well.

India Post also has plans to aggressively roll out ATMs across all the regions in the country. While 1,000 ATMs will be established in the first phase, by the end of 2015 it is proposed to install 2,800 ATMs. Initially the ATMs will be restricted to the postal network and card holders can avail of financial services from India Post only. As time goes by, India Post may consider providing interoperability with other banks.

One of the reasons why the post offices are making a strong case for banking activities are because currently their rural post offices are subsidised to the extent of 66% and the remote tribal post offices are subsidised up to 85%. While there is nothing much that can be done to rationalise the postal outlets due to universal service obligation, it is quite possible to leverage the network and get more revenue out of the existing network, an argument proposed by the Subramanian Committee (Subramaniam, 2014).

## FINANCIAL SERVICES OFFERED BY INDIA POST

### Savings

India Post already offers a bouquet of services mostly focussed on rural areas and on small customers. These services span savings products, risk cover products, remittances and third-party products. The fact that India Post as a government organisation enjoys trust and credibility with the customer adds to its importance. In addition, India Post has launched project arrow, which not only changes the physical look and feel of a postal outlet, but focusses on customer centricity, thereby gearing up the organisation to face competition even in the interior regions. The services covered under project arrow included savings services (reduction of transaction time at counters; adequate availability of stationery) and remittance services (delivery of money orders on day of receipt; ensuring adequate cash balance; extending the services of instant and electronic money order). The progress under this

**Table 7.2** **Balance outstanding with India Post on savings schemes**

| Region | Savings accounts | Recurring deposits | Time deposits (incl-NSS[1]) | Monthly income scheme | Senior citizen | Public provident fund | Total deposits (₹ billion) |
|---|---|---|---|---|---|---|---|
| North | 80.22 | 174.69 | 97.97 | 282.62 | 60.08 | 174.68 | 870.25 |
| North-east | 15.16 | 21.03 | 2.75 | 38.16 | 1.82 | 6.66 | 85.59 |
| East | 91.66 | 89.58 | 147.51 | 638.67 | 42.23 | 37.65 | 1,047.29 |
| Central | 113.58 | 165.14 | 76.69 | 259.52 | 21.40 | 54.48 | 690.81 |
| West | 53.99 | 88.15 | 72.42 | 477.42 | 45.64 | 123.30 | 860.92 |
| South | 73.90 | 200.02 | 49.33 | 321.84 | 53.52 | 68.62 | 767.23 |
| Base | 1.09 | 2.90 | 2.25 | 2.61 | .22 | .70 | 9.76 |
| Total savings balances | 429.59 | 741.51 | 448.93 | 2,020.84 | 224.91 | 466.08 | 4,331.85 |
| Add NSC[2] and KVP[3] | | | | | | | 1,818.33 |
| Grand total | | | | | | | 6,150.18 |

*Source:* Government of India (2015) Annual Report 2014–15, New Delhi: Department of Posts, Ministry of Communications and Information Technology, Government of India.

*Notes:* [1] NSS 1997 and NSS 2020 are National Savings Scheme.
[2] National Savings Certificate.
[3] Kisan Vikas Patra.

customer experience enhancement programme is being regularly measured.

India Post offered a multiple savings products, ranging from a plain vanilla savings account to accumulation savings products such as recurring deposits, time deposits and public provident funds. India Post had the second largest share in the institutional space as far as deposits collected, next only to the State Bank of India. What is even more important was that the entire deposit base of the postal network (except for parts of National Savings Certificates [NSCs] and Kisan Vikas Patra [KVP]) was based on individual deposit and not institutional deposits. Thus, the postal network had the largest number of individual accounts—349.1 million accounts as against the 309 million individual accounts of the State Bank group. The total amount of savings that India Post can accept from individuals is capped at ₹0.45 million. By this, India Post is ensuring that the entire deposit base of India Post is in the hands of individuals. The total number of individual account holders for the entire banking system stood at 415 million as of March 2014. The average balance in the individual accounts of the postal department was far lower than the banking system, thereby confirming that India Post was serving significantly smaller customers (Table 7.2).

## Remittances

India Post is one of the oldest players in the remittance market with its traditional product Money Order. In 2013–14, India Post handled 10.91 crore money orders bearing a value of ₹122.40 billion. In addition to the money order, India Post also played a large part in remittances of benefits from the GoI. While the payments for social security schemes such as Indira Gandhi National Old Age Pension Scheme, Indira Gandhi National Widow Pension Scheme, Indira Gandhi National Disability Pension Scheme and Indira Gandhi Matritva Sahyog Yojana were made either through money order (₹40.85 billion) or through post office savings accounts (₹14.94 billion). In case of wages under the Mahatma Gandhi National Rural Employment Guarantee Act (MGNREGA), the payment was made to the savings accounts directly (642 million beneficiaries with amounts of ₹114.03 billion). A total of 96,735 postal outlets were handling MGNREGA payments.

In instant domestic money transfer service, India Post offers an iMO (instant money order) for amounts ranging from ₹1,000 to ₹50,000 wherein the recipient could display a 16-digit iMO number and a photo identity and claim the amount instantaneously, even if the person does not have an account with either the post office or the bank. The service of iMO was available in 23,741 postal outlets as of March 2015.

International money transfer service (inward remittances) from 195 countries on a real-time basis was offered in association with Western Union in 9,943 post office locations, and Moneygram in 6,070 post office locations.

India Post has also launched the electronic Indian Postal Order (eIPO), which is largely used to file Right to Information (RTI) applications with the GoI. This facility was available both to citizens resident in India and to citizens residing outside the country.

### Third-party products

India Post is a point of presence agency for the National Pension Scheme (NPS). It is also retailing the products of the UTI Mutual Fund in about 2,000 postal outlets. In the past it has also sold gold coins as a third-party distributor for Reliance. The post offices were selling gold in sizes of 0.5 gram and 1 gram coins. It was available and also affordable at that size. So when India Post first introduced the sale of this gold, there was almost a riot because it was such a small size, added with the credibility of India Post. Nobody knew it was a third-party product being sold on behalf of Reliance.

### Insurance services

India Post provides two different types of insurance services. The PLI is a life insurance product that is open only to employees of government institutions and government undertakings such as civil and military employees, state and central government employees, employees of local bodies, government-aided educational institutions, cooperatives and universities. The maximum possible sum assured in PLI is restricted to ₹5 million. The RPLI product is offered to anybody and is aimed at the smaller clients, with the maximum sum assured restricted to ₹500,000 (Table 7.3). Under both the categories, there are several products the India Post offers. However, it is to be noted that India Post had only about 2.7% market share in the insurance sector (Subramaniam, 2014), thus indicating the potential for growth, given the reach.

## WHAT DOES THE PAYMENTS BANK LICENCE MEAN?

(Based on an interview with Smt Kalpana Tewari, Member, Postal Services Board, since retired.)

While India Post did not manage to get the universal bank licence, it has been granted an in-principle licence for operating a PB. In one sense, India Post is already a PB since it does the basic function of collecting savings (and remitting them to the treasury) and managing remittances. However, this licence actually means a significant step forward for India Post towards its foray into banking.

- Firstly, unlike the current function where savings are just put into the treasury, as a PB, India Post will have to manage the money by actually building up capabilities to invest in treasury products and manage the balance sheet. While the functions pertaining to savings are now being done as a division of India Post, this foray will have a separate balance sheet, network and staffing and thereby it will have the potential to prove the possibility of what India Post can do in banking.
- Secondly, PB gives a scope to India Post to play in the market; it can issue PPIs; focus on distribution of third-party products such as PLI, other insurance products, sell gold coins and even act as an agency for third-party credit products.
- Third, while India Post will continue its small savings schemes which basically go to the state governments, PB will leverage the India Post network to expand the savings market significantly, and bring PB into the mainstream market system. PB will be in competition with traditional and specialised financial institutions. PB may be able to offer better choices.
- Fourthly, savings collected by India Post is totally non-institutional savings. PB gives a scope to get into the local rural institutional market.
- Fifthly, due to leveraging of the India Post network, PB would be able to offer deep localisation. The postmaster is local, and most of the India Post business has been out of the premises of the postmaster. Therefore, this foray will also focus on the smallest customer, and would be in a better position to offer financial literacy.

**Table 7.3** Details of postal life insurance and rural postal life insurance policies

| Name of the scheme | Number of policies procured | Sum assured (₹ billion) | Aggregate of active policies | Aggregate sum assured (active policies ₹ billion) |
|---|---|---|---|---|
| Postal life insurance | 433,182 | 161.29 | 540,6093 | 1,022.76 |
| Rural postal life insurance | 871,462 | 67.12 | 1,501,4314 | 794.66 |
| Total | 1,304,644 | 228.31 | 2,042,1407 | 1,817.42 |

Source: Annual Report, Department of Posts.

- Sixthly, there is a good sense of the physical space available in the India Post network which gives PB an early advantage to spread to the nooks and corners of the country. While PB will be an independent entity, the customer touch and feel will be of India Post. While at the district level there would be a separate branch (initially co-located with the post office with sharing of infrastructure), at the customer level the current network will be leveraged.
- Seventhly, the extant investment in rolling out ATMs will be fully leveraged.
- Eighthly, on the human resources side, there will be rationalisation. The post offices in rural and tribal areas are currently heavily subsidised. With more business on the same network it may be leveraged much better to cut the departmental losses.

## IN CONCLUSION

In conclusion it could be said that India Post and its foray in the financial inclusion space are to be watched carefully. The department has the network, it is accessible to everybody and has had experience of remittances in the post with solid systems in place. While the banks are struggling with the BC network, India Post has been operating something similar for years. While the department has been incurring losses for years, this foray is expected to cut the losses of the department and leverage its sunk investment in the vast rural network much better. Traditionally India Post has been working with the smaller depositors and the smaller customer network in remoter regions than the banks and therefore its foray into banking holds a great hope for the cause of inclusive finance.

**APPENDIX 7.1**

**Scheme-wise/year-wise detail of outstanding balance of saving accounts with India Post (₹ billion) as of 31 March**

| Scheme | 2009 | 2010 | 2011 | 2012 | 2013 | 2014 | 2015 |
|---|---|---|---|---|---|---|---|
| Post Office Savings Bank | 226.90 | 264.58 | 301.01 | 340.70 | 378.50 | 430.17 | 474.28 |
| 1 Year Term Deposit | 144.93 | 180.49 | 182.76 | 168.69 | 213.36 | 273.43 | 361.53 |
| 2 Year Term Deposit | 11.12 | 12.30 | 13.68 | 13.11 | 14.75 | 17.67 | 20.31 |
| 3 Year Term Deposit | 36.90 | 37.81 | 42.68 | 42.07 | 39.89 | 39.15 | 41.42 |
| 4 Year Term Deposit | 69.70 | 45.13 | 45.33 | 50.04 | 62.09 | 76.89 | 94.31 |
| 5 Year Term Deposit | 650.72 | 628.18 | 612.50 | 626.61 | 679.62 | 741.49 | 745.13 |
| National Savings Certificate 1987 | 38.62 | 38.74 | 42.31 | 40.58 | 39.63 | 38.69 | 36.89 |
| National Savings Certificate 1992 | 5.65 | 5.77 | 4.78 | 4.07 | 3.26 | 2.77 | 2.32 |
| Monthly Income Scheme 1987 | 1,795.04 | 2,016.93 | 2,186.74 | 2,052.88 | 2,017.87 | 2,020.85 | 2,005.57 |
| Senior Citizen | 206.51 | 249.89 | 309.13 | 267.63 | 240.93 | 224.92 | 179.75 |
| MGNREGA | | | | 0 | 56 | 0 | 0 | 0 |
| Post Office CTD | | | | 0 | 6 | 0 | 6 | 8 |
| Others | 49 | 44 | 36 | 22 | 22 | 22 | 22 |
| Total | 3,186.58 | 3,480.26 | 3,741.28 | 3,607.22 | 3,690.12 | 3,866.31 | 3,961.81 |
| National Savings Certificate VI | −60 | −69 | −66 | −69 | −75 | −77 | −82 |
| National Savings Certificate VII | −43 | −51 | −43 | −49 | −64 | −50 | −53 |
| National Savings Certificate VIII | 553.09 | 547.76 | 546.42 | 550.69 | 647.19 | 750.86 | 856.08 |
| Indira Vikas Patra | 10.31 | 10.22 | 10.20 | 8.94 | 9.07 | 8.96 | 8.87 |
| Kisan Vikas Patra | 1,475.17 | 1,539.33 | 1,585.84 | 1,539.60 | 1,283.75 | 1,067.54 | 848.41 |
| Kisan Vikas Patra 2014 | | | | | | | 26.71 |
| Others | 59 | 56 | 60 | 65 | 20.25 | 56.49 | 95.38 |
| Total | 2,038.13 | 2,096.67 | 2,141.97 | 2,098.70 | 1,958.87 | 1,882.58 | 1,834.10 |
| Public Provident Fund | 234.02 | 260.96 | 315.83 | 359.93 | 411.21 | 466.08 | 527.48 |
| Grand Total | 5,458.73 | 5,837.89 | 6,199.08 | 6,065.85 | 6,060.20 | 6,214.97 | 6,323.39 |

*Source:* Director, Financial Services, IndiaPost.

**Total number of live accounts as on 31 March 2015**

| No. of live accounts 2014–15 | | | |
|---|---|---|---|
| Total no. of live accounts (excluding 0 balance MNREGA A/cs) | Total no. of certificates issued and discharged | Total no. of 0 balance of MNREGA accounts | Total outstanding balance of all schemes |
| 330.3 million | 71.3 million | 45.6 million | 6,323.39 billion |

### APPENDIX 7.2
### Recommendations of the Task Force on leveraging the post office network (Chair: T.S.R. Subramanian) pertaining to financial services

## INSURANCE SERVICES

- The current departmental organisation is not suitable for the conduct of the life insurance business of India Post. (Para 11.2.6.)
- The coverage of PLI may be extended by allowing members of the general public as well as government/PSU employees to buy PLI policies. (Para 11.2.7.)
- Operations under both the PLI and RPLI schemes may be brought under the purview of the new Corporation. (Para 11.2.9.)
- India Insurance should have an independent Board and operate at arm's length from the Department of Posts. (Para 11.2.9.)
- India Insurance should be allowed to extend a full bouquet of insurance services in both urban and rural areas as it sees fit on the basis of considerations of market profitability. (Para 11.2.9.)
- The life insurance activities of the Department of Posts should be hived off and converted into an independent corporate entity which may be designated as India Insurance or given some other suitable name. (Para 11.3.1.)
- India Insurance should be delinked from the Consolidated Fund of India. (Para 11.3.1.)
- The new corporate entity will initially be a 100% owned subsidiary of a (new) Holding Company, which will in turn be 100% owned by the India Post. (Para 11.3.1.)
- The new corporate entity would be fully regulatory complaint and will follow the norms as prescribed by the government and the IRDA. (Para 11.3.2.)
- In course of time, the Government of India in the Department of Posts may disinvest part of its holding and allow the new entity to raise resources through an IPO offering in the market. (Para 11.3.3.)
- The initial capitalisation cost and solvency requirements, estimated at ₹100 crores, should be funded from the current insurance portfolio of the Department of Posts. (Para 11.3.4.)
- In future, additional capital may be funded through available surpluses, market borrowing or disinvestment as provided for in the Articles of Association. (Para 11.3.4.)
- India Insurance will enter into an MoU with India Post setting out objectives to be achieved and broad parameters of action. (Para 11.5.1.)
- India Insurance will initially draw most of its personnel from the current strength of the Department of Posts, except for senior executives and experts as required. (Para 11.5.1.)
- Decisions on future inductions may be decided by the Board of Directors. (Para 11.5.1.)
- There shall be a transitional period of 1 to 3 years, during which preparatory steps will be completed and the new structure will be put in place. (Para 11.6.1.)
- These steps shall include incorporation of the new entity; transfer of resources and records; takeover of the business portfolio; training of personnel; expansion and diversification of the product basket; addition of corporate agents, banks, brokers to the distribution network; making operations IT driven; and institution of performance evaluation protocols. (Para 11.6.1.)
- India Insurance will also engage in the distribution of non-life insurance products of other insurance companies, including Motor, Fire, Marine, Engineering, Health, Personal Accident, Crop, Weather and Household Articles Insurance. (Para 11.7.1.)
- India Insurance will only distribute such products on behalf of other companies on a commission basis without incurring any insurance liability/risk in this regard. (Para 11.7.3.)

- As per the legal requirements, India Insurance may take up a Corporate Agency or Broker's Licence for its third-party business, depending on whether it chooses to distribute the products of one or more other insurance companies. (Para 11.7.4.)
- If India Insurance distributes the products of more than one company on a Broker's Licence, a separate company will have to be incorporated for this purpose. (Para 11.7.4.)
- India Insurance should become a distributor of non-life insurance products, to begin with as a Corporate Agent, with the option to convert it to a Broker's Licence after it gains experience and develops an appropriate personnel base. (Para 11.7.6.)
- The independent company(ies) owning the Broker's Licence to distribute, which can be a Private or Public Limited Company(ies), will be 100% owned by the Holding Company. (Para 11.7.6.)
- A systematic publicity campaign should be planned and executed by India Post, in collaboration with a professional advertising and PR company, to support the activities of the new entity, India Insurance. (Para 11.8.2.)

## MONEY REMITTANCE SERVICES

- India Post should strengthen its capabilities and diversify the range of products which it offers, paying particular attention to growth segments such as Card Based Money Transfers, Mobile Banking, Collection of EMIs and bill payments. (Para 12.2.1.)
- India Post may collaborate with the National Payments Corporation of India (NPCI) to develop new financial products based on the RuPay Indian domestic card scheme. (Para 12.2.2.)
- India Post may tie up with RuPay to boost the acceptability of the card, particularly in rural areas. (Para 12.2.3.)

## POST BANK OF INDIA

- The proposal is not to convert the PO Network into a Bank, but to set up a fully professional new Bank to further financial inclusion and meet the objectives of the Pradhan Mantri Jan Dhan Yojana, which specifically provides for the extension of credit to all Indians resident in every part of India, particularly in rural areas. (Para 13.1.9.)
- This opportunity for achieving universal financial inclusion via technology and the institutional reach of the PO Network must not be lost. There is admittedly a risk involved, as there is in any new venture into uncharted waters. The risk involved can and must be managed in the interests of the overall larger national objectives. (Para 13.1.12.)
- The PBI must be professionally managed and operated, with credit and other risks being handled by experienced experts hired from the market. In its own interest, its operations must be fully in line and compliant with RBI Guidelines. (Para 13.1.13.)
- A new institution, to be called the Post Bank of India or by some other suitable name, should be set up as a commercial bank offering the full spectrum of financial and banking services. (Para 13.2.2.)
- As the owner of the proposed PBI, the Government of India may take decisions as appropriate on structural and organisational issues and other details, including the funding requirements. (Para 13.2.2.)
- The Task Force is of the view that the PBI should be set up under an Act of Parliament and that establishing the PBI as a statutory institution and a Government Bank would enhance its credibility, insulate it from local pulls and greatly facilitate its operations. (Para 13.2.4.)
- It is essential to structure the proposed PBI in such a manner as to pre-empt the possibility of outside interests influencing its day-to-day operations. (Para 13.2.5.)
- The Task Force also recommends that the PBI should initially be set up as a Public Sector Bank wholly owned by the Government of India. (Para 13.2.6.)
- The initial capital requirement, estimated at ₹500 crores as per RBI requirements, would be fully funded by the Government. (Para 13.2.6.)
- After the Bank establishes itself in 3 to 5 years, the Board of Directors could take a view on floating an IPO to raise fresh capital. (Para 13.2.6.)
- The PBI will focus on fulfilling the Government's mandate of financial inclusion and on bringing the unbanked and under-banked segments of the population, particularly in rural, semi-rural and remote areas within the ambit of the formal monetised economy. (Para 13.2.7.)

- A view needs to be taken on how best to seamlessly integrate the earlier banking operations into the proposed new structure. The best and seamless method would be to fully absorb the POSB in the new proposed Bank (PBI). (Para 13.2.8.)
- The PBI will offer services including credit, which are beyond the remit of the POSB. (Para 13.2.9.)
- The PBI will develop financial products and services which are specifically tailored to the needs of the rural and urban unbanked population, if necessary in collaboration with other banks. (Para 13.2.9.)
- The PBI will function as a commercially viable and self-sustaining entity without the need for continuing government subsidies. (Para 13.2.10.)
- After the initial gestation period, it should generate its own resources and sustain itself in the competitive market environment. (Para 13.2.10.)
- The PBI should price its services on a cost plus basis and revise these rates from time to time, so that its operations do not become a continuing and increasing burden on the government exchequer. (Para 13.2.11.)
- The PBI will start with a Head Office Main Branch and will thereafter expand its operations by opening branch offices in the metro towns and state capitals to be manned by banking professionals. (Para 13.2.12.)
- The longer term objective would be to establish a Branch Office of the PBI in each District Headquarter over a 3- to 5-year period, to be operated mostly by banking professionals. (Para 13.2.12.)
- The 150,000-plus Departmental and Branch POs will act as Banking Correspondents for the PBI. (Para 13.2.12.)
- Careful consideration should be given to the various types, elements and levels of risk involved in the PBI's operations. (Para 13.3.1.)
- Robust System Protocols and Standard Operating Procedures should be put in place to manage these risks effectively. (Para 13.3.1.)
- The PBI should recruit/commission the services of banking experts to manage its credit, portfolio and market risks. (Para 13.3.3.)
- Appropriate management capabilities should be mobilised from the market and robust systems and processes should be put in place to ensure that non-performing assets are kept within acceptable limits. (Para 13.3.3.)
- It is neither necessary nor desirable to mandate a waiting period before the PBI enters into credit and lending operations. (Para 13.4.1.)
- The PBI should be constituted and begin working as a credit and lending bank immediately, without any trial/waiting/learning period. (Para 13.4.2.)
- The PBI should be set up as an independent statutory and corporate entity offering the full bouquet of banking services, including credit, to its customers. (Para 13.4.3.)
- The PBI will primarily target currently unbanked and under-banked customers in rural, semi-rural and remote areas, with a focus on providing small and affordable loans and simple deposit products. (Para 13.4.3.)
- Customers will be provided with full-fledged Savings Accounts, which can be retained even with zero balances, as provided for in the PMJDY. (Para 13.4.3.)
- Credit risks will be managed by hiring professionals from the banking sector and by developing and implementing robust protocols for building checks and balances in the system. (Para 13.4.3.)

## REFERENCES

*Economic Times* (2014). *RBI Grants in Principle Approval to IDFC, Bandhan for New Bank Licences*. Mumbai: *Economic Times*.

Government of India (GoI) (2015). *Annual Report 2014–15*. Department of Posts, Ministry of Communication and Information Technology.

Subramanian, T.S.R. (2014). *Report of the Task Force on Leveraging Post Office Network—Empowering Rural India*. New Delhi: Government of India, Department of Posts, Ministry of Communications and Information Technology.

Unnikrishnan, D. (2013). *Finance Ministry Opposes India Post's Banking Licence Plan*. New Delhi: HT Media.

# Review of self-help group bank linkage programme

## INTRODUCTION

The year 2015 seems to be a watershed for India in its quest to provide access to a wide range of financial services. The recent developments, in the last one year, have been fast paced giving a stronger path for financial inclusion in the country. While public sector banks do not take the story further after opening a large number of bank accounts under the PMJDY, the RBI has made provisions to issue licenses to SFBs and payment banks. This is arguably the first opportunity to some financial intermediaries to get involved in offering a complete range of financial services that a bank can offer. What does this mean for the hugely successful community based financial inclusion programmes? Has the discourse shifted significantly towards individualisation and bank led inclusion? This is an issue worth examining in the context of the community based programmes.

It is well known that the self-help group bank linkage programme (SHGBLP) emerged from the grassroots efforts of several NGOs across the country. In design, the SHGBLP was savings led; helped in aggregating the transactions of poorer women; created a transaction trail; and provided a basic level of discipline through regular meeting. The SHGBLP demonstrated the strength and power of social collaterals. Over a period the group-based collaterals of SHGs were even recognised by the RBI for the purposes of provisioning and other prudential norms.

The basic design of the SHGBLP had the concept of a group fund which was built up with the savings as well as the margins between the borrowing rates from the banks and the lending rates to the members as a buffer that absorbed the possible default costs of individual members, thus maintaining a high repayment rates to the lending institutions. In general, the SHGBLP spread faster in the southern states, with Andhra Pradesh, Telangana and Tamil Nadu

leading the numbers in both group formation, linkage and credit activities. Elsewhere in the country there were examples of success stories depending on how actively some of the NGOs promoted the concept of groups.

What is to be noted is that, by and large, the SHG-BLP was kept as a peoples' movement. The support of the state was largely in providing funding for the NGO for group formation, as well as creating a policy environment for SHGs to flourish. Some state governments linked some of the benefit schemes to be distributed through SHG (like the erstwhile Andhra Pradesh government's Deepam scheme that provided cooking gas connections to SHG members). However, in the past few years there has been an increasing participation of the state in the SHGBLP ever since the National Rural Livelihoods Mission (NRLM) was launched. With the launch of the scheme which kept SHGs as the centrepiece of community organisation and had a blueprint for the scale-up model—having federations at the village level (village organisation [VO]); at the district level (zilla samakhyas) and even a proposal to set up an apex development financial institution (DFI). In fact, the AP government went ahead and set up a federated cooperative (Streenidhi). It it can be seen that there is an increasing tendency to co-opt the SHG movement more as a state-promoted developmental plan. While this trend has been in the works for many years, it is important to take note of it—to understand the trajectory that the SHGBLP will take.

## REVIEW OF DEVELOPMENTS IN SHGBLP

The SHGBLP and the NRLM continued on their growth path of setting up community-based institutional structures and linking them with the banking system. While the number of groups grew marginally, the credit offtake for SHGs showed a sharp improvement, indicating that the linkage with NRLM has accelerated the credit deployment to SHG. However, the larger numbers showed that there were a far greater number of groups that were only saving and were not linked to the bank for credit, and the credit multiplier on savings had a great potential to improve.

The NRLM-based SHGs also continued the effort to provide support systems for enterprises to be set up. With the three-tier structure of SHGs, village organisations and district federations, it was expected that the support systems that were earlier being offered by NGOs will be offered from within the federal structure. The aspect of sustainability of these structures had to be examined in greater detail. National Bank for Agriculture and Rural Development (NABARD) has undertaken a programme of digitising the SHG records as a major initiative this year. There were attempts of achieving greater convergence between the old SHGs and the NRLM-linked SHGs and a greater convergence in approach between the Ministry of Rural Development (MoRD) and NABARD.

When the SHGBLP completed 20 years, in 2012 there was a review of the programme by NABARD, and at that time the thinking was to take the SHG-BLP to the next level. This was christened SHG-II (NABARD, 2012) and the strategy was based on identifying the following issues:

(a) inadequate outreach in many regions;
(b) delays in opening of SHG accounts and disbursement of loans;
(c) impounding of savings by banks as collateral;
(d) non-approval of repeat loans even when the first loans were repaid promptly;
(e) multiple membership and borrowings by SHG members within and outside SHGs; and
(f) limited banker interface and monitoring.

From the above diagnosis, NABARD initiated some changes at the product level:

(a) allowing voluntary savings so as to capture the increased financial flows from other activities like MGNREGA wages;
(b) encouraging SHG members to open individual bank accounts to facilitate them to graduate from community banking to individual banking; with commensurate financial education programme on managing the sophistication of this product:
(c) converting the loans to SHGs as cash credit/overdraft limits to ensure that repeat loans are not denied;

(d) enabling Joint Liability Groups (JLGs) within SHGs for the members of an SHG who may graduate faster and require higher levels of loans than required by other SHG members;
(e) improving Risk Mitigation Systems by self-rating; and
(f) building second-tier institutions.

While many of the issues identified were real issues, there has been no update on how the above strategy was rolled out by NABARD. For instance, allowing voluntary savings in groups was a concept that was already there. A study commissioned by NABARD during the year suggested that the capture of higher savings happened when the individual members in the groups set a dream goal, usually for purchase of gold or for education of children and also increased the trust levels within the groups (Kumar et al., undated). The progress under the SHGBLP (reviewed below) shows that the problems with linkage continue, particularly in certain regions. Individualisation of banking, which was identified rightly three years ago, has moved in a different direction. Later in this chapter, the impact and benefit of individualisation of banking will be discussed in detail.

## PROGRESS UNDER SHGBLP

Comparing the statistics for the period 2006–10 and the next five years of 2010 to 2015 the previous year's report noted that the growth of SHGs had plateaued. Table 8.1 gives the numbers of SHGs for the past four years and we can see that while there is little action on group formation, the activities of savings and loaning within the groups are showing growth.

In 2011, an ambitious NRLM was initiated which made SHGs as a foundational aspect in roll-out of the programme. Unlike the traditional group formation efforts where it would take about 6 months for the groups to go through the four-stage process of Forming-Storming-Norming and Performing (Kanitkar, 2002), the NRLM process tried to accelerate the programme. A classic group formation effort requires regular savings and internal lending which leads to a build-up of base capital as well as a transaction trail for even a savings-based linkage with the bank. The NRLM process tried to accelerate this by (a) providing the base capital in the form of a grant and (b) accelerating the linkage to the bank through active intervention and handholding support. The process designed by NRLM is given in Figure 8.1.

**Table 8.1 Overall progress under SHG bank linkage**

(Amount in billion/Numbers in million)

| Particulars | | 2011–12 | | 2012–13 | | 2013–14 | | 2014–15 | |
|---|---|---|---|---|---|---|---|---|---|
| | | No. of SHGs | Amount | No. of SHGs | Amount | No. of SHGs | Amount | No. of SHGs | Amount |
| SHGs savings with banks as on 31 March | Total SHGs | 7.96 | 65.51 | 7.32 | 82.17 | 7.43 | 98.97 | 7.71 | 113.07 |
| | | 6.7% | –6.7% | –8.1% | 25.4% | 1.53% | 20.45% | 3.76% | 14.28% |
| | Of which NRLM SGSY other Govt. programmes | 2.12 | 13.95 | 2.05 | 18.22 | 2.26 | 24.78 | 3.05 | 45.94 |
| | | 5.0% | –23.2% | –3.6% | 30.6% | 10.46% | 36.01% | 34.95% | 85.39% |
| | % of which NRLM SGSY other Govt. programmes to total | 26.7 | 21.3 | 28.0 | 22.2 | 30.45 | 25.03 | 39.55 | 40.63 |
| | All women SHGs | 6.30 | 51.04 | 5.94 | 65.15 | 6.25 | 80.13 | NA | NA |
| | | 3.3% | –3.7% | –5.7% | 27.6% | 5.27% | 22.99% | | |
| | Percentage of women Groups | 79.1 | 77.9 | 81.1 | 79.3 | 84.15 | 80.96 | NA | NA |
| Loans disbursed to SHGs during the year | Total SHGs | 1.15 | 165.35 | 1.22 | 205.85 | 1.37 | 240.17 | 1.64 | 303.34 |
| | | –4% | 13.7% | 6.3% | 24.5% | 12.02% | 16.67% | 19.7 | 26.30% |
| | Of which NRLM SGSY other Govt. programmes | 0.21 | 26.44 | 1.81 | 22.07 | 0.23 | 34.80 | 0.65 | 95.62 |
| | | –12.9% | 6.6% | –13.8% | –16.5% | 24.56% | 57.67% | 182.60% | 174.77% |
| | % of which NRLM SGSY other Govt. programmes to Total | 18.3 | 16.0 | 14.8 | 10.7 | 16.52 | 14.49 | 39.63 | 31.52 |
| | All women SHGs | 0.92 | 141.32 | 1.04 | 178.54 | 1.15 | 210.38 | NA | NA |
| | | –9.2% | 12.0% | 12.4% | 26.3% | 11.02% | 17.83% | | |
| | Percentage of women hroups | 80.4 | 85.5 | 85.1 | 86.7 | 84.3 | 87.6 | NA | NA |
| Loans outstanding against SHGs as on 31st March | Total SHGs | 4.35 | 363.40 | 4.45 | 393.75 | 4.20 | 429.28 | 4.49 | 526.31 |
| | | –9.0% | 16.4% | 2.2% | 8.4% | –5.71 | 9.02% | 6.45% | 22.6% |
| | Of which NRLM SGSY other Govt. programmes | 1.22 | 80.55 | 1.19 | 85.97 | 1.31 | 101.77 | 1.85 | 198.30 |
| | | –5.4% | 2.9% | –1.9% | 6.7% | 9.55% | 18.38% | 41.22% | 37.68% |
| | % of which NRLM SGSY other Govt. programmes to total | 27.9 | 22.2 | 26.8 | 21.8 | 31.1 | 23.7 | NA | NA |
| | All women SHGs | 3.65 | 304.65 | 3.76 | 328.40 | 3.40 | 361.52 | NA | NA |
| | | –8.4% | 16.6% | 2.9% | 7.8% | –9.34 | 10.08% | | |
| | Percentage of women groups | 83.8 | 83.8 | 84.4 | 83.3 | 81.2 | 84.2 | NA | NA |

Percentage numbers represent growth over previous years, indicate growth/decline over the previous year.

*Source:* Status of Microfinance in India, NABARD, Mumbai. Data for 2014–15 from Micro Credit Innovations Department, NABARD. The 2014–15 data is provisional.

In addition to the hand-holding support, the NRLM provided other forms of financial support for various activities. The following specific areas of financial support were available from NRLM:

- NRLM provides Revolving Fund (RF) to SHGs of ₹10,000–15,000 as corpus to meet the members' credit needs directly and as catalytic capital for leveraging repeat bank finance. RF is given

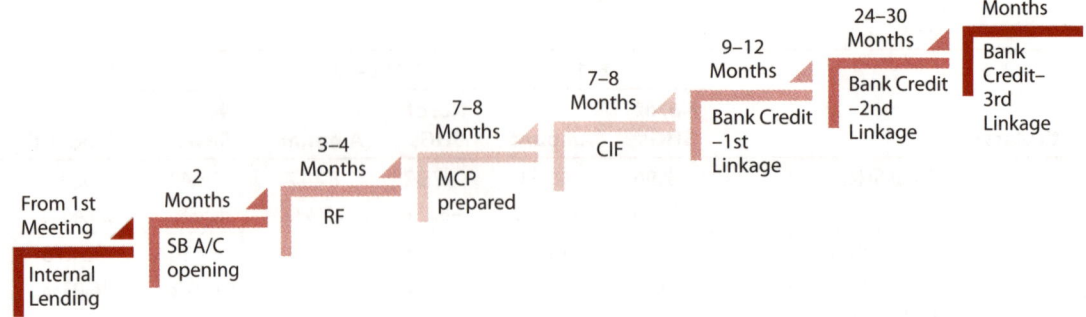

**Figure 8.1** Process of formation, growth and linkage of SHGs under NRLM

*Source:* NRLM website: http://aajeevika.gov.in/content/components/financial-inclusion, accessed on 26 August 2015.

to SHGs that have been practising 'Panchasutra' (regular meetings; regular savings; regular inter-loaning; timely repayment and up-to-date books of accounts).

- NRLM provides Community Investment Fund as seed capital to SHG Federations at cluster level to meet the credit needs of the members through the SHGs/Village Organisations and to meet the working capital needs of the collective activities at various levels.
- NRLM provides Vulnerability Reduction Fund to SHG Federations at village level to address vulnerabilities like food security, health security etc., and to meet the needs of the vulnerable persons in the village.[1]

## REGIONAL SPREAD OF SHGs

With the ambitious roll-out of NRLM, the expectations were twofold: (a) the activities under the SHGBLP will pick up steam and scale substantially

and (b) the bank loans, for SHGs, which were traditionally focussed on the southern region would be available more evenly across the country and the regional imbalance would be restored.

## SAVINGS

The data for the SHGs has shown an interesting trend. The data on total number of SHGs that are collecting savings (and thereby defining these as active SHGs) shows a reduction from 7.9 million groups in March 2011 to about 7.4 million groups in 2014. There is a gradual claw back to the earlier levels with the March 2015 numbers indicating about 7.7 million groups having savings. The relative share of the groups under NRLM has increased to near about 40% of the total groups in 2015. However, the regional balance shows a general increase in the number of SHGs in all regions; the southern region accounts not only for the growth in the number of groups but also shows a significantly higher amount of deposits (Table 8.2).

**Table 8.2** Number of SHGs with savings and amount of savings collected: 2010 and 2015

| Region | 31 March 2010 | | | 31 March 2015 | | |
| --- | --- | --- | --- | --- | --- | --- |
| | SHGs (millions) | Savings (₹ billion) | Ave savings/ group | SHGs (millions) | Savings (₹ billion) | Ave savings/ group |
| North | 0.35 | 3.42 | 9,723 | 0.36 | 2.80 | 7,748 |
| North-east | 0.29 | 1.22 | 4,164 | 0.33 | 1.49 | 4,468 |
| East | 1.37 | 11.20 | 8,151 | 1.53 | 22.84 | 14,979 |
| Central | 0.78 | 5.14 | 6,706 | 0.82 | 8.43 | 10,310 |
| West | 0.94 | 9.27 | 9,800 | 0.95 | 11.07 | 11.598 |
| South | 3.22 | 31.75 | 9,848 | 3.72 | 66.43 | 17,859 |
| Total | 6.95 | 61.99 | 8,915 | 7.71 | 113.07 | 14,660 |

*Source:* Status of Microfinance in India. Mumbai: NABARD. Data for 2014-15 is provisional and provided by MCID, NABARD.

[1] The above data is available at NRLM website: http://aajeevika.gov.in/content/components/financial-inclusion, accessed on 26 August 2015.

The savings amounts of the NRLM groups have grown at a faster pace than the general growth of non-NRLM groups up to 2015 (Table 8.1). However, the regional spread seems to indicate that there has been little impact of NRLM in reducing the regional skew. Data in Figure 8.2, shows that the share of groups (in terms of the number of SHGs) has grown from 46% to 48%, this growth coming at the cost of western region. Given that the absolute numbers of groups are not significantly going up, this growth in the relative share of the southern region should be seen with caution. It is to be examined if the groups formed on an accelerated basis by the NRLM process are sustainable over a longer duration or whether they are vulnerable.

In addition to the spread of active groups concentrated in the southern region, the absolute amount of savings of the groups is also concentrated in south. This is understandable if we assume that the southern groups are older, have had the habit of savings for longer and therefore the average amount of savings per group is much larger than the other parts of the region. However, what is interesting to note is not just the disproportionately high share in the overall savings in 2010, but the increased share of savings coming from the southern region in 2015. As can be seen from the panels in Figure 8.3, the five southern states account for 59% of the savings of SHGs across the country.

## Loans

While the process of financial inclusion starts when the groups start their savings and start internal lending, the real linkage with the formal sector for the groups is said to happen only when they start getting loans from the formal banking sector. Therefore, it is important to look at the numbers

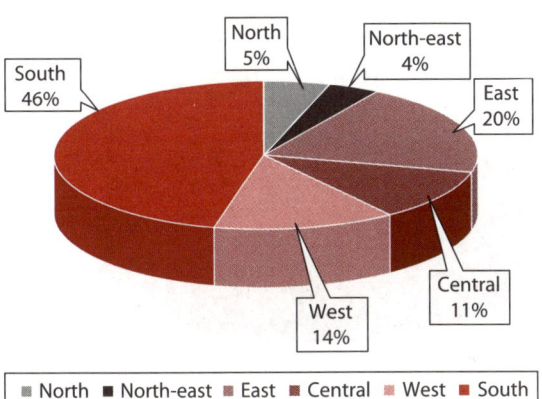

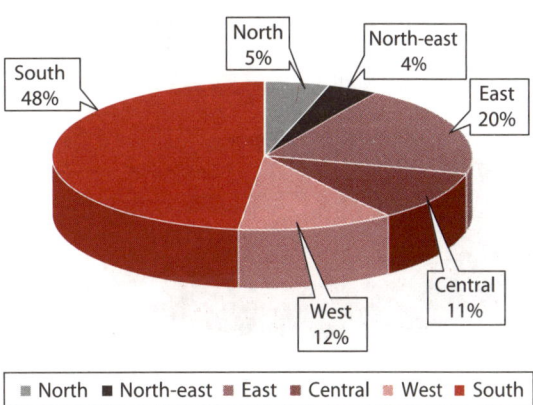

**Figure 8.2** Region-wise distribution of SHGs collecting savings in 2010 and 2015

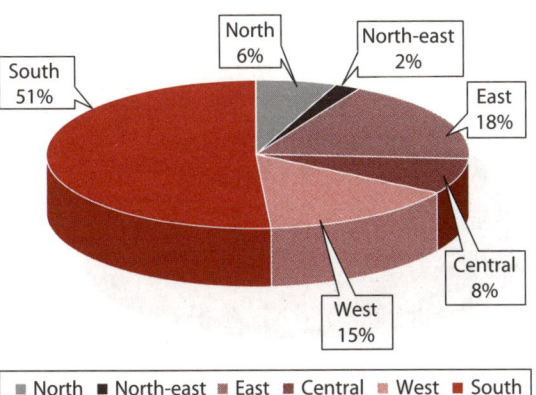

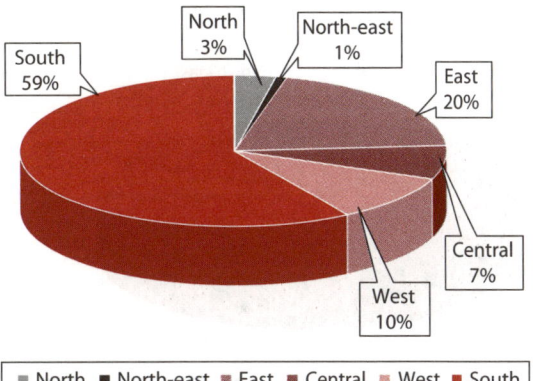

**Figure 8.3** Region-wise savings balances with SHGs in 2010 and 2015

pertaining to the loans, which is an indication of (a) connection with the bank and the bank reposing faith on the customers and (b) investing those amounts (usually) in income-generating activities. A perusal of the data shows some interesting trends on the overall:

(a) In the first two years of NRLM starting 2011 there is not much lending coming in from the formal banking sector to the subset of SHGs that are under NRLM, the numbers for 2014–15 show a significant growth in the NRLM sub-segment of lending both in the number of groups lent and the amounts lent for the NRLM-recognised SHGs (see Table 8.1).

(b) The proportion of groups that are enjoying the increased access, however, goes back to south (see Figure 8.4), with a larger proportion of the SHGs getting loans from the formal banking system.

(c) The amounts of loan given to the groups in the south take a whopping 79% of all the loans given to SHGs and this is a significant increase from the proportion given to SHGs in 2010 when it was 76% of the loan amounts (see panels in Figure 8.5).

(d) The number of accounts outstanding and the amounts outstanding in those accounts at the end of 2010 and 2015, respectively also show similar trends (see Figures 8.6 and 8.7).

The last bit of data that is of importance is the region-wise credit multiplier which can be seen in Figure 8.8. While it appears that the north-east has the best credit multiplier (₹5.85 of loan for every rupee of savings) it is to be noted that the entire north-eastern numbers are calculated on a very low base. The region accounts for only 2% of the country's SHG activity on all parameters. If the numbers of north-east can be glossed over for a moment, then

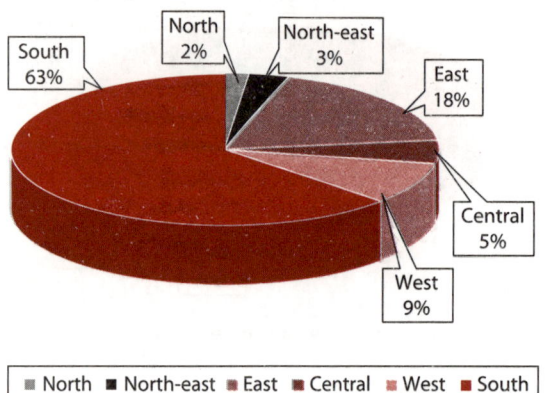

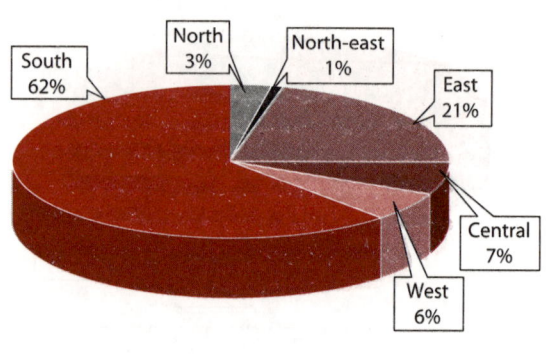

**Figure 8.4** Loans disbursed to SHGs in 2010 and 2015

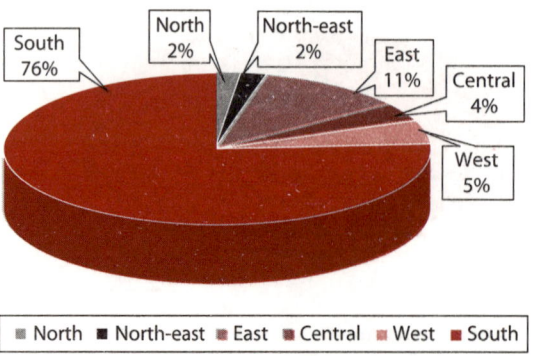

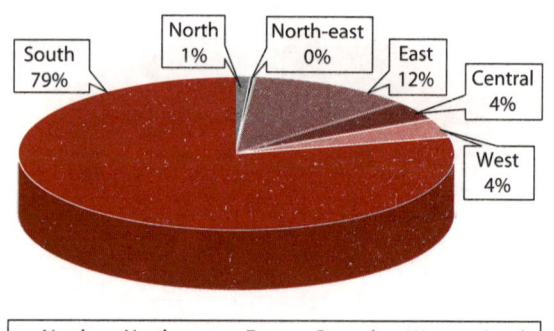

**Figure 8.5** Loan amounts disbursed to SHGs in 2010 and 2015

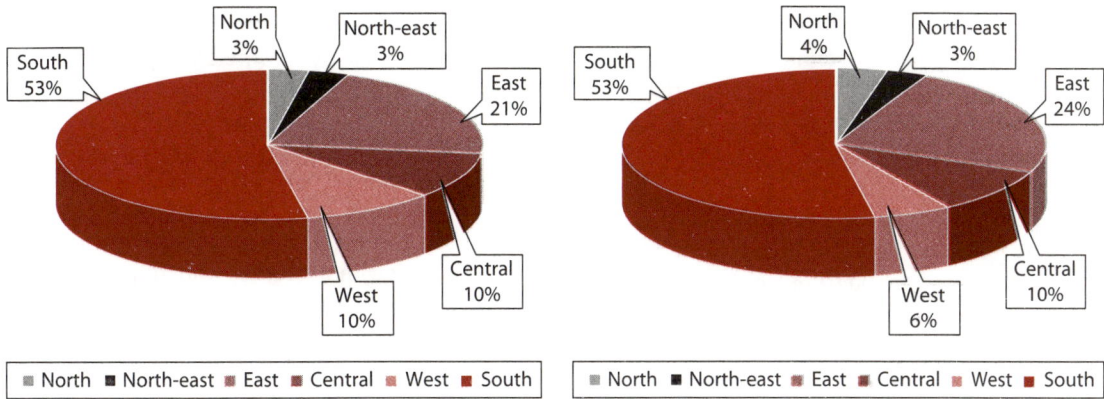

**Figure 8.6**  Number of SHG accounts outstanding as on 31 March 2010 and 2015

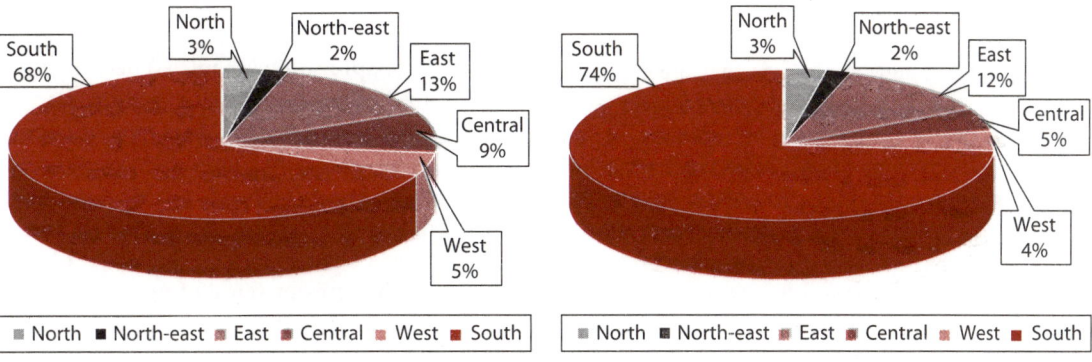

**Figure 8.7**  Loan amounts outstanding with SHGs as on 31 March 2010 and 2015

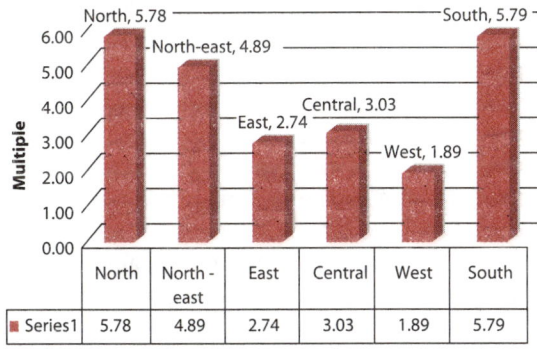

**Figure 8.8**  Region-wise credit multiple of savings (savings*loan) in 2015

the story that is narrated is that the multiplier for south is the highest and that of the west is 1.76. There is much scope for the banks to offer greater amounts of credit in states other than the southern India.

Given the above data and the trends, it was possibly appropriate for NRLM to express concern that the bank linkage programme is not taking off in providing the loan multipliers in the newer states and therefore to examine an apex refinance institution for SHGs.

From the time NABARD was set up in 1982 there has been no direct intervention in creating new institutions in the financial inclusion space. There were attempts in the past few years by the MoRD to set up an apex Developmental Financial Institution (DFI) to focus on the women's SHG movement; it never fructified. In 2014, the MoRD appointed a committee (Chair: Ms Usha Thorat, former Deputy Governor, RBI) to advise on the feasibility of setting up a DFI for focussed growth of inclusive finance through the women's SHG movement (MoRD, GoI, 2014). The committee identified that there were two elements of gaps in the institutional architecture for inclusive finance through the SHGs. The first is: development of the ecosystem that makes the financial system, particularly the banks, comfortable to transact with the community-based systems like SHGs and their federal organisations. The second is: the actual transactional aspects pertaining to providing loans and other financial products.

---

**Box 8.1 To set up a DFI for SHGs or not? The recommendations of the Usha Thorat Committee**

The committee did not encourage of setting up of a DFI while appreciating the issues that were brought up for discussion. It instead suggested a setting up of a specialised agency that will purely address the ecosystem in which the financial structure would be comfortable in engaging with the community-based SHGs. The ecosystem needs were identified as issues pertaining to capacity building and training (so that the bankers could appreciate the ground-level complexities); credit guarantee arrangements to provide a comfort factor for lending and increase the risk appetite; a rating mechanism that would objectively evaluate the quality of the portfolio; a securitisation system that will help the insular SHG portfolio to discover its worth in the financial markets; research, consumer protection issues and so on. While the committee identified that this could be done within the existing departmental architecture of NABARD—an institution that has been dealing with the community-based organisations in the past—it found the need for focussed action and therefore suggested a separate agency as a subsidiary of NABARD.

On the transactional issue of providing access to finance, the committee was of the view that the existing institutional architecture of NABARD Financial Services (NABFINS) as a specialised subsidiary of NABARD was filling in this space and suggested more such institutions be set up on a regional basis.

---

In general, the Ministry of Finance and the RBI have held the view that new apex financial institutions do not add value and the initiatives should be more in strengthening the retail part of the portfolio. This was also reflective in the views that these agencies had expressed vis-à-vis the proposal to set up an apex DFI for SHGs. Not only was this the view

of these agencies in the instance of this particular proposal, the regulator has held this view for a while now. Therefore, it was evident that there were no big institutional initiatives in the DFI space for more than three decades.

## BEYOND SHGs: CONVERGENCE WITH VARIOUS INITIATIVES

The SHGBLP is being promoted by three distinct efforts—starting with the NGOs who initially promoted the groups; the groups encouraged by NABARD through the banking system and the efforts of mobilisation by NRLM. In addition, the massive roll-out of PMJDY would be touching the households of the SHG members and some of them may become eligible for the DBT scheme over a period of time. An examination of the data put out by NABARD has consistently distinguished between the SHGs that were promoted outside of the government schemes and the SHGs that were linked with the state-sponsored schemes. There might be a reason to do this—because the SHGs under the state-sponsored schemes had other 'noise' factors like subsidies and subventions. However, in the light of aggressive orientation towards individualisation of banking transactions under the PMJDY, there may be a need to look at the aspect of convergence with a greater sense of urgency and ensure that the diverse efforts undertaken add up to something substantial.

While data on the SHGBLP linked to the banking system is available, the independent efforts may go unreported. In addition, there are fairly large institutions such as NABFINS, Sanghamithra Rural Financial Services and Kalanjiam Development Financial Services that are actively working with the SHGs where banks have not been supporting. All these efforts need coordination.

The need for convergence is articulated several times. The Usha Thorat Committee report provides a framework for a coordination mechanism between the ministry and NABARD, and with the induction of members representing the NGO and the second-tier institutions other than banks, this could be achieved.

As far as the NRLM is concerned, the government is proposing to create an arrangement of establishing a committee on financing SHG sector in NABARD. This committee would be headed by the secretary of Rural Development. This committee would primarily focus on MGNREGA workers, SHG members and would try to bring them under the purview of formal banking structure thus accelerating the whole notion of Financial Inclusion.

The committee will create processes wherein banks would be equally encouraged to fund the SHG structures as well. The ministry is looking forward to launch a number of campaigns, to sensitise the banks on the need to fund the SHGs.

There may be a need for more institutions like NABFINS that specialise in funding SHGs to come up in areas where SHGs are underfinanced. With the requirements for achieving priority sector targets becoming more stringent, and the financial markets maturing to accept securitisation deals and the potential for opening of trading of the PSL obligations through PSL certificates, there may be a possibility of more specialised institutions taking the portfolio off the balance sheet of the mainstream banks. While the new SFBs come with a deep belief in the JLG model of MFIs, they are also eminently suited to look at these linkages with a greater attention to detail.

Finally, it may be important to involve bankers in the conversations on the bank linkage programme. Usually in such forums, bankers are conspicuous by their absence.

One reason why the bankers might be unwilling to lend to SHGs may be because of the belief that a large chunk of the credit goes for consumption under the SHG structure. However, if the fact that poverty is a multidimensional issue is articulated and be addressed accordingly, there is scope for better penetration. The MoRD would be using data provided by the various departments to design the interventions. It will be an integrated model where the focus would be on a number of aspects of well-being starting with education, health, sanitation, credit linkage, etc. These themes could be merged with the Gram Panchayat Plan with SHGs having an institutional partnership with the Panchayat Raj Institutions. This convergence will dovetail the individual household economy (both consumption expenditure and productive investments and income thereof) and make the groups more robust and reliable.

The MoRD hopes that through this process non-farm activities would be supported and encouraged. For example, in states such as Tamil Nadu, agricultural production has created a space wherein the banking sector is also confident about funding them. Eventually such an approach also paves the way for further credit flow in terms of non-farm-based activities as well. NRLM is also aiming to move beyond the purist approach and would want to look at SHGs which are outside the realm of NRLM. NRLM will continue to support the SHGs to make them viable in the long run.

The idea is to provide unified code/number for each household which will help in capturing data that measures the extent and kind of deprivations that the household has to suffer. Once this is done, NRLM with its approach of saturation would be able to provide necessary assistance and support. The idea is that if the data capture process is adequate and there is enough evidence, the SHG lending proportion will grow up substantially. This approach looks at data at the client level as against the other recommendations of creating an external institutional eco-system. The MoRD believes that among the states, Bihar seems to display huge potential under this context where the tendency of borrowing from MFIs has gone down in the recent past given the higher rates of interests. The next focus states to roll this out in the coming year would be Odisha, Chhattisgarh, Madhya Pradesh, Rajasthan and Himachal Pradesh.

## FEDERAL STRUCTURES

While most of the SHG movement has been a single-tier structure—functional linkages to the bank for financial transactions, and linkages with the NGO for promotional support—in the past few years there have been attempts to create a federal structure for the SHGs in order to strengthen them. While discussing the federal structures in the SHGBLP, it is important to draw lessons from the multi-tier cooperative system to see how it may pan out.

As per the last estimate available there were in all 178,664 federations in India (ILRT, 2014). These federations performed multiple roles of providing financial intermediation, providing support services, providing livelihood enhancement services and so on. For instance, Myrada, one of the strongest Self-Help Group Promoting Institutions in Karnataka, has had community resource centres that provide support to the groups. Similarly, Dhan Foundation also has the federal organisations in the Kalanjiam family that provide other financial services like insurance which cannot be offered at a group level. Thus, some of these efforts have indicated that there is a need for a federal structure which could have a specialised role.

The design of NRLM envisages the formation of both the Village Organisation (federal structure for all the SHGs in a given village) and a District Federation. The idea of the NRLM structure is similar to the other federal structures—holding bulk funds and acting as intermediaries to the grass-roots formations. While the federal structures give the advantage of transaction aggregation and thus scale, they also add a layer of cost. In the cooperative structure it is more than amply demonstrated that the federal structures could lead to significant problem of imbalances, if the margins in the intermediary structures are not sufficient to cover the administrative and default risks. In case of SHG federations, this risk seems to have been mitigated by providing for better margins, as well as revenue generation through fee-based activities. But with increasing emphasis on subvention being transferred to the individuals the viability of the federal structures may be under question.

NABARD commissioned a study on the need and effectiveness of SHG Federations. The study undertaken by the Institute of Livelihood Research and Training (IRLT) concluded that:

(a) Members reported some incremental benefits in terms of income, upgraded production skills and enhanced ability to manage risks.
(b) SHG Federations were primarily offering financial intermediation services. The other services were offered by a very small number of SHG Federations.
(c) SHG Federations offering financial intermediation services as a primary activity in general did not seem to look beyond to offer non-financial services.
(d) There were some questions about the sustainability of SHG Federations that were not undertaking financial intermediation.
(e) Being a part of the federal structure did not affect the autonomy of the SHGs.

With the above findings, it may be useful for NRLM to look at the design of the three-tier structure and sharply define the roles and the financial flows in these structures to justify their existence and sustainability.

## INDIVIDUALISATION OF FINANCIAL INCLUSION AND ITS IMPLICATIONS FOR SHGBLP

While the SHG2 programme enunciated by NABARD recognised the need for looking beyond groups as far as the financial inclusion agenda was concerned, the articulation was more in terms of examining the needs of individuals both in savings and credit requirements and transcending the group for the limited purpose of what the group could not achieve. However, from 2012, times have changed

significantly at the ground level. The articulation of the financial inclusion agenda through banks as the primary drivers has picked up speed. While this was articulated very clearly when the RBI asked the banks to draw up board-approved financial inclusion plans to cover all the villages with habitation of more than 2,000, it has come into sharper focus with the PMJDY.

The initiative of broadening the definition of financial inclusion from opening of individual accounts and getting access to a formal source was expanded and articulated in specific terms when the RBI redefined inclusion to have not only savings (both current and accumulative savings with an overdraft facility) but also to include access to term/working capital loan, a remittance product and a risk mitigation product.

However, as discussed earlier, the articulation of the RBI was more about providing the access points within a reasonable distance from the client. However, under the PMJDY, the same has been translated into actionable target of opening accounts that may have most of the features described above.

While the SHG2 programme articulated the issue of direct access to banking structure in the form of opening/reviving a no-frills account, the PMJDY has rearticulated this differently and has completely bypassed the community structures to reach out to the client as directly as possible. In the spirit of the SHG2 programme, NABARD has also embarked on an ambitious pilot to digitise SHG records thereby making the financial behaviour of SHG available to the banks. In addition, the credit bureaus are also re-engineering their programmes to capture the credit history of SHG members as individuals so that it could be appropriately mapped for the purposes of providing greater information for other players to understand the indebtedness of the client. All these initiatives seem to be taking the inclusion agenda towards individualisation and moving away from the community-based structures. The question that emanates is: should this be seen as the beginning of the end of the community-based financial inclusion programmes like the SHGs?

---

**Box 8.2 Digitisation of SHGs**

One of the initiatives taken up by NABARD this year is to run a pilot programme on digitisation of SHGs. This pilot to be executed over a period of two years will first be tried out in Ramgarh district in Jharkhand and Dhule in Maharashtra, with a target of digitising 75,000 SHGs. The broad objectives of the digitisation programme are:

1. Integrating SHG members with the national financial inclusion agenda
2. Improving the quality of interface between SHG members and banks for efficient and hassle-free delivery of banking services
3. Facilitating convergence of delivery system with SHGs using Aadhaar
4. The upliftment in economic level of the SHG members, mostly poor rural women, by these measures will facilitate increasing the outreach of PMJDY
5. Financial inclusion in poor households

The digitisation process is expected to bring in the following benefits:

- Main-streaming of SHG members with financial inclusion agenda enabling access to wider range of financial services
- Digitisation of SHG accounts will increase bankers' comfort in credit appraisal and linkage of SHGs
- Automatic and accurate rating of SHGs will be available online for banks
- Mapping of persons not covered under Aadhaar platform and bringing them under Aadhaar fold
- Ease of transfer of social benefits and DBT through Aadhaar-linked accounts and convergence with other government benefits
- A comprehensive information base and robust MIS can be developed about poor community coverage, which may facilitate suitable interventions and convergence of other programme for social and financial empowerment
- It will help in identifying suitable interventions and support for proper nurturing and strengthening of SHGs

*Source:* Project on Digitisation of Self-Help Groups, Brochure published by NABARD.

In a workshop organised at NABARD to understand the status of SHGBLP, one of the themes discussed was the implications of the individualisation and the implication of financial inclusion initiatives outside of the SHGBLP on the SHG movement. The group took into account the following issues that were emerging:

1. Almost universal coverage of Aadhaar enrolment leading to provision of 'identity' to the customer—one of the most significant functions that the SHG was doing;
2. Move towards payments of MGNREGA wages and other benefits including cooking gas subsidy directly to the bank accounts of the beneficiaries;
3. The setting up of PBs that would accelerate the individual customer's linkage with the formal banking system;
4. The launch of PMJDY where the individual in the household was the focus.

While the group acknowledged the above trends, in general the impression amongst the participants was that the SHGBLP was here to stay for a while and these efforts at individualisation stated above would make the movement stronger than weaker. The arguments that were set forth to indicate that the movement would emerge stronger as a result of the above initiatives were as follows:

1. While Aadhaar helped in establishing the identity, the digitisation effort would help in creating an objectively verifiable transaction trail which would help the bankers to understand the underlying risk much better than just blindly going by the performance of the group.
2. It was also pointed out that under the PMJDY it was most likely that the accounts were opened in the name of men, while most of the members of the SHGBLP were women.
3. Digitisation would help in easy upload of individual data to the credit bureaus thereby increasing the confidence level of bankers in dealing with this portfolio. It is also an effective tool for managing information and also for completing the customer loop through a confirmatory SMS. This will help in moving the groups away from capture by the elite and prominent leaders.
4. Digitisation would also help agencies such as NABARD to follow up on banks and bankers that are not catering to groups, and help in monitoring the deposit capture by banks. This will also help in monitoring the new phenomenon of 'equal distribution' within the groups and help the support agencies in taking immediate corrective action.
5. In spite of Aadhaar and transaction trail, the ticket sizes of the individual loans of SHGs were so small that the main banking world might crowd them out and ration the credit. SHG was a good place to aggregate transactions, while continuing to understand the ground-level risk through

transaction trail. The data on the loan sizes are an indication that the average loan size of a typical SHG loan is still small and therefore aggregation will continue to be attractive to bankers.

6. While the data on the opening of individual accounts under the PMJDY was coming in, the question was about the extent of coverage given that there might be multiple accounts of a person in multiple banks. The de-duplication effort was not complete. Therefore, people could potentially be left out in this campaign, and the role of SHGs did not diminish.

7. A study undertaken by Shri Kshetra Dharmasthala Rural Development Programme (SKDRDP)—which is still underway—shows an early indication that a substantial number of women who were members of SHGs did not have PMJDY accounts, thereby indicating that for women-centric savings and credit programmes, SHG might be a better intervention.

8. If the digitisation helped in opening of accounts with a debit card, the transactions of the SHG could also move towards a cashless settlement on a much larger scale, where the loans as well as the repayments could be directly made to the bank account. This will involve the bank in the transactions, but not in the risks associated with the transactions.

9. With PBs coming in, it could be an opportunity for SHGs to act as BCs for banks, as well as for distribution of third-party financial products.

10. There were tolerance limits for the groups. The group guarantee would not work beyond a loan limit of ₹1 million per group. The current scale of lending was mostly conducive for consumption smoothening and petty enterprise; however, if serious entrepreneurship

had to come out, the size of the loan had to go up. For this, having a transaction trail would really help in moving the customer as a direct borrower from the bank.

In general, it was felt that individualisation—capture of data at the individual level—would not harm the group process, but it would enhance the flow of credit and other financial services to the members. The individualisation has not taken away the primary function of social collateral as well as transaction aggregation, both of which provide immense value to the banks.

## NPA LEVELS IN SHGBLP: A DISCUSSION

The average NPA levels of the entire portfolio was at 7.40% cutting across the source of the loans. The lowest NPA level was in the southern region at 5.98% and the highest was in the central region at 16.48%. The case being made for greater engagement of the banks in regions other than south, with the roll-out of NRLM gets somewhat weakened when the data of NPA is examined. While the private sector banks as a source of loans had the lowest levels of NPA (overall 1.05%), their own exposure to the SHG sector was also pretty low, with their share being at around 8% of the exposure of the banking sector. Even with the private sector, the highest level of NPAs came from Nagaland, though it is important to mention that this was on a very small base.

In general, the RRBs being regional and local institutions had lower level of NPAs than the commercial banks except for the central region, which brought their overall averages down (Figure 8.9). These numbers clearly indicate the effect of rapid roll-out of groups (represented by a much better

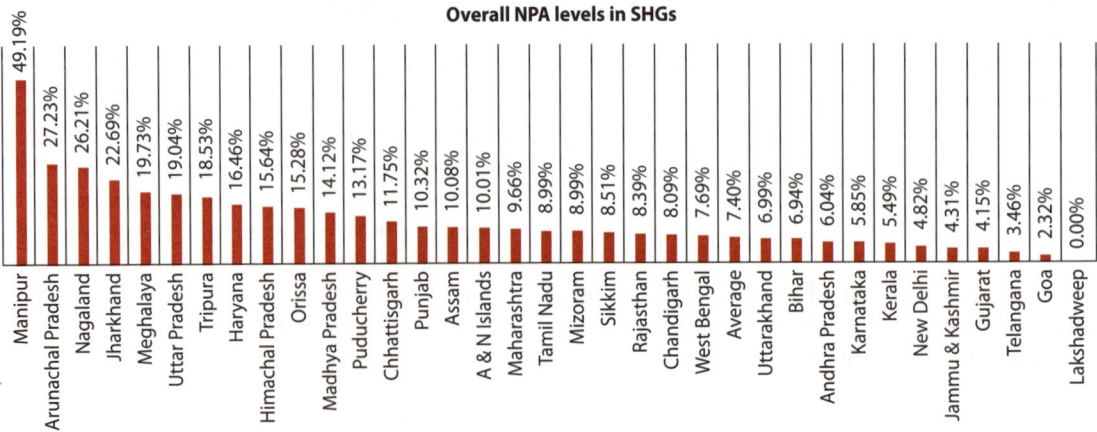

**Figure 8.9** NPA levels in SHGs stacked according to states

*Source:* NABARD (2014).

regional spread in terms of group numbers) and the amount of hand holding and support to be provided. The rapid roll-out of NRLM in other regions has possibly led to a growth in the number of SHGs possibly without a concurrent capacity-building programme undertaken by passionate NGOs. The results are there to see, the groups do not get linked, and when they do, there are defaults thereby making the case of SHGBLP weak.

## CONCLUDING NOTES

While the SHGBLP has grown significantly over the years, it is clear from the data that the meaningful linkage is happening only in the southern part of the country. While efforts to promote and help SHGs to save are happening across the nation, the meaningful embedding with the banking system is yet to be seen. Early setbacks with high NPAs in low penetration areas do not help the cause. It is also pertinent to note that in areas where there are high levels of NPAs in SHGs—in the eastern, central and north-eastern parts—the MFIs are growing and are managing better recovery. There might be some lessons for the roll-out of SHGBLP in getting process improvements to ensure that the linkage programme is meaningful.

### APPENDIX 8.1
### Progress under microfinance—savings of SHGs with banks

| | Region-wise/State-wise/Agency-wise position as on 31 March 2015 (₹ in million) | | | | | | | | | |
|---|---|---|---|---|---|---|---|---|---|---|
| | Public commercial banks | | Private commercial banks | | Regional rural banks | | Cooperative banks | | Total | |
| Region/State | No. of SHGs | Savings amount | No. of SHGs | Savings amount | No. of SHGs | Savings amount | No. of SHGs | Savings amount | No. of SHGs | Savings amount |
| **NORTH** | | | | | | | | | | |
| Chandigarh | 90 | 0.42 | — | — | — | — | — | — | 90 | 0.42 |
| Haryana | 19,654 | 160.72 | 1,185 | 8.72 | 17,013 | 164.68 | 3,801 | 30.99 | 41,653 | 365.11 |
| HP | 14,209 | 93.82 | 61 | 0.53 | 9,267 | 74.60 | 14,302 | 95.97 | 37,839 | 264.92 |
| J&K | 1,060 | 8.51 | 5,154 | 29.34 | — | — | — | — | 6,214 | 37.84 |
| New Delhi | 3,177 | 78.79 | 129 | 0.10 | — | — | — | — | 3,306 | 78.90 |
| Punjab | 11,074 | 135.17 | 1,406 | 2.69 | 6,941 | 45.70 | 6,455 | 39.96 | 25,876 | 223.52 |
| Rajasthan | 82,953 | 746.88 | 23,855 | 209.64 | 64,602 | 456.95 | 74,505 | 412.04 | 245,915 | 1,825.50 |
| Total | 132,217 | 1,224.30 | 31,790 | 251.01 | 97,823 | 741.93 | 99,063 | 578.97 | 360,893 | 2,796.21 |
| **NORTH-EAST** | | | | | | | | | | |
| Assam | 74,540 | 708.46 | 288 | 1.79 | 192,215 | 448.02 | 25,190 | 26.86 | 292,233 | 1,185.13 |
| Arunachal | 873 | 7.67 | — | — | 1,399 | 10.26 | 1,079 | 7.64 | 3,351 | 25.57 |
| Manipur | 4,229 | 11.92 | — | — | 6,473 | 7.77 | — | — | 10,702 | 19.69 |
| Meghalaya | 1,313 | 11.01 | 4 | 0.05 | 4,035 | 51.24 | 2,558 | 23.98 | 7,910 | 86.27 |
| Mizoram | 200 | 0.67 | — | — | 6,784 | 29.51 | 517 | 1.18 | 7,501 | 31.35 |
| Nagaland | 2,862 | 27.26 | 25 | 0.07 | — | — | — | — | 2,887 | 27.33 |
| Sikkim | 1,149 | 15.97 | 1 | 0.02 | — | — | 240 | 7.26 | 1,390 | 23.26 |
| Tripura | 8,280 | 95.05 | — | — | — | — | — | — | 8,280 | 95.05 |
| Total | 93,446 | 878.00 | 318 | 1.92 | 210,906 | 546.79 | 29,584 | 66.92 | 334,254 | 1,493.64 |
| **EAST** | | | | | | | | | | |
| A&N | 295 | 2.01 | — | — | — | — | 4,703 | 10.52 | 4,998 | 12.53 |
| Bihar | 131,782 | 1,403.56 | 3,425 | 68.11 | 89,270 | 1,495.06 | — | — | 224,477 | 2,966.73 |
| Jharkhand | 49,536 | 627.10 | 150 | 0.48 | 32,668 | 223.94 | 28 | 0.10 | 82,382 | 851.63 |

*(Continued)*

*(Continued)*

| Region/State | Public commercial banks | | Private commercial banks | | Regional rural banks | | Cooperative banks | | Total | |
|---|---|---|---|---|---|---|---|---|---|---|
| | No. of SHGs | Savings amount | No. of SHGs | Savings amount | No. of SHGs | Savings amount | No. of SHGs | Savings amount | No. of SHGs | Savings amount |
| Odisha | 179,418 | 2,441.68 | 20,882 | 85.87 | 170,916 | 1,793.59 | 80,920 | 650.10 | 452,136 | 4,971.23 |
| West Bengal | 245,872 | 4,582.69 | 3,606 | 36.58 | 182,110 | 3,559.99 | 329,597 | 5,864.76 | 761,185 | 14,044.02 |
| Total | 606,903 | 9,057.04 | 28,063 | 191.04 | 474,964 | 7,072.58 | 415,248 | 6,525.48 | 1,525,178 | 22,846.14 |
| **CENTRAL** | | | | | | | | | | |
| Chhattisgarh | 30,672 | 478.84 | 603 | 3.82 | 92,794 | 1,281.40 | 24,386 | 94.03 | 148,455 | 1,858.09 |
| MP | 65,906 | 710.92 | 17,268 | 122.93 | 135,030 | 1,651.12 | 7,711 | 28.16 | 225,915 | 2,513.12 |
| UP | 114,540 | 2,142.41 | 12,362 | 136.59 | 264,348 | 1,273.76 | 1,033 | 3.59 | 392,283 | 3,556.35 |
| Uttarakhand | 11,216 | 214.45 | 226 | 0.49 | 20,415 | 153.39 | 19,212 | 135.55 | 51,069 | 503.87 |
| Total | 222,334 | 3,546.61 | 30,459 | 263.83 | 512,587 | 4,359.67 | 52,342 | 261.32 | 817,722 | 8,431.43 |
| **WEST** | | | | | | | | | | |
| Goa | 3,430 | 38.81 | 458 | 1.80 | — | — | 3,565 | 79.33 | 7,453 | 119.94 |
| Gujarat | 119,831 | 931.43 | 11,289 | 177.64 | 51,454 | 450.91 | 33,687 | 208.11 | 216,261 | 1,768.08 |
| Maharashtra | 261,114 | 2,481.11 | 60,845 | 601.09 | 115,329 | 1,566.44 | 293,679 | 4,535.29 | 730,967 | 9,183.93 |
| Total | 384,375 | 3,451.34 | 72,592 | 780.53 | 166,783 | 2,017.35 | 330,931 | 4,822.72 | 954,681 | 11,071.95 |
| **SOUTH** | | | | | | | | | | |
| AP | 599,650 | 21,672.43 | 11,099 | 1.14 | 256,758 | 4,048.76 | 17,000 | 572.67 | 884,507 | 26,295.00 |
| Karnataka | 348,235 | 6,650.46 | 44,466 | 430.25 | 129,690 | 1,297.81 | 211,929 | 4,777.69 | 734,320 | 13,156.21 |
| Kerala | 441,389 | 4,823.53 | 29,760 | 282.19 | 51,332 | 729.70 | 62,995 | 617.07 | 585,476 | 6,452.49 |
| Lakshadweep | 231 | 64.89 | — | — | — | — | — | — | 231 | 64.89 |
| Puducherry | 9,557 | 86.89 | 6 | 0.21 | 3,717 | 43.98 | 3,370 | 24.79 | 16,650 | 155.86 |
| Tamil Nadu | 575,475 | 6,472.54 | 169,495 | 1,375.19 | 74,848 | 533.89 | 167,733 | 1,966.88 | 987,551 | 10,348.50 |
| Telangana | 319,133 | 7,274.70 | 12 | 1.69 | 181,907 | 2,073.29 | 10,138 | 611.65 | 511,190 | 9,961.33 |
| Total | 2,293,670 | 47,045.45 | 254,838 | 3,090.66 | 698,252 | 8,727.42 | 473,165 | 8,570.75 | 3,719,925 | 66,434.28 |
| Grand Total | 3,732,945 | 65,202.75 | 418,060 | 3,579.00 | 2,161,315 | 23,465.74 | 1,400,333 | 20,826.16 | 7,712,653 | 113,073.64 |

*Source:* MCID, NABARD, 2015.

### APPENDIX 8.2
### Progress under microfinance—bank loans disbursed during the year 2014–15

| Region/State | Public commercial banks | | Private commercial banks | | Regional rural banks | | Cooperative banks | | Total | |
|---|---|---|---|---|---|---|---|---|---|---|
| | No. of SHGs | Loans disbursed | No. of SHGs | Loans disbursed | No. of SHGs | Loans disbursed | No. of SHGs | Loans disbursed | No. of SHGs | Loans disbursed |
| **NORTH** | | | | | | | | | | |
| Chandigarh | 7 | 1.18 | — | — | — | — | — | — | 7 | 1.18 |
| Haryana | 979 | 136.29 | 866 | 205.78 | 454 | 49.70 | 224 | 14.23 | 2,523 | 406.00 |
| HP | 936 | 177.99 | 87 | 20.02 | 697 | 78.30 | 2,138 | 246.77 | 3,858 | 523.08 |

*(Continued)*

(Continued)

| Region/State | Public commercial banks | | Private commercial banks | | Regional rural banks | | Cooperative banks | | Total | |
|---|---|---|---|---|---|---|---|---|---|---|
| | No. of SHGs | Loans disbursed | No. of SHGs | Loans disbursed | No. of SHGs | Loans disbursed | No. of SHGs | Loans disbursed | No. of SHGs | Loans disbursed |
| J&K | 403 | 24.51 | 1,504 | 95.27 | — | — | — | — | 1,907 | 119.78 |
| New Delhi | 90 | 16.56 | — | — | — | — | — | — | 90 | 16.56 |
| Punjab | 487 | 129.28 | 1,041 | 185.42 | 914 | 67.64 | 227 | 20.88 | 2,669 | 403.21 |
| Rajasthan | 2,232 | 177.66 | 9,310 | 1,806.34 | 3,735 | 274.42 | 17,317 | 628.91 | 32,594 | 2,887.33 |
| Total | 5,134 | 663.46 | 12,808 | 2,312.83 | 5,800 | 470.06 | 19,906 | 910.78 | 43,648 | 4,357.13 |
| **NORTH-EAST** | | | | | | | | | | |
| Assam | 5,025 | 565.39 | 55 | 2.85 | 11,709 | 793.80 | 410 | 13.48 | 17,199 | 1,375.51 |
| Arunachal | 13 | 4.57 | — | — | 9 | 1.67 | 6 | 1.43 | 28 | 7.66 |
| Manipur | 52 | 4.05 | — | — | 120 | 11.08 | — | — | 172 | 15.13 |
| Meghalaya | 15 | 1.50 | — | — | 68 | 4.60 | 11 | 1.69 | 94 | 7.80 |
| Mizoram | 5 | 0.91 | — | — | 356 | 35.60 | 1 | 0.70 | 362 | 37.21 |
| Nagaland | 69 | 15.06 | — | — | — | — | — | — | 69 | 15.06 |
| Sikkim | 95 | 3.10 | — | — | — | — | 6 | 0.89 | 101 | 3.99 |
| Tripura | 400 | 27.13 | — | — | — | — | — | — | 400 | 27.13 |
| Total | 5,674 | 621.70 | 55 | 2.85 | 12,262 | 846.76 | 434 | 18.19 | 18,425 | 1,489.49 |
| **EAST** | | | | | | | | | | |
| A&N | 20 | 7.17 | — | — | — | — | 244 | 34.59 | 264 | 41.76 |
| Bihar | 16,922 | 935.79 | 3,246 | 873.37 | 44,954 | 2,928.13 | — | — | 65,122 | 4,737.28 |
| Jharkhand | 2,738 | 617.97 | 13 | 1.62 | 1,808 | 84.48 | 8 | 4.49 | 4,567 | 708.57 |
| Odisha | 19,278 | 2,079.99 | 12,287 | 2,233.31 | 25,417 | 5,428.04 | 65,576 | 3,312.00 | 1,22,558 | 13,053.34 |
| West Bengal | 42,389 | 4,064.00 | 2,550 | 449.69 | 54,333 | 6,879.64 | 60,249 | 5,547.70 | 159,521 | 16,941.03 |
| Total | 81,347 | 7,704.92 | 18,096 | 3,557.98 | 126,512 | 15,320.28 | 126,077 | 8,898.79 | 352,032 | 35,481.98 |
| **CENTRAL** | | | | | | | | | | |
| Chhattisgarh | 3,590 | 364.63 | 500 | 72.62 | 7,066 | 567.70 | 6,203 | 108.39 | 17,359 | 1,113.34 |
| MP | 12,286 | 1,119.56 | 10,741 | 1,570.84 | 6,767 | 346.77 | 61 | 13.60 | 29,855 | 3,050.77 |
| UP | 14,017 | 3,418.83 | 9,007 | 2,114.07 | 35,701 | 1,495.51 | 221 | 0.07 | 58,946 | 7,028.47 |
| Uttarakhand | 688 | 62.21 | 206 | 43.37 | 1,266 | 107.94 | 902 | 131.28 | 3,062 | 344.80 |
| Total | 30,581 | 4,965.23 | 20,454 | 3,800.90 | 50,800 | 2,517.92 | 7,387 | 253.33 | 109,222 | 11,537.38 |
| **WEST** | | | | | | | | | | |
| Goa | 346 | 56.63 | 183 | 48.60 | — | — | 274 | 76.58 | 803 | 181.81 |
| Gujarat | 9,530 | 799.14 | 6,843 | 1,304.29 | 4,778 | 405.04 | 1,425 | 148.14 | 22,576 | 2,656.61 |
| Maharashtra | 17,783 | 2,284.72 | 32,205 | 4,527.09 | 9,467 | 1,150.75 | 14,886 | 964.51 | 74,341 | 8,927.07 |
| Total | 27,659 | 3,140.49 | 39,231 | 5,879.99 | 14,245 | 1,555.79 | 16,585 | 1,189.24 | 97,720 | 11,765.50 |
| **SOUTH** | | | | | | | | | | |
| AP | 142,890 | 36,002.87 | — | — | 131,582 | 19,430.86 | 2,780 | 797.75 | 2,77,252 | 56,231.48 |
| Karnataka | 155,003 | 50,142.69 | 22,880 | 5,598.17 | 38,225 | 7,027.68 | 26,596 | 5,390.70 | 242,704 | 68,159.24 |
| Kerala | 39,661 | 8,635.10 | 9,735 | 2,290.04 | 10,525 | 2,200.30 | 17,173 | 2,020.74 | 77,094 | 15,146.17 |

*(Continued)*

*(Continued)*

| | Region-wise/State-wise/Agency-wise position as on 31 March 2015 (₹ in million) | | | | | | | | | |
|---|---|---|---|---|---|---|---|---|---|---|
| | Public commercial banks | | Private commercial banks | | Regional rural banks | | Cooperative banks | | Total | |
| Region/State | No. of SHGs | Loans disbursed | No. of SHGs | Loans disbursed | No. of SHGs | Loans disbursed | No. of SHGs | Loans disbursed | No. of SHGs | Loans disbursed |
| Lakshadweep | — | — | — | — | — | — | — | — | — | — |
| Puducherry | 871 | 219.59 | — | — | 502 | 110.26 | 154 | 44.26 | 1,527 | 374.11 |
| Tamil Nadu | 69,480 | 17,283.66 | 47,039 | 13,954.93 | 17,570 | 5,558.03 | 28,911 | 5,007.13 | 163,000 | 41,803.74 |
| Telangana | 144,564 | 34,076.12 | — | — | 114,116 | 22,214.28 | 2,372 | 705.30 | 261,052 | 56,995.70 |
| Total | 552,469 | 146,360.02 | 79,654 | 21,843.14 | 312,520 | 56,541.41 | 77,986 | 13,965.88 | 1,022,629 | 238,710.45 |
| Grand Total | 702,864 | 163,455.82 | 170,298 | 37,397.69 | 522,139 | 77,252.22 | 248,375 | 25,236.21 | 1,643,676 | 303,341.93 |

*Source:* MCID, NABARD, 2015

## APPENDIX 8.3
### Progress under microfinance—bank loans outstanding as on 31 March 2015

| | Public commercial banks | | Private commercial banks | | Regional rural banks | | Cooperative banks | | Total | |
|---|---|---|---|---|---|---|---|---|---|---|
| Region/State | No. of SHGs | Loans O/S amount (million) | No. of SHGs | Loans O/S amount (million) | No. of SHGs | Loans O/S amount (million) | No. of SHGs | Loans O/S amount (million) | No. of SHGs | Loans O/S amount (million) |
| **NORTH** | | | | | | | | | | |
| Chandigarh | 72 | 9.28 | — | — | — | — | — | — | 72 | 9.28 |
| Haryana | 12,088 | 1,391.41 | 869 | 150.75 | 5,901 | 670.00 | 723 | 50.54 | 19,581 | 2,262.71 |
| HP | 6,097 | 449.35 | 91 | 16.30 | 6,150 | 217.10 | 6,189 | 444.56 | 18,527 | 1,127.31 |
| J&K | 944 | 44.70 | 1,299 | 67.45 | — | — | — | — | 2,243 | 112.14 |
| New Delhi | 1,030 | 267.51 | — | — | — | — | — | — | 1,030 | 267.51 |
| Punjab | 8,036 | 1,142.91 | 1,112 | 161.64 | 4,079 | 191.61 | 2,618 | 84.51 | 15,845 | 1,580.68 |
| Rajasthan | 69,872 | 6,877.62 | 14,148 | 2,059.51 | 17,422 | 1,111.83 | 18,165 | 752.95 | 119,607 | 10,801.90 |
| Total | 98,139 | 10,182.78 | 17,519 | 2,455.65 | 33,552 | 2,190.54 | 27,695 | 1,332.56 | 176,905 | 16,161.54 |
| **NORTH-EAST** | | | | | | | | | | |
| Assam | 49,221 | 3,085.49 | 80 | 2.17 | 55,423 | 3,019.10 | 4,100 | 151.92 | 108,824 | 6,258.68 |
| Arunachal | 136 | 14.38 | — | — | 133 | 11.53 | 39 | 7.64 | 308 | 33.55 |
| Manipur | 1,464 | 56.59 | — | — | 1,183 | 43.84 | — | — | 2,647 | 100.43 |
| Meghalaya | 749 | 36.83 | — | — | 744 | 77.37 | 411 | 17.57 | 1,904 | 131.76 |
| Mizoram | 91 | 11.28 | — | — | 1,024 | 126.00 | 25 | 3.47 | 1,140 | 140.74 |
| Nagaland | 1,398 | 95.40 | 6 | 0.21 | — | — | — | — | 1,404 | 95.62 |
| Sikkim | 567 | 58.21 | — | — | — | — | 42 | 3.33 | 609 | 61.54 |
| Tripura | 6,412 | 481.86 | — | — | — | — | — | — | 6,412 | 481.86 |
| Total | 60,038 | 3,840.03 | 86 | 2.38 | 58,507 | 3,277.84 | 4,617 | 183.92 | 123,248 | 7,304.17 |
| **EAST** | | | | | | | | | | |
| A&N | 107 | 7.57 | — | — | — | — | 913 | 51.90 | 1,020 | 59.47 |
| Bihar | 92,952 | 5,246.02 | 3,737 | 789.44 | 92,652 | 4,232.12 | — | — | 189,341 | 10,267.57 |

*(Continued)*

(Continued)

| Region/State | Public commercial banks | | Private commercial banks | | Regional rural banks | | Cooperative banks | | Total | |
|---|---|---|---|---|---|---|---|---|---|---|
| | No. of SHGs | Loans O/S amount (million) | No. of SHGs | Loans O/S amount (million) | No. of SHGs | Loans O/S amount (million) | No. of SHGs | Loans O/S amount (million) | No. of SHGs | Loans O/S amount (million) |
| Jharkhand | 28,993 | 3,592.66 | 9 | 0.86 | 28,862 | 647.14 | 8 | 4.37 | 57,872 | 4,245.03 |
| Odisha | 113,393 | 8,153.09 | 16,451 | 2,156.66 | 77,692 | 7,684.60 | 28,604 | 1,368.90 | 236,140 | 19,363.25 |
| West Bengal | 177,964 | 8,105.36 | 3,216 | 347.93 | 150,575 | 12,688.95 | 253,431 | 7,525.13 | 585,186 | 28,667.37 |
| Total | 413,409 | 25,104.69 | 23,413 | 3,294.89 | 349,781 | 25,252.80 | 282,956 | 8,950.30 | 1,069,559 | 62,602.68 |
| **CENTRAL** | | | | | | | | | | |
| Chhattisgarh | 16,039 | 1,021.10 | 515 | 61.99 | 62,745 | 1,214.60 | 10,488 | 73.19 | 89,787 | 2,370.88 |
| MP | 37,624 | 3,054.82 | 13,085 | 1,518.82 | 45,416 | 1,276.65 | 1,628 | 34.80 | 97,753 | 5,885.09 |
| UP | 73,130 | 6,979.90 | 11,390 | 1,925.87 | 137,237 | 6,803.12 | 119 | 7.83 | 221,876 | 15,716.72 |
| Uttarakhand | 9,552 | 773.04 | 228 | 37.73 | 8,516 | 310.56 | 10,658 | 477.32 | 28,954 | 1,598.65 |
| Total | 136,345 | 11,828.86 | 25,218 | 3,544.41 | 253,914 | 9,604.93 | 22,893 | 593.13 | 438,370 | 25,571.34 |
| **WEST** | | | | | | | | | | |
| Goa | 1,662 | 149.25 | 254 | 43.46 | — | — | 1,098 | 104.20 | 3,014 | 296.91 |
| Gujarat | 41,671 | 2,824.31 | 9,519 | 1,406.18 | 12,290 | 497.84 | 2,059 | 158.31 | 65,539 | 4,886.64 |
| Maharashtra | 74,753 | 6,205.17 | 50,122 | 5,512.97 | 35,852 | 2,701.45 | 42,195 | 1,336.04 | 202,922 | 15,755.63 |
| Total | 118,086 | 9,178.73 | 59,895 | 6,962.61 | 48,142 | 3,199.29 | 45,352 | 1,598.55 | 271,475 | 20,939.18 |
| **SOUTH** | | | | | | | | | | |
| AP | 574,396 | 112,387.21 | 70 | 2.01 | 221,877 | 44,728.58 | 14,546 | 1,891.49 | 810,889 | 159,009.29 |
| Karnataka | 357,216 | 40,167.39 | 29,799 | 5,824.70 | 74,391 | 9,885.51 | 84,951 | 7,015.54 | 546,357 | 62,893.15 |
| Kerala | 89,590 | 16,360.88 | 14,053 | 2,254.07 | 23,818 | 2,241.10 | 15,909 | 2,558.91 | 143,370 | 23,414.96 |
| Lakshadweep | 14 | 0.43 | — | — | — | — | — | — | 14 | 0.43 |
| Puducherry | 3,804 | 493.90 | — | — | 1,407 | 151.88 | 881 | 67.43 | 6,092 | 713.20 |
| Tamil Nadu | 234,589 | 34,535.15 | 72,938 | 17,450.86 | 33,650 | 4,138.31 | 86,030 | 7,686.97 | 427,207 | 63,811.29 |
| Telangana | 291,705 | 50,712.19 | — | — | 173,235 | 22,824.60 | 7,592 | 1,258.99 | 472,532 | 74,795.77 |
| Total | 1,551,314 | 254,657.14 | 116,860 | 25,531.65 | 528,378 | 83,969.97 | 209,909 | 20,479.33 | 2,406,461 | 384,638.09 |
| Grand Total | 2,377,331 | 314,792.23 | 242,991 | 41,791.59 | 1,272,274 | 127,495.37 | 593,422 | 33,137.80 | 4,486,018 | 517,216.99 |

*Source:* MCID, NABARD, 2015.

## State-wise and bank type-wise NPA levels of SHGs

| Region/State | Public sector commercial banks | | | Private sector commercial banks | | | Regional rural banks | | | Cooperative banks | | | Total | | |
|---|---|---|---|---|---|---|---|---|---|---|---|---|---|---|---|
| | Loan amount OS against SHGs | Amount of GNPA against SHGs | NPA %age to loan OS | Loan amount OS against SHGs | Amount of GNPA against SHGs | NPA %age to loan OS | Loan amount OS against SHGs | Amount of GNPA against SHGs | NPA %age to loan OS | Loan amount OS against SHGs | Amount of GNPA against SHGs | NPA %age to loan OS | Loan amount OS against SHGs | Amount of GNPA against SHGs | NPA as %age to loan OS |
| **NORTH** | | | | | | | | | | | | | | | |
| Chandigarh | 9.28 | 0.75 | 8.09 | 0.00 | 0.00 | 0.00 | 0.00 | 0.00 | 0.00 | 0.00 | 0.00 | 0.00 | 9.28 | 0.75 | 8.09 |
| Haryana | 1,391.41 | 266.14 | 19.13 | 150.75 | 0.36 | 0.24 | 670.00 | 65.70 | 9.81 | 50.54 | 40.25 | 79.63 | 2,262.71 | 372.44 | 16.46 |
| HP | 449.35 | 49.95 | 11.12 | 16.30 | 0.00 | 0.00 | 217.10 | 33.70 | 15.52 | 444.56 | 92.63 | 20.84 | 1,127.31 | 176.28 | 15.64 |
| J&K | 44.70 | 4.52 | 10.12 | 67.45 | 0.32 | 0.00 | 0.00 | 0.00 | 0.00 | 0.00 | 0.00 | 0.00 | 112.14 | 4.84 | 4.31 |
| New Delhi | 267.51 | 12.89 | 4.82 | 0.00 | 0.00 | 0.00 | 0.00 | 0.00 | 0.00 | 0.00 | 0.00 | 0.00 | 267.51 | 12.89 | 4.82 |
| Punjab | 1,142.91 | 131.35 | 11.49 | 161.64 | 0.02 | 0.01 | 191.61 | 12.33 | 6.44 | 84.51 | 19.36 | 22.91 | 1,580.68 | 163.06 | 10.32 |
| Rajasthan | 6,877.62 | 561.09 | 8.16 | 2,059.5 | 46.70 | 2.27 | 1,111.83 | 172.75 | 15.54 | 752.95 | 125.66 | 16.69 | 10,801.90 | 906.20 | 8.39 |
| Total | 10,182.78 | 1,026.7 | 10.08 | 2,455.7 | 47.39 | 1.93 | 2,190.54 | 284.49 | 12.99 | 1,332.56 | 277.90 | 20.85 | 16,161.54 | 1,636.46 | 10.13 |
| **NORTH-EAST** | | | | | | | | | | | | | | | |
| Assam | 3,085.49 | 483.97 | 15.69 | 2.17 | 0.14 | 6.46 | 3,019.10 | 82.39 | 2.73 | 151.92 | 64.48 | 42.44 | 6,258.68 | 630.98 | 10.08 |
| Arunachal | 14.38 | 3.36 | 23.35 | 0.00 | 0.00 | 0.00 | 11.53 | 3.79 | 32.86 | 7.64 | 1.99 | 26.02 | 33.55 | 9.13 | 27.23 |
| Manipur | 56.59 | 29.89 | 52.82 | 0.00 | 0.00 | 0.00 | 43.84 | 19.51 | 44.50 | 0.00 | 0.00 | | 100.43 | 49.40 | 49.19 |
| Meghalaya | 36.83 | 16.27 | 44.18 | 0.00 | 0.00 | 0.00 | 77.37 | 9.73 | 12.57 | 17.57 | 0.00 | 0.00 | 131.76 | 26.00 | 19.73 |
| Mizoram | 11.28 | 2.34 | 20.79 | 0.00 | 0.00 | 0.00 | 126.00 | 10.31 | 0.00 | 3.47 | 0.00 | 0.00 | 140.74 | 12.66 | 8.99 |
| Nagaland | 95.40 | 24.93 | 26.13 | 0.21 | 0.13 | 62.62 | 0.00 | 0.00 | 0.00 | 0.00 | 0.00 | 0.00 | 95.62 | 25.06 | 26.21 |
| Sikkim | 58.21 | 3.91 | 6.72 | 0.00 | 0.00 | 0.00 | 0.00 | 0.00 | 0.00 | 3.33 | 1.33 | 39.86 | 61.54 | 5.24 | 8.51 |
| Tripura | 481.86 | 89.28 | 18.53 | 0.00 | 0.00 | 0.00 | 0.00 | 0.00 | 0.00 | 0.00 | 0.00 | 0.00 | 481.86 | 89.28 | 18.53 |
| Total | 3,840.03 | 653.94 | 17.03 | 2.38 | 0.27 | 11.50 | 3,277.84 | 125.73 | 3.84 | 183.92 | 67.80 | 36.86 | 7,304.17 | 847.74 | 11.61 |

**EAST**

| | C1 | C2 | C3 | C4 | C5 | C6 | C7 | C8 | C9 | C10 | C11 | C12 | C13 | C14 | C15 |
|---|---|---|---|---|---|---|---|---|---|---|---|---|---|---|---|
| A&N | 7.57 | 0.63 | 8.33 | 0.00 | 0.00 | 0.00 | 0.00 | 0.00 | 0.00 | 51.90 | 5.32 | 10.25 | 59.47 | 5.95 | 10.01 |
| Bihar | 5,246.02 | 634.08 | 12.09 | 789.44 | 0.00 | 0.00 | 4,232.12 | 78.95 | 1.87 | 0.00 | 0.00 | 0.00 | 10,267.57 | 713.03 | 6.94 |
| Jharkhand | 3,592.66 | 387.25 | 10.78 | 0.86 | 0.00 | 0.00 | 647.14 | 345.29 | 53.36 | 4.37 | 230.70 | 0.00 | 4,245.03 | 963.24 | 22.69 |
| Odisha | 8,153.09 | 1,686.2 | 20.68 | 2,156.7 | 0.41 | 0.02 | 7,684.60 | 1,273.0 | 16.57 | 1,368.90 | 0.00 | 0.00 | 19,363.25 | 2,959.62 | 15.28 |
| WB | 8,105.36 | 1,031.6 | 12.73 | 347.93 | 0.00 | 0.00 | 12,688.95 | 832.49 | 6.56 | 7,525.13 | 341.87 | 4.54 | 28,667.37 | 2,205.92 | 7.69 |
| Total | 25,104.69 | 3,739.7 | 14.90 | 3,294.9 | 0.41 | 0.01 | 25,252.80 | 2,529.8 | 10.02 | 8,950.30 | 577.90 | 6.46 | 62,602.68 | 6,847.76 | 10.94 |

**Central**

| | C1 | C2 | C3 | C4 | C5 | C6 | C7 | C8 | C9 | C10 | C11 | C12 | C13 | C14 | C15 |
|---|---|---|---|---|---|---|---|---|---|---|---|---|---|---|---|
| Chhattisgarh | 1,021.10 | 152.57 | 14.94 | 61.99 | 1.11 | 1.79 | 1,214.60 | 110.70 | 9.11 | 73.19 | 14.13 | 19.31 | 2,370.88 | 278.51 | 11.75 |
| MP | 3,054.82 | 600.02 | 19.64 | 1,518.8 | 5.10 | 0.34 | 1,276.65 | 222.80 | 17.45 | 34.80 | 3.10 | 8.92 | 5,885.09 | 831.02 | 14.12 |
| UP | 6,979.90 | 1,104.3 | 15.82 | 1,925.9 | 0.00 | 0.00 | 6,803.12 | 1,882.4 | 27.67 | 7.83 | 6.50 | 83.04 | 15,716.72 | 2,993.20 | 19.04 |
| Uttarakhand | 773.04 | 55.92 | 7.23 | 37.73 | 0.00 | 0.00 | 310.56 | 24.61 | 7.92 | 477.32 | 31.21 | 6.54 | 1,598.65 | 111.74 | 6.99 |
| Total | 11,828.86 | 1,912.8 | 16.17 | 3,544.4 | 6.20 | 0.00 | 9,604.93 | 2,240.6 | 23.33 | 593.13 | 54.95 | 9.26 | 25,571.34 | 4,214.47 | 16.46 |

**West**

| | C1 | C2 | C3 | C4 | C5 | C6 | C7 | C8 | C9 | C10 | C11 | C12 | C13 | C14 | C15 |
|---|---|---|---|---|---|---|---|---|---|---|---|---|---|---|---|
| Goa | 149.25 | 2.76 | 1.85 | 43.46 | 0.13 | 0.29 | 0.00 | 0.00 | 0.00 | 104.20 | 3.99 | 3.83 | 296.91 | 6.88 | 2.32 |
| Gujarat | 2,824.31 | 132.56 | 4.69 | 1,406.2 | 1.25 | 0.09 | 497.84 | 38.60 | 7.75 | 158.31 | 30.56 | 19.30 | 4,886.64 | 202.97 | 4.15 |
| Maharashtra | 6,205.17 | 936.04 | 15.08 | 5,512.9 | 3.20 | 0.06 | 2,701.45 | 240.44 | 8.90 | 1,336.04 | 342.08 | 25.60 | 15,755.63 | 1,521.75 | 9.66 |
| Total | 9,178.73 | 1071.4 | 11.67 | 6,962.6 | 4.58 | 0.07 | 3,199.29 | 279.04 | 8.72 | 1,598.55 | 376.63 | 23.56 | 20,939.18 | 1,731.60 | 8.27 |

**SOUTH**

| | C1 | C2 | C3 | C4 | C5 | C6 | C7 | C8 | C9 | C10 | C11 | C12 | C13 | C14 | C15 |
|---|---|---|---|---|---|---|---|---|---|---|---|---|---|---|---|
| AP | 112,387.2 | 7646.4 | 6.80 | 2.01 | 2.01 | 100 | 44,728.58 | 1708.0 | 3.82 | 1,891.49 | 251.30 | 13.29 | 159,009.3 | 9,607.69 | 6.04 |
| Karnataka | 40,167.39 | 820.49 | 2.04 | 5,824.7 | 16.32 | 0.28 | 9,885.51 | 2507.8 | 25.37 | 7,015.54 | 331.65 | 4.73 | 62,893.15 | 3,676.21 | 5.85 |
| Kerala | 16,360.88 | 941.89 | 5.76 | 2,254.1 | 18.50 | 0.82 | 2,241.10 | 78.60 | 3.51 | 2,558.91 | 245.32 | 9.59 | 23,414.96 | 1,284.31 | 5.49 |
| Lakshadwip | 0.43 | 0.00 | 0.00 | 0.00 | 0.00 | 0.00 | 0.00 | 0.00 | 0.00 | 0.00 | 0.00 | 0.00 | 0.43 | 0.00 | 0.00 |
| Puducherry | 493.90 | 88.13 | 17.84 | 0.00 | 0.00 | 0.00 | 151.88 | 5.78 | 3.81 | 67.43 | 0.00 | 0.00 | 713.20 | 93.91 | 13.17 |
| Tamil Nadu | 34,535.15 | 4,552.6 | 13.18 | 17,450 | 341.2 | 1.96 | 4,138.31 | 285.76 | 6.91 | 7,686.97 | 559.10 | 7.27 | 63,811.29 | 5,738.64 | 8.99 |
| Telangana | 50,712.19 | 1,887.7 | 3.72 | 0.00 | 0.00 | | 22,824.60 | 609.95 | 2.67 | 1,258.99 | 89.18 | 7.08 | 74,795.77 | 2,586.79 | 3.46 |
| Total | 254,657 | 15,937 | 6.26 | 25,531 | 378.1 | 1.48 | 83,970 | 5,196 | 6.19 | 20,479.33 | 1,476.6 | 7.21 | 384,638.1 | 22,987.55 | 5.98 |
| Grand Total | 314,792 | 24,341 | 7.73 | 41,791 | 436 | 1.05 | 127,495 | 10,655 | 8.36 | 33,137.80 | 2,831.7 | 8.55 | 517,216 | 38,265.58 | 7.40 |

*Source: MCID, NABARD, 2015.*

## REFERENCES

Institute of Livelihood Research and Training (ILRT) (2014). SHG Federations as Livelihood Supporting Organisations. Hyderabad: ILRT.

Kanitkar, Ajit (2002). Exploring empowerment and leadership at the grassroots: social entrepreneurship in the SHG movement in India. In Fisher, Thomas and Sriram MS (eds). *Beyond Microcredit: Putting Development Back into Microfinance.* New Delhi: SAGE Publications, pp. 234–262.

Kumar, Lakshmi, Vijayalakshmi, C., and Raghuraman, S. (undated). *Role of Voluntary Savings in SHG/SHG Members: An Analysis in Tamilnadu and Karnataka.* Chennai: Institute for Financial Management and Reserch.

NABARD (2014). *SHG2: Revisiting SHG Bank Linkage Programme.* MCID, NABARD. Mumbai: NABARD.

Thorat, Usha (2014). *Report of the Expert Group on Setting up of a Developmental Financial Institution for Women SHGs.* New Delhi: Government of India, Ministry of Rural Development.

# Review of microfinance

On 19 August 2015, Religare Institutional Research put out a document titled 'India Microfinance: Crisis Brewing—Sell SKSM', advising its subscribers and clients to sell shares of the only publicly listed company SKS Microfinance. While the advisory was only about one listed entity, the analysis was about the entire sector drawing from international examples of crises and indicating that the Indian Microfinance was headed for another 2010 like crisis, though the firm identified the risks from within the sector rather than from outside forces, thereby indicating that political risk was not the only risk for microfinance. There have been rumblings of whether the microfinance sector is heating up and whether there should be any cause for concern.

The situation in the microfinance sector is not necessarily comparable to 2010, when the Andhra Pradesh government promulgated an ordinance and later passed a law on how private sector microfinance firms could operate in the state, leading to a huge crisis amongst the top microfinance firms who were concentrated in that state.

The situation has changed because of changes in the regulatory architecture and in the overall ecosystem. The regulatory architecture requires all MFIs operating as NBFC-MFIs to seek a separate registration and follow the norms laid out in the master circular pertaining to NBFC-MFIs. These norms are aimed at addressing the three problems identified with the MFI crisis in 2010—multiple lending, excessive interest rates and coercive recovery practices. The regulatory frame has restrictions on margins; caps on loan size and tenor and of loans per borrower. There is also an advisory on the fair practices code to be followed by the MFIs; and this code has additional elements specific to MFIs over and above the advisory given to NBFCs in general (RBI, 2015).

The ecosystem has matured into having officially recognised self-regulatory organisations; having a credit bureau that provides indebtedness data and enhanced scrutiny by analysts tracking the sector—not only for the sole listed MFIs but also others who are in the market either for further equity infusion and raising debt or for securitisation of the existing portfolio. The question therefore is, whether there is indeed a crisis in the MF sector, or as a competing analyst Anand Rathi's advisory to its clients on the 27th August (in response to Religare) 'Robust growth rate ahead; superior return ratios; maintain buy'.

## MICROFINANCE DURING THE YEAR

By June 2015, there were 65 institutions licensed by the RBI as NBFC-MFIs (Table 9.1). While collectively their footprint was across the country, it is interesting to note the regional spread of the headquarters of the MFIs.

**Table 9.1 MFIs in India**

| Headquarters | Number of MFIs |
|---|---|
| South (Bangalore, Srinivasapura, Haveri, Chennai, Tiruchirapalli, Madurai, Theni, Coimbatore, Palani, Chittoor, Hyderabad) | 28 |
| East (Kolkata, Howrah, Michael Nagar, Bhubaneshwar, Rajgangpur) | 10 |
| West (Mumbai, Pune, Latur, Ahmedabad, Vadodara) | 12 |
| North (Delhi, Jaipur, Jalandhar) | 9 |
| Central (Varanasi, Lucknow) | 3 |
| North-east (Guwahati, Chhaygaon) | 3 |
| Total | 65* |

*Includes Bandhan, which converted to a Bank during the year.
*Source:* RBI. Accessed from https://rbi.org.in/Scripts/BS_NBFCList.aspx on 31 August 2015.

Microfinance sector grew at a sharp pace during the year. The highlights are given in Box 9.1. The sector continued to be profitable and as the numbers indicate, the growth happened with the deepening of the engagement. The investors reposed faith in the MFIs, with the industry attracting a total of ₹29 billion in equity investment, thereby providing adequate risk capital to have a robust gross loan portfolio (GLP).

---

**Box 9.1 Highlights of MFI performance (March 2015)**

- As of 30 June, 2015, MFIs provided microcredit to over 31.1 million clients.*
- The aggregate GLP of MFIs stood at ₹421.06 billion (excluding non-performing portfolio at risk [PAR] > 180 days) portfolio (₹30 billion in Andhra Pradesh).
- Of the GLP, around 12% represented off-balance sheet assets at ₹46.73 billion; for the first quarter ₹8.43 billion of the GLP was securitised.
- Annual disbursements (loan amount) in FY 2014–15 increased by 55% to ₹545.91 compared to that in FY 2013–14. The disbursements in the first quarter April–June 2015 were ₹159 billion.
- Total number of loans disbursed by MFIs grew by 37% in FY 2014–15 compared to FY 2013–14 reaching 33.43 million. The number of loans disbursed in the first quarter April–June 2015 was 9 million accounts.
- Funding to MFIs (in FY 2014–15) grew by 84% compared with FY 2013–14; the funding for the first quarter April–June 2015 was ₹38.23 billion.
- PAR figures (PAR 30, 90, 180) remained under 1% for FY 2014–15 and for the first quarter of 2015–16.
- Average loan amount disbursed per account was ₹16,327 in March 2015 and was ₹17,848 in June 2015.
- The MFIs cover 32 states/union territories (489 districts).
- MFIs' geographical coverage on GLP was south at 31%, east at 29%, north at 4%, west at 13%, north-east at 4% and central at 18%.
- Productivity ratios for MFIs continued to improve. GLP per branch was at ₹38.03 million, up by 49% over FY 2013–14 and ₹41.7 million as of quarter ending June 2015.

- Insurance (credit life) to over 36.36 million clients (37.8 million as of June 2015) with sum insured of ₹670.50 billion (₹757.64 billion for June 2015) was extended through MFI network.
- Pension accounts were extended to over 1.87 million (1.70 million as of June 2015) clients through MFI network.

*Client numbers may not represent 'unique' clients given that a client might have borrowed from multiple institutions.

*Source:* MFIN Micrometer Nos. 13 and 14.

On the regulatory side, there were minor changes in the notification, allowing the MFIs to lend up to ₹100,000 per client as against the extant cap of ₹50,000 per client allowing the MFIs to deepen their engagement with their existing clients. The spread of the MFI activity was getting more even, with the eastern sector leading the growth after the south.

---

**Box 9.2 Governor Rajan on NBFC-MFI guidelines**

*Professor Sriram:* The next thing I want to talk to you is about MFIs. Prior to 2010 they were growing at a very fast pace. Then the Andhra Pradesh episode happened and then the RBI set up the Malegam Committee. I think the RBI announcement came on the same day as the Andhra Pradesh ordinance. So, possibly the RBI was anticipating a crisis because if you look at the date it was the exact same date as the Chandigarh board meeting. Based on the report of the committee, there are stringent norms laid out on MFIs. Some of these possibly are still necessary, but some of these are difficult to implement like income, asset size, number of loans, etc. Number of loans is of course possible to monitor.

*Dr Rajan:* That I have said that there has been some substantial improvement in monitoring the over-indebtedness of the individual.

*Professor Sriram:* That is true but there are a couple of things—85% of the qualifying assets (portfolio) has to be in a defined category of households with ₹60,000 income in rural areas and ₹120,000 income in urban areas. Such norms lead to a large amount of misreporting. It also becomes worthless data for their own data mining purposes.

*Dr Rajan:* What we need to do is liberalise. We are trying to develop a norm for NBFCs as a whole. See, the problem comes when some NBFCs get regulatory preferences. For example, lending to NBFC-MFI counts as priority sector. If we say that lending to any NBFC against microfinance loans, should count as priority sector, then the entire privilege for NBFC-MFI vanishes. So that is probably something that we could examine. And that will alleviate this problem of having to micro-manage the structure of the MFIs.

*Professor Sriram:* Yes, because 85% is also a difficult ratio to maintain, given that some of these clients actually graduate and there is a fair mid-level market developed.

*Dr Rajan:* Yes I know. We are trying to move away from creating these silos for NBFCs, to make it continuous. If you are 95% in equipment financing, you are treated as thus and such. But if you are 70% into MFI financing …, so you should get privileges based on what you do, rather than because of the institution you are categorised as. That's all. We shouldn't have 0/1 categories.

The RBI announced draft guidelines for setting up SFBs, opening a window for many of the MFIs to convert themselves into banks. Of the 65, Bandhan Microfinance already had received an in-principle licence to convert into a universal bank and by August 2015 Bandhan was operational as a bank. Of the 64, 21 NBFC-MFIs had applied for a licence to operate as an SFB (including two MFIs that wanted to merge into a bank). With nearly a third of the MFIs wanting to be SFBs, the aspirational road map for NBFC-MFIs was clear. The RBI has indicated that the licences for SFBs and universal banks would eventually be available on-tap, thus opening up the possibilities for these organisations to move towards that aspiration.

The year for microfinance was marked by two significant events. One of the MFIs is Bandhan which started its operations as an NGO, transformed to an NBFC, registered itself as an NBFC-MFI in 2011 and finally became a full-fledged universal bank in August 2015. While the process of transformation to a bank required many changes in the NBFC, two things were marked out in the transformation—the commitment of Bandhan to continue with the microfinance activities through a dedicated vertical and absorbing all the employees of the MFI into the bank. The other event was the granting of in-principle licences to operate as SFBs to eight MFIs, thus bringing them also into the banking fold and holding out promise for the others to eventually aspire to become regulated banks offering a bouquet of services to the customers.

The investors seemed to be reposing greater faith in MFIs than ever before. As against a total equity investments of ₹7.48 billion that flowed into the MFI sector last year (April 2014 to July 2014), this year the total inflow in the form of equity was almost four times at ₹29.51 billion (August 2014 to July 2015) (Table 9.2). While this amount included about ₹11 billion in Bandhan which was known to become a bank, the equity inflow is still impressive at ₹18 billion after excluding it. What might be important to note is that the most significant investments have come into organisations that were aspiring to be SFBs (Janalakshmi, Aarohan, Utkarsh, Satin, Ujjivan and Equitas); and of the list only two

**Table 9.2 Equity infusion in MFIs—August 2014 to July 2015**

| Month of announcement | MFI name | Equity infusion (₹ in million) | Investors |
|---|---|---|---|
| November 2014 | Equitas | 3,250 | DEG (German Development Finance Co; Creation Investments; FMO; IFC; CDC and IFIF) |
| November 2014 | Janalakshmi | 6,100 | TPG Asia; Alpha TC Holdings; Morgan Stanley; Gawa Microfinance Fund; Mizuho Securities |
| December 2014 | Utkarsh | 1,320 | CDC; Lok Capital; IFC; NMI; and Aavishkar |
| March 2015 | Ujjivan | 6,000 | CX Partners; CDC; NewQuest Asia; Bajaj Holdings; IFC; and Elevar Equity |
| March 2015 | Aarohan | 600 | Tano Capital |
| April 2015 | Annapurna Microfinance | 250 | SIDBI Venture capital |
| May 2015 | Bandhan | 10,950 | IFC; SIDBI; and GIC Singapore |
| June 2015 | Satin | 513 | SBI FMO |
| June 2015 | Fusion | 530 | Belgian Investment Company and Oikocredit |
| Total | | 29,513 | |

*Source:* VCCircle. http://www.vccircle.com/finance-microfinance, accessed on 31 August 2015.

MFIs had not applied for an SFB licence (Annapurna and Fusion). Therefore, the equity flow into the MFIs might also be based on expectations.

## CHANGE OF OWNERSHIP/ PROMOTERS

During the year 2014–15 there were some realignments in the ownership patterns of the MFIs, which are listed below:

- Disha Microfin based out of Ahmedabad and Future Financial Services based out of Chittor (Andhra Pradesh) came together to form Fincare Disha to operate under a single brand and platform to offer a range of financial services. (*Source:* Fincare website http://www.fincare.com/)
- Mannapuram acquired majority stake in the Coimbatore-based Asirvad Microfinance with operations in Kerala, Tamilnadu, Odisha and Gujarat. (*Source:* VCCircle)
- Muthoot Fincorp demerged its microfinance business and set up a separate entity Muthoot Microfin.
- SKS Trust Advisors who were managing the mutual benefit trusts of SKS borrowers and the original promoters of SKS Microfinance fully exited from the company by selling their stake in the open market. The severance with all connections with Vikram Akula, the promoter of SKSNGO, was complete and the company now has a diversified ownership and possibly may be called a company run by professionals with no identifiable promoters. (*Source:* VCCircle)
- SKS Trust Advisors acquired about 70% stake in Outreach Financial Services, a start-up that is

adopting the BC model and partnering with banks. The company was renamed as Vaya Finserve.
- With equity infusion as shown in Table 9.2, the relative shares of the promoters would have undergone a significant change. Figure 9.1 shows the shareholdings of some of the large MFIs, where the private equity and venture capital investors have a majority stake and a significant presence on the boards.

---

**Box 9.3 Governance of MFIs: a study by MicroSave**

A study undertaken by MicroSave during the year 2015 about the governance of MFIs found the quality of governance in MFIs to be adequate.

The key findings of the study were classified into four categories.

On Board Composition and Structure the report indicated that the MFIs had done well in expanding their size of the boards to the optimal level. The issue on which the report had some reservations was about the representation of professional members on not-for-profit MFIs and the gap levels in board members with deep knowledge of risk management practices on the boards. The issue of CEOs also occupying the Chairperson's position was flagged by the report.

The report was not very flattering about the Board Administration and Procedures, particularly on how the sub-committees of the board work and called for more formalisation of the processes. The report suggested that nominee directors on the boards representing investors

---

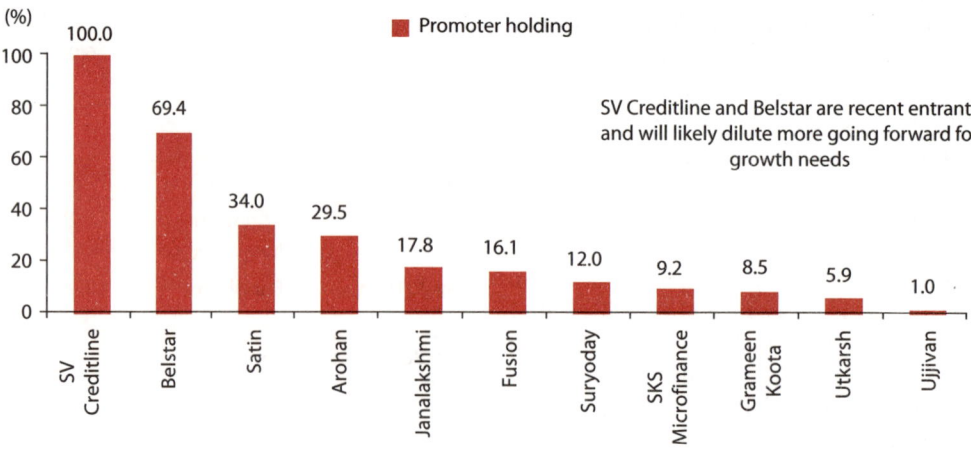

**Figure 9.1** Promoter holdings in large MFIs

*Source:* India Microfinance: Crisis Brewing—Sell SKSM Report by Parag Jariwala and Vikesh Mehta, available at http://rakesh-jhunjhunwala.in/stock_research/StocksDB/topic/religare-report-on-india-microfinance-crisis-brewing-sell-sksm/india-microfinance-sector-report-19aug15/#dlcenter

brought in significant improvement in quality of the processes.

In the section on Commitment to Roles and Responsibilities the report notes with satisfaction the involvement of the board in strategy formulation. However, the report noted that on responsible finance-related matters the boards restricted themselves to the regulatory requirements and did not go beyond. This is a matter of concern, given the current growth rate of MFIs and the observation needs to be taken seriously. The report also noted that the process of performance evaluation of the CEO was generally on pre-specified documented parameters, and there was hardly any evaluation of the board itself. There was also no effort to build the capacities of the board members.

The most damning part of the report, was about Responsible Finance where most MFIs had codes, and policies laid out. However, the report notes that many boards did not actively pursue the implementation and monitoring of responsible finance initiatives. The report noted that the boards did not adequately distinguish between social performance and corporate social responsibility. Basically the report suggested that these boards were pursuing a single bottom-line agenda rather than a double bottom-line agenda.

*Source:* Governance Practices among Microfinance Institutions in India. MicroSave, June 2015.

## GROWTH OF MFIS DURING THE YEAR[1]

The spread of MFIs across the country was impressive. As per the data made available by CRIF Highmark, there were only 110 districts of the total 676 districts where MFI-like activity was not happening. MFIs were present in 32 states and union territories and in 489 districts. In about 430 (see Table 9.3) districts in the country there were five or more institutions (including banks) offering MFI-like products—basically loans on the basis of a Joint Liability Group (JLG).

Apart from the geographic spread, the year witnessed very significant growth in the loan disburs-

[1] This segment solely relies on the data of the 50 MFIs that form the database of MFIN. Together, these 50 MFIs represent 90% of the non-SHG business in the country and are subject to the oversight of MFIN as an SRO. The SHG segment of the business was discussed in Chapter 8, and the other not-for-profit MFIs and MFIs that are not members of MFIN are discussed to the extent data is available in the public domain.

**Table 9.3** **District details of number of institutions offering MF-like loan facility**

| Number of institutions with JLG products | Number of districts |
| --- | --- |
| 0 or not available | 110 |
| Less than 2 | 50 |
| 3–5 institutions | 85 |
| More than 5 institutions | 430 |
| Total | 676 |

*Source:* CRIF Highmark.

als by MFIs, and as of 31 March 2015, the MFIs had a GLP of over ₹400 billion. A part of this portfolio (about ₹46 billion) were not on the books of the MFI, but were under the management of the MFIs. Of the ₹46 billion, ₹5.36 billion was originated by the MFIs acting as BCs to a bank. About ₹41.37 billion were originated by the MFIs but were sold to the banks. Going forward, the securitisation deals are likely to increase with the new stringent priority sector norms coming into place and these norms being applicable to foreign banks as well. The new priority sector norms have a sub-target of 8% of the ANBC to be given as loans to small and marginal farmers and 7.5% of the ANBC to be given as loan to micro-enterprises. MFIs—whether urban or rural focussed—are the most appropriate institutions to originate these loans and there would be a significant demand for their portfolio in times to come.

The increased investment into the Microfinance Sector and the general bullishness were not without reason. After the 2010 crisis, the sector that went into a bit of a setback bounced back on very strong growth numbers. From a GLP of ₹168.13 billion in 2011–12 the portfolio grew by about 2.5 times (Figure 9.2).

Amidst the growth story of microfinance across the country, the crisis that originated in the

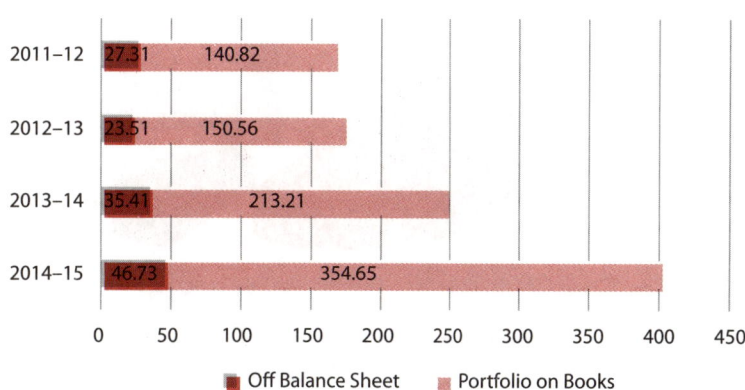

**Figure 9.2** Growth of MFI portfolio post 2010

undivided state of Andhra Pradesh (AP) in 2010 continued to have its effects, with microfinance activity almost coming to a complete stop. A state that had a GLP of ₹86 billion (representing almost half of the GLP across the country), 12.64 million clients, 5,235 branches and near about 40,000 employees was reduced to a number that was not worth reckoning. Given that there is one large state (now bifurcated into two) is out of bounds for MFIs, the growth elsewhere is particularly impressive. As a result of the AP crisis, five large MFIs went into a corporate debt restructuring (CDR) programme with their lenders. Of those one of the MFIs—Trident Microfin—liquidated and four other MFIs—Share, Spandana Spoorthy, Asmitha and BSFL—continue to be under the CDR package. While most of the MFIs have tried to recover from the AP crisis by growing outside the state, the recovery has been slow and difficult.

If one goes back to history and examines the spread of microfinance in 2010 before the AP government intervened with its ordinance (and later Act), the picture was as given in Figure 9.3, where the client outreach as well as the loan portfolio was heavily concentrated in AP. At that time, the report lamented that the microfinance had not spread wide and the exposure in other regions was limited. Of particular importance was the lack of coverage in north, north-east and the central regions of the country. If the crisis had not happened, the picture might have remained the same, but a result of the crisis was that the share of south shrank substantially. While there was not much of an offtake in the north and north-east, the fall in the relative share of south was largely compensated by an increase in the relative share of the central region and marginal increases in western and southern regions.

The spread of SHGs had a similar distribution in 2010 and as the movement grew, the south kept its share in physical outreach and had a deeper engagement as far as portfolio was concerned. This was partly explained by possible replacement of MFI loans with SHG loans. While the bank credit to SHGs grew by 84% from 2009–10 to 2014–15, the credit to AP and Telangana SHGs grew by 99%. In a way one can say that the crisis in AP turned out to be good to the other parts of the country as seen below. As the MFI sector was largely dominated by the for-profit NBFC-MFIs, the only way they could survive was probably to ring-fence the AP portfolio and grow outside. While the MFIs that had concentrated exposure to AP wilted under the defaults, the other MFIs quickly diversified and grew outside of AP. The private sector market-oriented MFIs have shown resilience and growth in the light of the AP adversity, while the state-led SHG movement has continued to grow in comfort zones.

If the spread of MFIs were to be classified into the four regions of north, east, south and west as done by MFIN, it would appear that the growth of the MFIs was even. However, if the classification was as per the zonal distribution adopted by the RBI, which adds two more zones—north-east and central, then the spread would not look as even. East contributes to more than 30% of the market share, ahead of south on all parameters and this is largely because of the absence of action in Telangana and AP. This is a significant point given that traditionally the formal banking parameters have been lagging in the east. But there is no MFI otherwise evenly distributed across regions both in terms of outreach and in terms of deployment of credit. What is interesting to note is that while south leads the numbers in terms of the number of branches (33%) and GLP

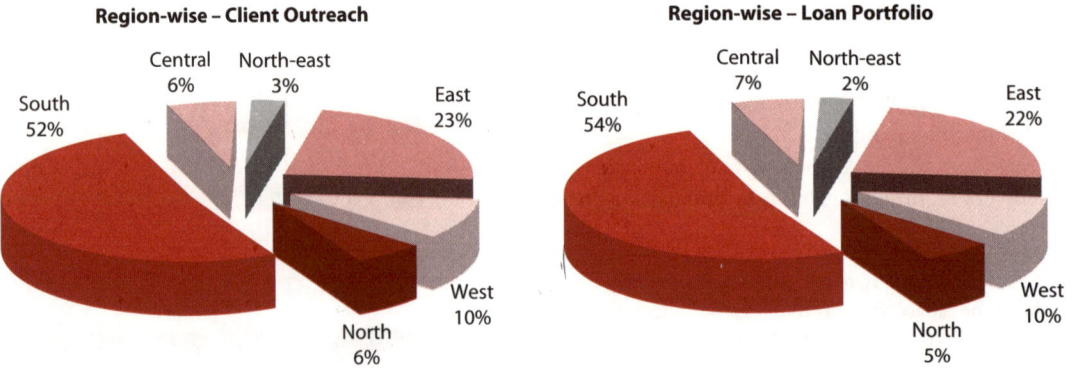

**Figure 9.3** Client outreach and loan outstanding of MFIs in 2010

*Source:* Champatiray, Amulya Krishna; Agarwal, Parul; and Sadhu, Santadarshan (2010): Map of Microfinance Distribution in India. Chennai: IFMR Centre for Microfinance.

at 31%, the incremental growth in terms of the portfolio was coming from the eastern region. The most important number to watch is the average loan disbursed as given in the panel (Figure 9.4). It appears that the average loan size in the southern region is the least, possibly representing saturation and maturity while the north-east, north and eastern regions are showing aggressive growth.

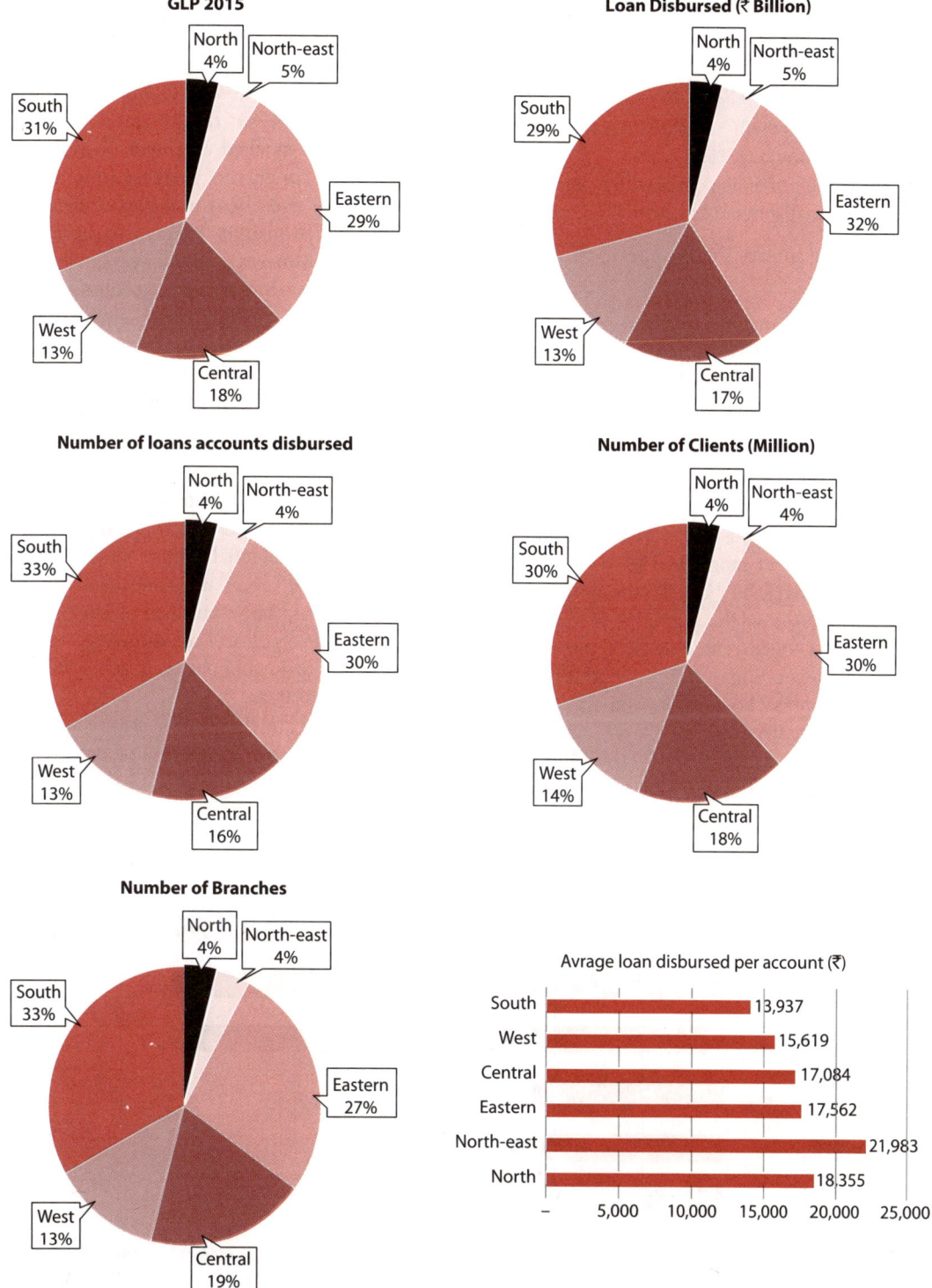

**Figure 9.4** Regional spread of the MFIs

## A DEEPER LOOK AT THE DATA

Going by the spirit of the analysis given out by Religare, which indicated that the MFI sector was headed for a 2010-like crisis (though the risk not emanating from the political side), it was important to look at the data closely to draw some inferences.

A look at the more detailed numbers provided by MFIN in its quarterly publication MFIN Micrometer shows the following trends:

- The portfolio growth rate in the last year has been a phenomenal 63%.
- This growth in portfolio comes with a concurrent growth in loan disbursements which grew at 55%.

However, the interesting numbers are the following:

- The number of branches of MFIs grew by 8%.
- The staff strength of MFIs grew by 20%.
- The number of clients grew by 29%.
- The number of loans grew by 37%.

While the above numbers are for all the MFIs spread across the 32 states and union territories, MFIN has provided for detailed data for MFIs in 19 states which is being used for the analysis below. These MFIs represent more than 95% of the MFI GLP reported to MFIN. Figure 9.5 shows that there is a drastic increase in the amounts of loans disbursed without a concurrent increase in the number of loans and clients. Worse still the workforce that is servicing this portfolio is growing at a fraction of the disbursement rate.

Table 9.4 gives the details of how the MFIs grew in the most important states. The state-wise data given by MFIN represents 97% of the GLP reported. The state-wise data indicates a very phenomenal growth in some large states, where a large number of MFIs are operating. To put the data in Table 9.4 in perspective, the year on year (YoY) growth rates between 2013–14 and 2014–15 are computed in percentage terms and represented in Table 9.5.

A perusal of the percentage growth rates in Table 9.5 shows that while the GLP grew by 62% in the select 19 states, the loan disbursements grew by a whopping 82%. Of the 19 states (including UTs), six regions clocked a growth of more than 100% without a concurrent increase in branch offices, employees and client numbers, indicating a deepening of relationships. This is also represented by the significant increase in the average loan disbursed and outstanding per loan account.

This growth rate needs a closer look to understand whether the growth that is coming is too rapid, and might be causing a systemic risk of over-indebtedness, particularly in certain regions. In raising these questions, the following factors need due consideration (Kumar, 2015):

- It is a myth that there are no political risks. Given that all the customers are clearly identified as poor, there is always a potential vulnerability.
- It is a myth that urban areas are insulated from political risks—a large number of clients in an urban slum are a political constituency.
- Group liabilities do not hold as effectively in urban areas as in rural areas.
- Sudden burst of growth in urban areas is worrying.
- The funding for MFIs is coming from multiple channels—leveraging of the balance sheet,

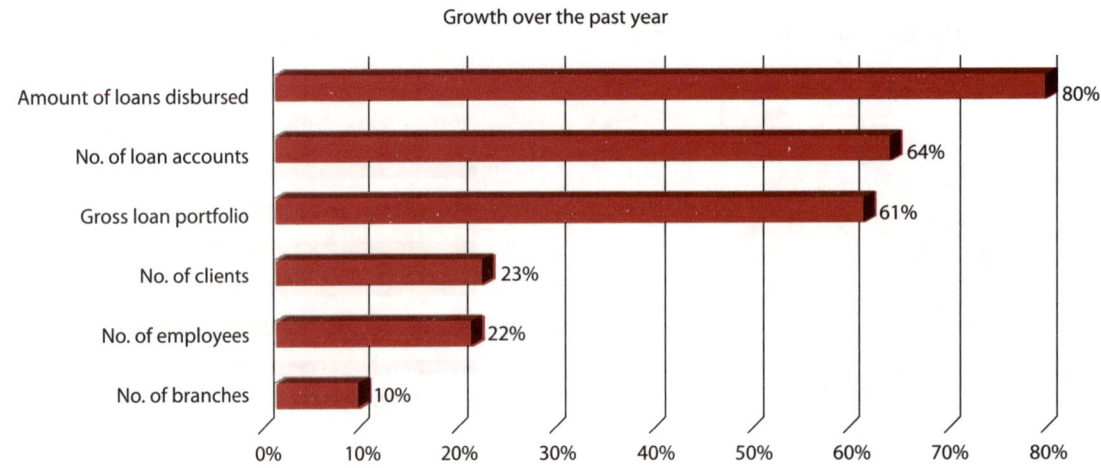

**Figure 9.5** Growth of MFIs from 2013–14 to 2014–15

**Table 9.4 State-wise details of MFIs for 2014–15**

| State | MFI (Nos.) | Gross loan portfolio (₹ billion) | | Number of clients | | Number of branches | | Number of employees | | Loans disbursed (₹ billion) | | Number of loan accounts disbursed | |
|---|---|---|---|---|---|---|---|---|---|---|---|---|---|
| | | 2013–14 | 2014–15 | 2013–14 | 2014–15 | 2013–14 | 2014–15 | 2013–14 | 2014–15 | 2013–14 | 2014–15 | 2013–14 | 2014–15 |
| West Bengal | 13 | 38.85 | 60.19 | 3,886,914 | 4,579,767 | 1,363 | 1,362 | 9,749 | 9,453 | 53.31 | 92.31 | 3,223,665 | 4,771,783 |
| Tamil Nadu | 19 | 37.86 | 57.00 | 3,825,377 | 4,868,056 | 1,250 | 1,281 | 9,358 | 11,002 | 45.96 | 69.41 | 3,350,517 | 4,604,561 |
| Karnataka | 21 | 26.21 | 43.7 | 2,492,444 | 2,942,949 | 881 | 1,040 | 7,228 | 9,936 | 27.39 | 57.15 | 2,494,619 | 4,744,317 |
| Maharashtra | 27 | 23.67 | 38.72 | 2,362,155 | 3,020,680 | 784 | 960 | 5,916 | 8,186 | 26.26 | 50.47 | 1,863,391 | 3,380,705 |
| UP | 17 | 19.96 | 33.91 | 1,839,875 | 2,392,318 | 692 | 820 | 4,969 | 6,413 | 25.12 | 42.3 | 1,427,622 | 2,407,308 |
| Bihar | 19 | 15.56 | 27.23 | 1,725,668 | 2,134,493 | 624 | 723 | 4,166 | 5,045 | 18.32 | 41.15 | 1,141,207 | 2,380,907 |
| MP | 27 | 14.93 | 24.91 | 1,706,541 | 2,073,357 | 670 | 817 | 4,396 | 5,531 | 18.64 | 33.49 | 1,331,173 | 2,027,558 |
| Assam | 7 | 11.13 | 20.87 | 877,920 | 1,334,806 | 313 | 419 | 2,014 | 2,814 | 15.52 | 28.74 | 866,752 | 1,307,563 |
| Odisha | 14 | 10.98 | 19.3 | 1,468,654 | 1,673,288 | 518 | 575 | 3,106 | 3,866 | 9.68 | 27.52 | 707,112 | 1,933,399 |
| Kerala | 8 | 10.31 | 17.65 | 902,514 | 1,023,933 | 260 | 295 | 2,494 | 2,912 | 12.8 | 21.39 | 790,037 | 1,305,474 |
| Gujarat | 19 | 7.5 | 12.42 | 719,410 | 1,083,431 | 295 | 426 | 2,197 | 3,015 | 9.81 | 15.79 | 623,832 | 861,662 |
| Rajasthan | 14 | 5.82 | 8.62 | 645,151 | 687,177 | 246 | 263 | 1,742 | 2,035 | 5.9 | 11.95 | 346,800 | 694,665 |
| Jharkhand | 14 | 3.36 | 5.66 | 436,136 | 512,579 | 155 | 197 | 1,067 | 1,415 | 3.43 | 8.83 | 238,521 | 582,980 |
| Chhattisgarh | 14 | 3.27 | 5.44 | 364,386 | 471,781 | 186 | 237 | 1,093 | 1,486 | 4.4 | 7.69 | 307,612 | 476,708 |
| Haryana | 12 | 2.12 | 4.55 | 203,440 | 313,269 | 76 | 111 | 582 | 1,061 | 2.33 | 5.92 | 130,792 | 330,195 |
| Uttarakhand | 12 | 2.51 | 4.39 | 244,206 | 301,798 | 76 | 98 | 543 | 688 | 4.76 | 5.67 | 271,718 | 306,849 |
| Delhi | 10 | 2.98 | 4.24 | 214,980 | 257,006 | 61 | 65 | 1,158 | 1,347 | 3.83 | 5.09 | 166,324 | 226,054 |
| Puducherry | 9 | 0.69 | 1.13 | 74,781 | 91,934 | 15 | 18 | 135 | 176 | 0.88 | 1.42 | 66,884 | 90,170 |
| AP and Telangana | 6 | 3.63 | 0.86 | 365,657 | 122,574 | 1,054 | 753 | 3,365 | 3,015 | 1.9 | 2.22 | 87,493 | 132,412 |
| Total | | 241.3 | 390.79 | 24,356,209 | 29,885,196 | 9,519 | 10,460 | 65,278 | 79,396 | 290.24 | 528.51 | 19,436,071 | 32,565,270 |

*Source:* MFIN Micrometer, Issue 13, 31 March 2015. Accessed at: http://mfinindia.org/wp-content/uploads/2015/micrometer/Micrometer%20Issue%2013_Q4%20FY%2014-15_21st%20May%20 2015.pdf on 2 September 2015.

**Table 9.5**  Year on year growth rates of MFI activities in 2013–14 and 2014–15

| State | MFI (Nos.) | GLP (₹ billion) | Client (Nos.) | Branches (No.) | Employees (No.) | Loans disbursed (₹ billion) | Loan accounts disbursed (No.) | Average loan disbursed per account (₹) |
|---|---|---|---|---|---|---|---|---|
| West Bengal | 13 | 55% | 18% | 0% | –3% | 73% | 48% | 17% |
| Tamil Nadu | 19 | 51% | 27% | 2% | 18% | 51% | 37% | 10% |
| Karnataka | 21 | 67% | 18% | 18% | 37% | 109% | 90% | 10% |
| Maharashtra | 27 | 64% | 28% | 22% | 38% | 92% | 81% | 6% |
| UP | 17 | 70% | 30% | 18% | 29% | 68% | 69% | 0% |
| Bihar | 19 | 75% | 24% | 16% | 21% | 125% | 109% | 8% |
| MP | 27 | 67% | 21% | 22% | 26% | 80% | 52% | 18% |
| Assam | 7 | 88% | 52% | 34% | 40% | 85% | 51% | 23% |
| Odisha | 14 | 76% | 14% | 11% | 24% | 184% | 173% | 4% |
| Kerala | 8 | 71% | 13% | 13% | 17% | 67% | 65% | 1% |
| Gujarat | 19 | 66% | 51% | 44% | 37% | 61% | 38% | 17% |
| Rajasthan | 14 | 48% | 7% | 7% | 17% | 103% | 100% | 1% |
| Jharkhand | 14 | 68% | 18% | 27% | 33% | 157% | 144% | 5% |
| Chhattisgarh | 14 | 66% | 29% | 27% | 36% | 75% | 55% | 13% |
| Haryana | 12 | 115% | 54% | 46% | 82% | 154% | 152% | 1% |
| Uttarakhand | 12 | 75% | 24% | 29% | 27% | 19% | 13% | 6% |
| Delhi | 10 | 42% | 20% | 7% | 16% | 33% | 36% | –2% |
| Pondicherry | 9 | 64% | 23% | 20% | 30% | 61% | 35% | 19% |
| AP | 6 | –76% | –66% | –29% | –10% | 17% | 51% | –23% |
| Total | | 62% | 23% | 10% | 22% | 82% | 68% | 6% |

*Source:* Computed by the author from Table 9.4.

securitisation, equity infusion, debentures—each of these going through different concerns and different set of questions.

- Banks (including private sector banks) are putting in serious money into the business directly and this portfolio goes unreported in the microfinance segment of the credit bureau. In general, banks use different credit bureau (CIBIL) while the microfinance sector largely uses two credit bureaus (Equifax and CRIF Highmark).
- In MFIs that have gone down in the past, there have been issues of promoter-related fraud and governance and management dominated by promoters, with lesser stake in the organisation.
- In some MFIs the clients seem to have a stake through the Mutual Benefit Trust route, without the attendant personal returns on the equity stake, making a significant stake faceless.
- The obsession with zero delinquency creates perverse incentive systems for the field staff, and does not provide a timely feedback loop from the field that can trigger mid-course correction.

There might be incentives for the field staff to deliberately misreport the data to the credit bureau to achieve performance targets, thereby creating a risk.

- MFI sector is one sector where there is lender-led collateral damage. A clear case in point was BASIX which followed a more benevolent model of microfinance that got caught in the AP crossfire.

The MCril Microfinance Review 2014 (MCril, 2014) using the same indicators—of aggressive growth, low delinquency, high employee productivity, increased investment and high valuations and increasing profitability—also sounded a warning bell early in 2015. However, the sector has grown even more aggressively after the report was out. The mitigating factor in this fast growth according to MCril was the opening up of opportunity for SFBs and now that this has become a reality, the space is to be watched.

This is important to examine because of the significant growth of the MFIs to be seen with the very significant capital inflows into the sector during the past years, easy availability of loans from the banking sector, helping the MFIs to leverage and the rapid growth percentages being obtained on a much larger base. This growth is also happening while one of the largest markets for MFIs—Andhra Pradesh and Telangana—has almost dried out.

While there are adequate safeguards because of the two lender norms and the credit bureaus existing, there still may be some issues that may have to be considered. The data obtained from CRIF Highmark shows that there are 160 districts in the country where there is little or no microfinance activity, and 430 districts in the country where more than five institutions are present with a microfinance-like loan product, given on the basis of a group formation and a group guarantee. The CRIF Highmark database includes banks operating in these districts having an MFI-like product with JLGs. The data from CRIF Highmark is given in Table 9.3.

The 430 districts identified above should be examined closely to understand whether the sector is headed towards another round of excessive lending. The justification for waving a red flag is as follows:

- The growth is happening without concurrent increase in number of clients.
- The average loan size (in terms of both disbursement and outstanding) is increasing.
- This growth is happening during a period when the RBI had not increased the per borrower loan limit. The limit was increased in April 2015 and the data pertains to year ending March 2015.
- The banks are not bound by the upper limit and the two loan norms are applicable to NBFC-MFI and they are also operating in the same area as the MFIs.
- While the MFIs predominantly use the credit bureaus such as CRIF Highmark and Equifax, banks largely use CIBIL database for their enquiry. It is possible that the databases do not show an existing borrower as a borrower due to mismatch of spellings, address and identity papers. Even with this caveat and the caveat provided by MFIN that the client numbers might not represent 'unique' clients, there is deepening of engagement and this aspect needs to be considered.
- The SHG data is still in the process of digitisation and most of the credit bureaus do not have robust numbers for the SHG.
- This growth follows the aggressive investments that have come in the past year, and the MFIs may be under pressure to perform and also quickly deploy the resources they have raised.

---

**Box 9.4 Why is it difficult for 2010 to repeat itself?**

While there is much discussion on whether the industry is growing at an unstainable pace, the situation has changed fundamentally in the larger ecosystem that might provide adequate checks and balances from the situation going out of hands. Some of the factors that preceded the MFI crisis in AP in 2010 can be seen such as high levels of investment coming in at high valuations, and large number of MFIs operating in a single area. Therefore, the rumblings that the growth rates, the valuations, etc., could be leading to aggressive lending and client-level indebtedness may be well founded.

However, there are multiple mitigating factors that can provide a corrective framework. As the RBI recognised self-regulatory organisation, MFIN is charged with undertaking the following functions:

- Surveillance
- Dispute resolution
- Grievance redressal
- Knowledge dissemination and training
- Managing data

MFIN has already a robust system of collecting and disseminating data with fair degree of granularity. The data cuts are available in the public domain with a two-month lag and at a granularity of a state, and MFI. Going forward, MFIN is working on collecting data at the district level. MFIN also has a helpline and is able to track complaints and have field presence. MFIN has a self-regulation committee which is firewalled from the regular function as an industry association.

In addition to MFIN there are at least two credit bureaus that are working actively in this space and all loans being given out are being queried. CRIF Highmark, for instance, has shared the data on high percentages of inquiries being rejected for being non-compliant, which in itself is a strong indicator of aggressive behaviour and this could be tracked down.

The most important aspect is that with Bandhan moving out of the space to become a universal bank and with eight other MFIs getting an in-principle licence to set up an SFB—particularly the ones that were growing aggressively and fast—there would be a bit of a slowdown as these institutions gear up for the transition phase. Therefore, it

> is quite likely that in spite of the aggressive growth, there are some natural circuit breakers that slow down the industry and help the MFI sector to take a pause and reflect.

Considering the above argument, it is imperative that this data is broken up further and examined carefully. When the overall numbers are computed using the MFIN database, the following aspects stand out. The outreach parameters in terms of how many clients a loan officer is handling and the number of clients per branch have been range-bound. However, a look at the business parameters indicates something startling (Figure 9.6). With a stable outreach parameters, the business parameters (loans per branch, per employee, average loan outstanding) all show dramatic growth—implying that the growth is coming without concurrent deployment of the physical parameters needed. This is a matter of concern, unless there has been a deployment of a new methodology or technology that makes the loaning process gain efficiency.

The numbers given in Figure 9.6 indicate an increasing concentration in existing areas, a slightly better expansion of client base, possibly overlapping loans for the clients but more importantly deepening of relationship with the client. That such a growth is coming from deepening relationships is something that needs to be looked at with caution.

However, when the data is examined from different cuts—the states where largest number of MFIs are present; or for that matter statistics of the fastest growing MFIs and the largest MFIs—the pattern does not seem to indicate that there is deepening with the clients. The broad district parameters and the state parameters seem to be within a reasonable range. Therefore, if there is indeed a crisis brewing, then this data would come out only when we have data on clients borrowing from multiple sources and have the number of unique clients of the MFIs put together. That can be accomplished with the data from the credit bureaus.

## GROWTH OF MFIs AND INCLUSIX

While the growth could be analysed on various parameters such as GLP, loans disbursed, number of branches, clients and employees, the top states that emerged were West Bengal, Tamil Nadu, Karnataka, Maharashtra, Uttar Pradesh, Madhya Pradesh and Bihar. Their relative position is given in Table 9.6. From the data it is clearly seen that but for Karnataka and Tamil Nadu which had relatively high Inclusix scores and a high ranking on Inclusix, all other states where MFIs were present were in states that had a low Inclusix score.

But, the data is not strictly comparable because the Inclusix score is based on data for 2013. However, the fact that this MFI activity is happening in areas with a low Inclusix score, and that Inclusix is including MFI data in its scores indicate that these would contribute to improving the scores of the states in the future editions. While the MFI data given above are based on parameters which represent data on a stable state (employees, branches, existing portfolio balances and total disbursements), one parameter that would be interesting to note is where the incremental growth is coming from. While these growth rates are happening on a very low base, this is only indicative of the entry of many MFIs into these regions that had very low Inclusix scores. That data is given in Table 9.7.

## GRANULAR ANALYSIS

Data provided by CRIF Highmark—one of the major credit bureaus—shows some patterns that could be used in analysing whether an area is heating up

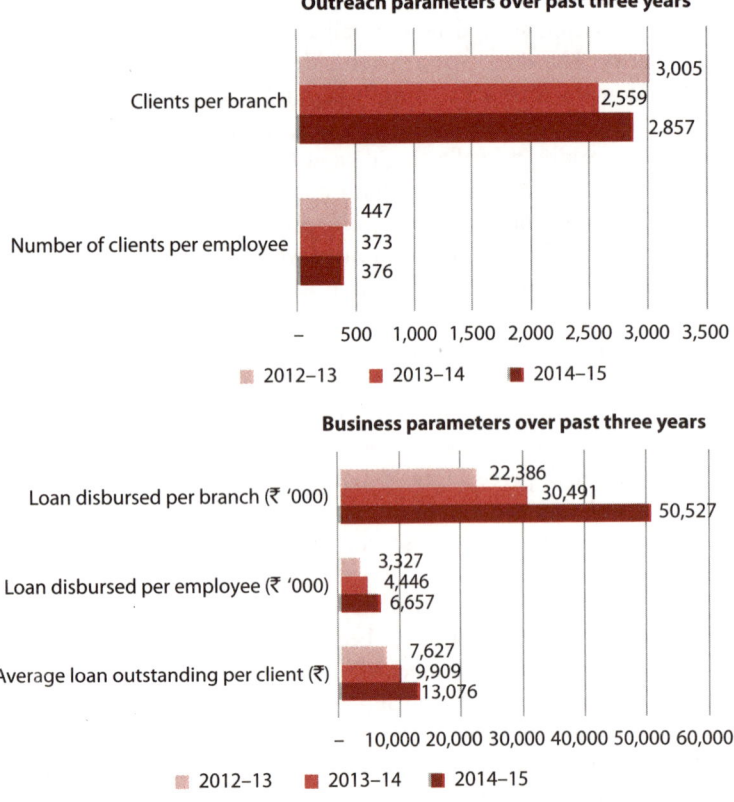

**Figure 9.6** Growth of MFI sector physical and business parameters

**Table 9.6 MFI activities: the top states**

| State | March 2015 | | | June 2015 | | | | | CRISIL Inclusix score and position |
|---|---|---|---|---|---|---|---|---|---|
| | GLP, loans given and branches | Clients (No.) | Employees (No.) | GLP | Loans given | Branches | Clients (No.) | Employees (No.) | |
| West Bengal | 1 | 2 | 3 | 1 | 1 | 1 | 2 | 2 | 46.6 (19) |
| Tamil Nadu | 2 | 1 | 1 | 2 | 2 | 2 | 1 | 1 | 79.2 (3) |
| Karnataka | 3 | 4 | 2 | 3 | 3 | 3 | 4 | 3 | 74.4 (6) |
| Maharashtra | 4 | 3 | 4 | 4 | 4 | 4 | 3 | 4 | 49 (17) |
| UP | 5 | 5 | 5 | 5 | 6 (Bihar is 5) | 6 | 5 | 5 | 40.1 (26) |
| MP | 7 (Bihar is 6) | | | 7 (Bihar is 6) | 7 | 5 | 6 | 7 (Bihar is 6) | 40.5 (25) |

*Source:* MFIN Micrometer, Nos. 13 and 14 for MFI data and CRISIL Inclusix Volume III for Inclusix data.

**Table 9.7 Top states with the highest gross loan portfolio growth rate of MFIs**

| | Growth position in 2014 | Growth position in Q1 of 2015 | Inclusix score and position as of 2013 |
|---|---|---|---|
| Mizoram | 1 | 3 | 42.6 (24) |
| Manipur | 2 | 2 | 21.6 (35) |
| Jammu & Kashmir | 3 | | 45.2 (21) |
| Himachal Pradesh | 4 | 1 | 60.5 (11) |
| Punjab | 5 | 7 | 50.7 (12) |
| Haryana | 6 | 4 | 53.2 (16) |
| Odisha | 7 | 5 | 55.2 (14) |
| Chhattisgarh | 15 | 6 | 35.4 (31) |
| Sikkim | 14 | 8 | 46.8 (18) |
| Gujarat | 16 | 9 | 45.0 (20) |

*Source:* MFIN Micrometer, Nos. 13 and 14 for MFI data and CRISIL Inclusix Volume III for Inclusix data.

with too many suppliers of credit. In some districts, the data indicates as many as 57 providers operating. A caveat is in order. The CRIF Highmark data includes all formal lenders in the area (including banks) using the group methodology to lend. For instance, the data in Table 9.8 presents a relatively higher percentage of inquiries showing pre-existing loans and borrowers who are not compliant in very high growth and deep penetration states like Tamil Nadu, Karnataka, Odisha, Madhya Pradesh and West Bengal. The state averages might be somewhat coloured by low averages from some districts. Therefore, it might be useful to look at the same data broken down into districts.

From Table 9.9 it is evident that the districts that have the largest number of borrowers also tend to give adverse credit bureau reports. Similarly, Table 9.10 gives numbers of MFIs in a district and it is evident that the more the number of MFIs operating in a district, the more the instances of inquiries

on ineligible borrowers. These could be the districts where the data and identity of the borrowers could be masked in order to get a clearance. The fact that about 8% of the borrowers on whom inquiry was made had a loan with two or more MFIs (which makes the borrower ineligible to borrow) shows that it is possible to get through the bureaus if the filters applied by the bureaus are not very tight, leading to a potential domino default in some districts.

The year was really good for the microfinance sector, as it attracted unprecedented investments; grew at a rapid pace; fully got over the crisis in Andhra Pradesh and maintained the health of the portfolio with PAR more than 30 days (PAR > 30) being maintained at less than 1%. There were rumblings in the sector that a bubble was building up and possibly this is not without reason. There were at least 32 districts where the number of operators exceeded 30, and as the data above shows, the inquiry results showed a very high degree of overlap,

**Table 9.8  Credit bureau inquiry results for states and union territories**

| State/ Union territories | Pre-existing loan | Non-compliant | Active loans with 2 MFIs | Active loans with 3 MFIs | Active loans with 4 MFIs | Active loans with 4 MFIs | Pre-existing default | Outstanding > ₹50,000 |
|---|---|---|---|---|---|---|---|---|
| Tamil Nadu | 55.74 | 8.57 | 4.03 | 0.75 | 0.16 | 0.06 | 3.25 | 0.31 |
| Puducherry | 55.33 | 6.14 | 3.36 | 0.44 | 0.07 | 0.01 | 2.09 | 0.17 |
| Karnataka | 48.59 | 8.55 | 3.93 | 0.98 | 0.21 | 0.06 | 1.70 | 1.67 |
| Odisha | 47.79 | 5.70 | 2.54 | 0.31 | 0.05 | 0.01 | 2.66 | 0.13 |
| Madhya Pradesh | 47.12 | 6.13 | 2.65 | 0.74 | 0.22 | 0.11 | 1.55 | 0.86 |
| West Bengal | 46.48 | 7.12 | 2.73 | 0.33 | 0.04 | 0.01 | 3.31 | 0.70 |
| Maharashtra | 46.46 | 8.97 | 3.63 | 0.95 | 0.24 | 0.08 | 3.20 | 0.88 |
| Gujarat | 44.73 | 7.02 | 3.25 | 0.74 | 0.15 | 0.03 | 2.44 | 0.40 |
| Goa | 43.02 | 4.61 | 2.12 | 0.22 | 0.01 | 0.00 | 0.91 | 1.35 |
| New Delhi | 42.87 | 6.52 | 2.83 | 0.56 | 0.09 | 0.02 | 2.02 | 1.01 |
| Manipur | 42.73 | 1.80 | 1.78 | 0.01 | 0.00 | 0.00 | 0.00 | 0.00 |
| Himachal | 41.69 | 4.91 | 0.35 | 0.03 | 0.00 | 0.00 | 4.50 | 0.03 |
| Rajasthan | 40.28 | 6.64 | 2.39 | 0.63 | 0.13 | 0.04 | 2.36 | 1.08 |
| Uttar Pradesh | 39.90 | 4.57 | 1.91 | 0.38 | 0.08 | 0.02 | 1.24 | 0.92 |
| Sikkim | 39.88 | 1.32 | 0.08 | 0.00 | 0.00 | 0.00 | 0.82 | 0.43 |
| Uttarakhand | 39.43 | 7.17 | 2.41 | 0.51 | 0.10 | 0.02 | 1.86 | 2.28 |
| Bihar | 37.77 | 4.16 | 2.11 | 0.39 | 0.07 | 0.02 | 0.92 | 0.65 |
| Jharkhand | 35.61 | 5.29 | 2.44 | 0.42 | 0.06 | 0.01 | 2.01 | 0.34 |
| Meghalaya | 34.62 | 6.56 | 2.37 | 0.04 | 0.00 | 0.00 | 2.63 | 1.53 |
| Kerala | 31.47 | 4.09 | 2.22 | 0.26 | 0.02 | 0.00 | 1.08 | 0.50 |
| Chhattisgarh | 29.40 | 2.86 | 0.95 | 0.12 | 0.02 | 0.00 | 1.58 | 0.18 |
| Haryana | 29.15 | 3.80 | 1.02 | 0.18 | 0.03 | 0.00 | 1.65 | 0.92 |
| Tripura | 21.52 | 1.33 | 0.35 | 0.01 | 0.00 | 0.00 | 0.34 | 0.63 |
| Punjab | 19.59 | 3.96 | 0.66 | 0.09 | 0.00 | 0.00 | 1.47 | 1.74 |
| Chandigarh | 15.82 | 0.37 | 0.05 | 0.00 | 0.00 | 0.00 | 0.19 | 0.14 |
| Assam | 13.57 | 2.95 | 0.32 | 0.04 | 0.00 | 0.00 | 2.17 | 0.42 |

*Source:* CRIF Highmark.

*Note:* The figures are in percentages. These figures indicate the results when an inquiry is made for providing a new loan to the customer. A high number would indicate a larger number of inquiries are being made in case of existing borrowers. Inquiries are also turning out results about ineligible borrowers.

**Table 9.9  Credit bureau inquiry results on districts**

| Districts by number of borrowers | Pre-existing loan | Non-compliant | Active loans with 2 MFIs | Active loans with 3 MFIs | Active loans with 4 MFIs | Active loans with 4 MFIs | Pre-existing default | Outstanding > ₹50,000 |
|---|---|---|---|---|---|---|---|---|
| Top 50 districts | 55.84 | 9.28 | 4.32 | 1.02 | 0.24 | 2.61 | 0.09 | 1.00 |
| District position 51–100 | 51.50 | 8.39 | 3.89 | 0.95 | 0.22 | 2.06 | 0.07 | 1.20 |
| District position 101–150 | 46.51 | 6.84 | 3.17 | 0.70 | 0.15 | 1.81 | 0.04 | 0.96 |
| District position 151–200 | 45.56 | 6.39 | 2.92 | 0.62 | 0.13 | 1.87 | 0.04 | 0.82 |

*(Continued)*

*(Continued)*

| Districts by number of borrowers | Pre-existing loan | Non-compliant | Active loans with 2 MFIs | Active loans with 3 MFIs | Active loans with 4 MFIs | Active loans with 4 MFIs | Pre-existing default | Outstanding > ₹50,000 |
|---|---|---|---|---|---|---|---|---|
| District position 201–250 | 38.69 | 6.04 | 2.14 | 0.43 | 0.09 | 2.59 | 0.02 | 0.76 |
| District position 251–300 | 36.52 | 4.77 | 1.74 | 0.31 | 0.06 | 1.89 | 0.02 | 0.74 |
| District position 301–350 | 33.84 | 4.27 | 1.58 | 0.28 | 0.06 | 1.69 | 0.02 | 0.64 |
| District position 351–400 | 30.41 | 3.97 | 1.26 | 0.19 | 0.03 | 1.88 | 0.00 | 0.61 |
| District position 401–450 | 26.35 | 3.00 | 0.93 | 0.08 | 0.01 | 1.53 | 0.00 | 0.45 |
| District position 451–473 | 27.55 | 2.70 | 0.90 | 0.06 | 0.00 | 1.59 | 0.00 | 0.15 |

*Source:* CRIF Highmark.
*Note:* The figures are in percentages. These figures indicate the results when an inquiry is made for providing a new loan to the customer. A high number would indicate a larger number of inquiries are being made in case of existing borrowers. Inquiries are also turning out results about ineligible borrowers.

**Table 9.10  Credit bureau inquiry results on districts classified by MFI presence**

| Districts by number of MFIs | Pre-existing loan | Non-compliant | Active loans with 2 MFIs | Active loans with 3 MFIs | Active loans with 4 MFIs | Active loans with 4 MFIs | Pre-existing default | Outstanding > ₹50,000 |
|---|---|---|---|---|---|---|---|---|
| >30 MFIs | 55.21 | 9.24 | 4.28 | 1.10 | 0.31 | 2.40 | 0.13 | 1.01 |
| 26–30 MFIs | 54.17 | 8.84 | 4.08 | 1.03 | 0.24 | 2.46 | 0.09 | 0.93 |
| 21–25 MFIs | 48.75 | 7.88 | 3.43 | 0.83 | 0.20 | 2.33 | 0.07 | 1.03 |
| 16–20 MFIs | 44.42 | 6.41 | 2.81 | 0.60 | 0.11 | 1.88 | 0.03 | 0.98 |
| 11–15 MFIS | 37.68 | 4.72 | 1.87 | 0.30 | 0.05 | 1.90 | 0.01 | 0.60 |
| 6–10 MFIs | 27.89 | 3.54 | 1.20 | 0.11 | 0.01 | 1.58 | 0.00 | 0.65 |
| 0–5 MFIs | 19.00 | 3.18 | 0.36 | 0.02 | 0.00 | 2.30 | 0.00 | 0.50 |

*Source:* CRIF Highmark.
*Note:* The figures are in percentages. These figures indicate the results when an inquiry is made for providing a new loan to the customer. A high number would indicate a larger number of inquiries are being made in case of existing borrowers. Inquiries are also turning out results about ineligible borrowers.

indicating that the same set of borrowers was approaching multiple agencies.

With the stipulations of the RBI on the two-lender norm as well as a cap on the loan amount, the larger data does not seem to indicate any clear pattern of over-lending. However, granular data on the districts accessed from the credit bureau indicates that these fears are not unfounded. An analysis of the number of unique borrowers as a proportion of the population of economically active women (as per census 2011) also indicates that the high growth regions have the proportions averaging 18%, with average loan disbursements touching ₹30,000 per borrower. In these districts the ratio of the number of loans to unique borrowers is about 1.5%, with many borrowers in the 3rd cycle. These numbers need to be watched carefully by the credit bureaus with tighter controls, particularly considering the fast pace of growth of the MFIs in the past years.

Going forward, the issue becomes even more involved. This is because apart from Bandhan (which has commenced operations as a universal bank), eight other MFIs have been given an in-principle approval to set up SFBs and the new banks would not be governed by the NBFC-MFI restrictions but most likely will be operating with similar clients and in the same area. Therefore, the indebtedness number in areas where there is rapid growth as well as intensity of MFI presence needs to be watched much more carefully not only by the credit bureaus, but also by the self-regulatory organisation MFIN and by the regulator—the RBI.

In the interregnum, there could be individual organisations that may face some turbulence if they have been unable to build in internal systems to manage this growth. It was interesting to note that this growth was happening at a fairly high base and as the sector moves forward there are more opportunities. Amidst all the concerns about a rapid growth, what is important to note is the spread of MFIs in areas that have got a low Inclusix score. While there is a data lag between the data for MFIs which is current and the Inclusix score which is for 2013, it is still a positive step forward in moving into difficult and unbanked areas.

This was a year when one of the largest MFIs became a commercial bank. As a result of Bandhan's exit, the size of the microfinance portfolio would shrink by a quarter (as per the March 2015 figures). However, this might be made up by the rapid growth exhibited by the next set of players. The impact of the SFB licences is to be seen.

More data on the MFIs on various cuts is given in the appendices of this chapter.

**APPENDIX 9.1**
**Highlights of MFI portfolio: March 2015**

Highlights portfolio

- MFIs (grouped by portfolio size) with highest growth rates are shown in the charts.

- Growth in glp has been broadly spread across various states and with few exceptions, all states have growth rates of 50% or above.

- States with highest growth in portfolio are Manipur, Himachal Pradesh, Jammu & Kashmir, albeit from a low base.

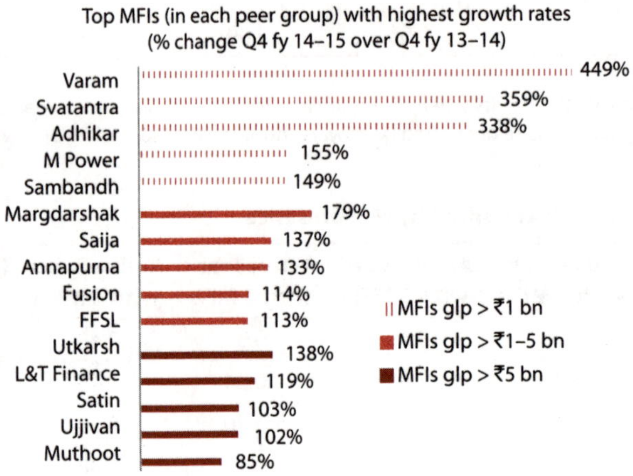

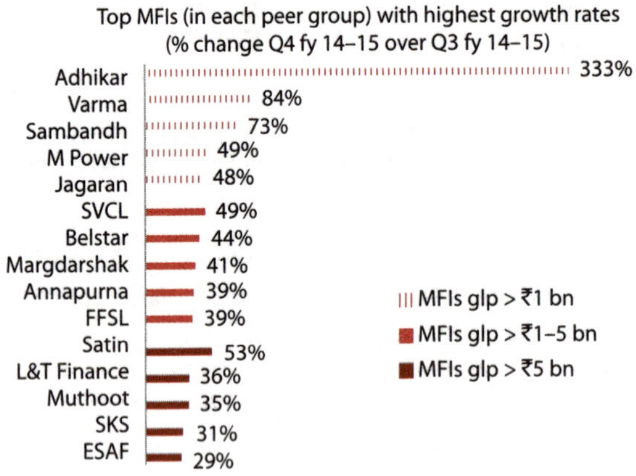

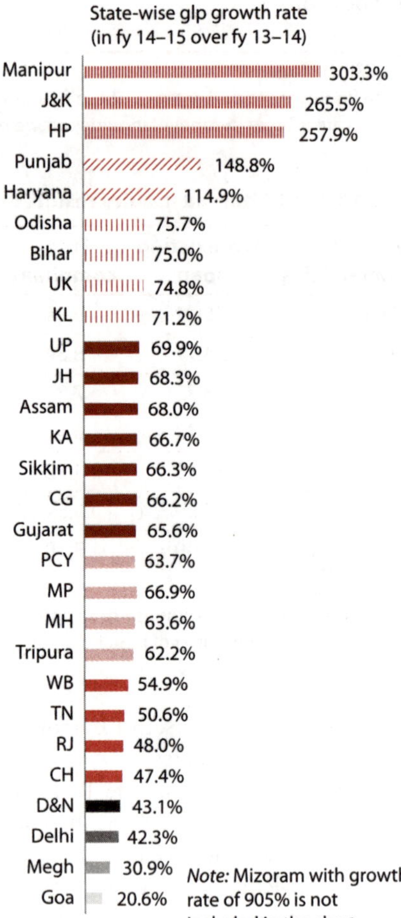

**Top MFIs (in each peer group) with highest growth rates**
(% change Q4 fy 14–15 over Q4 fy 13–14)

|  |  |
|-----|--------|
| Varam | 449% |
| Svatantra | 359% |
| Adhikar | 338% |
| M Power | 155% |
| Sambandh | 149% |
| Margdarshak | 179% |
| Saija | 137% |
| Annapurna | 133% |
| Fusion | 114% |
| FFSL | 113% |
| Utkarsh | 138% |
| L&T Finance | 119% |
| Satin | 103% |
| Ujjivan | 102% |
| Muthoot | 85% |

‖ MFIs glp > ₹1 bn
■ MFIs glp > ₹1–5 bn
■ MFIs glp > ₹5 bn

**Top MFIs (in each peer group) with highest growth rates**
(% change Q4 fy 14–15 over Q3 fy 14–15)

|  |  |
|-----|--------|
| Adhikar | 333% |
| Varma | 84% |
| Sambandh | 73% |
| M Power | 49% |
| Jagaran | 48% |
| SVCL | 49% |
| Belstar | 44% |
| Margdarshak | 41% |
| Annapurna | 39% |
| FFSL | 39% |
| Satin | 53% |
| L&T Finance | 36% |
| Muthoot | 35% |
| SKS | 31% |
| ESAF | 29% |

‖‖ MFIs glp > ₹1 bn
■ MFIs glp > ₹1–5 bn
■ MFIs glp > ₹5 bn

**State-wise glp growth rate**
(in fy 14–15 over fy 13–14)

|  |  |
|-------|--------|
| Manipur | 303.3% |
| J&K | 265.5% |
| HP | 257.9% |
| Punjab | 148.8% |
| Haryana | 114.9% |
| Odisha | 75.7% |
| Bihar | 75.0% |
| UK | 74.8% |
| KL | 71.2% |
| UP | 69.9% |
| JH | 68.3% |
| Assam | 68.0% |
| KA | 66.7% |
| Sikkim | 66.3% |
| CG | 66.2% |
| Gujarat | 65.6% |
| PCY | 63.7% |
| MP | 66.9% |
| MH | 63.6% |
| Tripura | 62.2% |
| WB | 54.9% |
| TN | 50.6% |
| RJ | 48.0% |
| CH | 47.4% |
| D&N | 43.1% |
| Delhi | 42.3% |
| Megh | 30.9% |
| Goa | 20.6% |

*Note:* Mizoram with growth rate of 905% is not included in the chart

fy, financial year; glp, gross loan portfolio

*Source:* MFIN Micrometer 13. New Delhi: Microfinance Institutions Network.

## APPENDIX 9.2
## Highlights of MFI outreach: March 2015

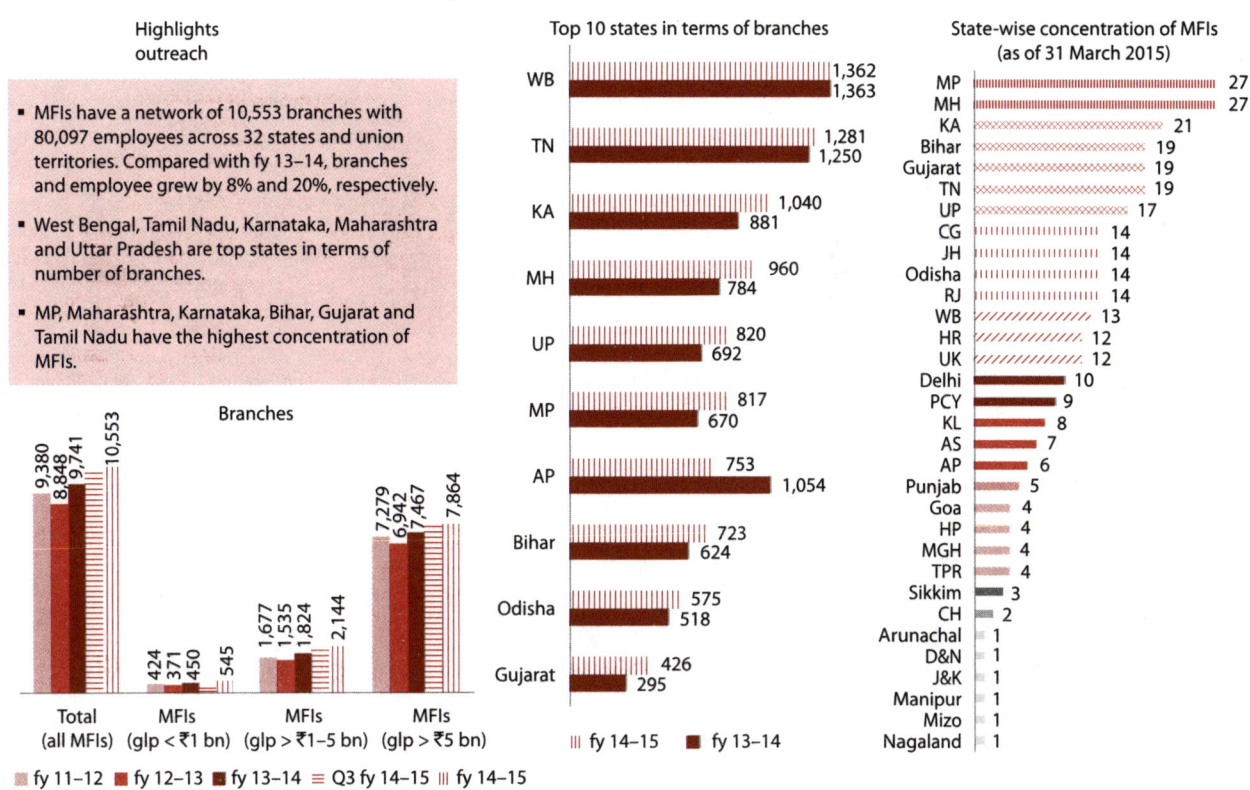

**Highlights outreach**

- MFIs have a network of 10,553 branches with 80,097 employees across 32 states and union territories. Compared with fy 13–14, branches and employee grew by 8% and 20%, respectively.

- West Bengal, Tamil Nadu, Karnataka, Maharashtra and Uttar Pradesh are top states in terms of number of branches.

- MP, Maharashtra, Karnataka, Bihar, Gujarat and Tamil Nadu have the highest concentration of MFIs.

*Source:* MFIN Micrometer 13. New Delhi: Microfinance Institutions Network.

## APPENDIX 9.3
## Highlights of MFI loan disbursals: March 2015

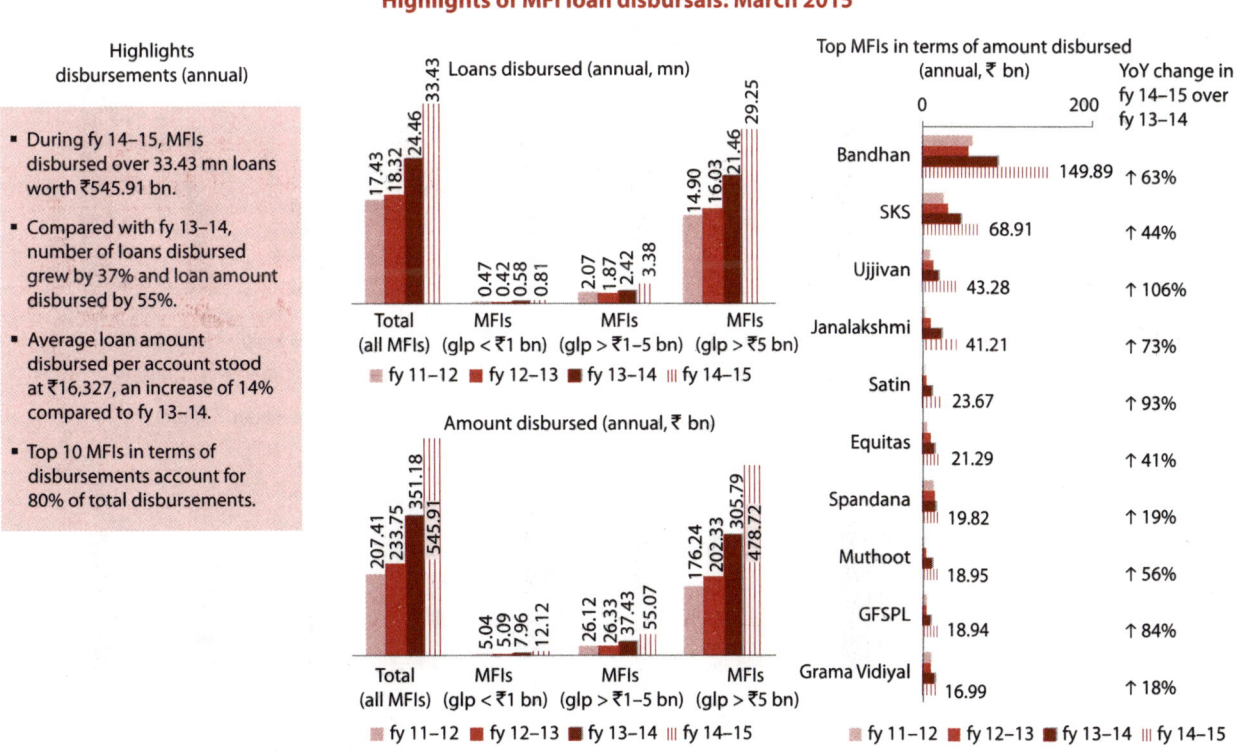

**Highlights disbursements (annual)**

- During fy 14–15, MFIs disbursed over 33.43 mn loans worth ₹545.91 bn.

- Compared with fy 13–14, number of loans disbursed grew by 37% and loan amount disbursed by 55%.

- Average loan amount disbursed per account stood at ₹16,327, an increase of 14% compared to fy 13–14.

- Top 10 MFIs in terms of disbursements account for 80% of total disbursements.

*Source:* MFIN Micrometer 13. New Delhi: Microfinance Institutions Network.

## APPENDIX 9.4
### Highlights of MFI debt funding: March 2015

**Highlights debt funding (annual)**

- During fy 14–15, MFIs received a total of ₹276.82 bn in debt funding (from Banks and other Financial Institutions). This represents a growth of 84% as compared to fy 13–14.

- 78% of the funding come from Banks and rest from other financial institutions (FIs).

- Securitisation of MFIs' portfolio increased by 39% compared with fy 13–14.

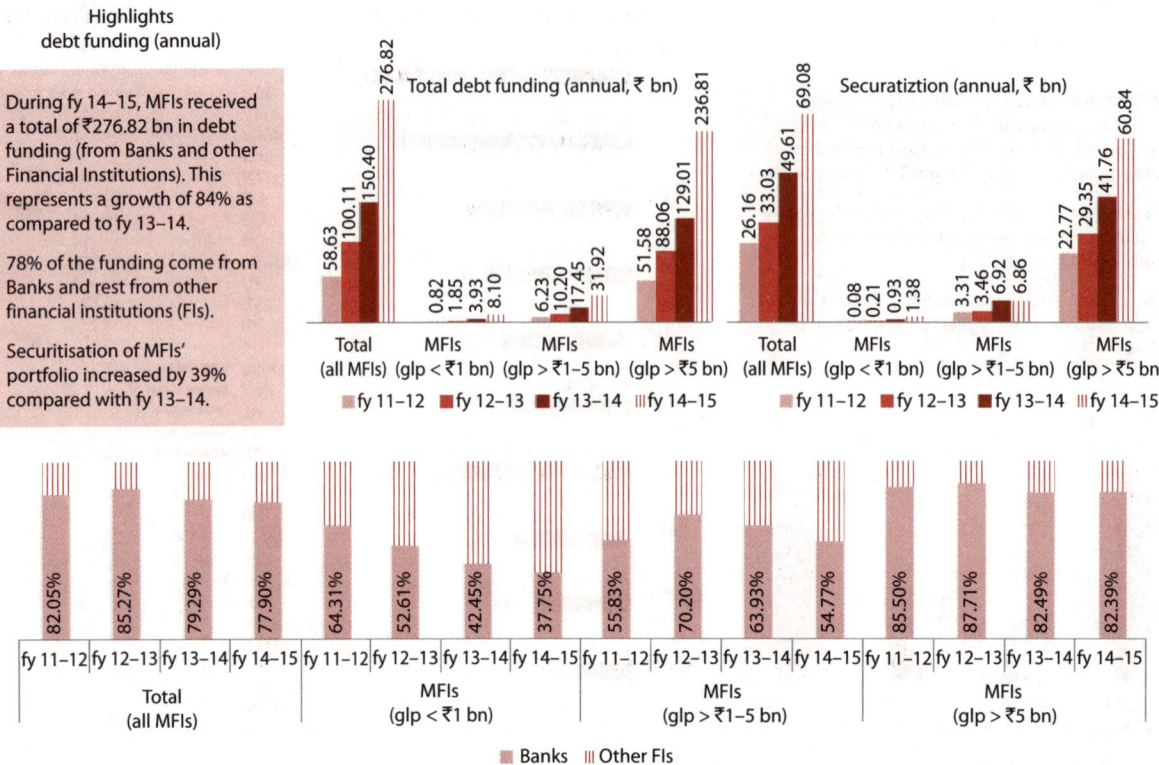

*Source:* MFIN Micrometer 13. New Delhi: Microfinance Institutions Network.

## APPENDIX 9.5
### Productivity of MFIs: March 2015

**Highlights productivity ratios**

- Productivity ratios have been improving. Clients per loan officer ratio and clients per branch ratio increased by 9% and 19% respectively over fy 13–14.

- However, there is greater increase in glp ratios. The glp per loan officer and glp per branch increased by 36% and 49% respectively over fy 13–14.

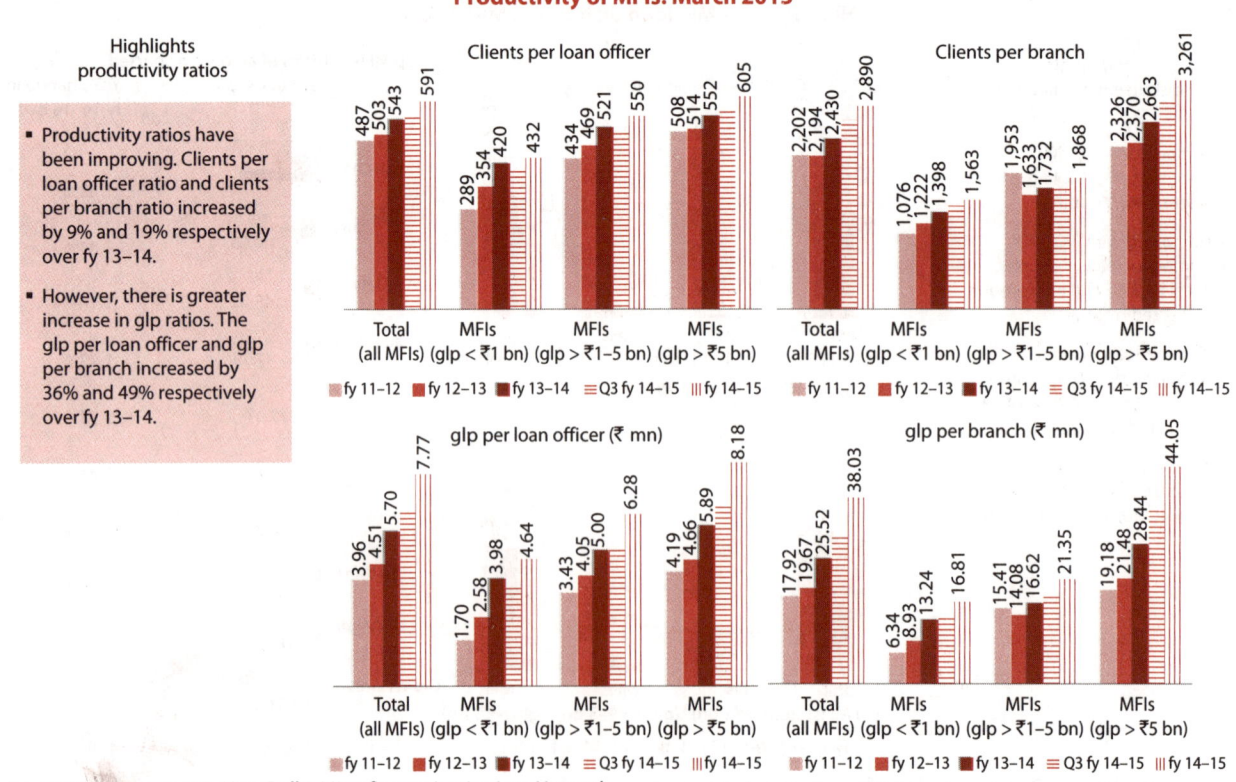

*Source:* MFIN Micrometer 13. New Delhi: Microfinance Institutions Network.

**APPENDIX 9.6**
**State- and union territory-wise credit bureau data for June 2015**

| State/ Union territory | Unique borrowers/ economi- cally active women | Number of active loans/ unique borrower | Loan amount disbursed/ unique borrower (₹) | Loan out- standing/ unique borrower | Overdue percent (amount) | Overdue percent (accounts) | % clients in cycle 1 | % clients in cycle cycle 2 | % clients in cycle cycle 3+ |
|---|---|---|---|---|---|---|---|---|---|
| Tamil Nadu | 20.32% | 1.56 | 28,970 | 18,028 | 2.79% | 4.02% | 61.38% | 20.99% | 17.63% |
| New Delhi | 17.67% | 1.04 | 26,474 | 16,948 | 2.37% | 3.56% | 77.53% | 18.73% | 3.75% |
| Puducherry | 17.51% | 1.53 | 30,181 | 20,079 | 0.83% | 1.67% | 65.03% | 23.69% | 11.27% |
| Assam | 13.13% | 1.11 | 32,476 | 23,058 | 0.88% | 2.06% | 82.71% | 7.34% | 9.95% |
| Karnataka | 12.91% | 1.77 | 34,391 | 21,713 | 2.35% | 3.08% | 60.75% | 18.84% | 20.40% |
| Odisha | 12.45% | 1.48 | 28,452 | 17,872 | 4.92% | 6.79% | 54.62% | 22.38% | 23.00% |
| West Bengal | 12.36% | 1.23 | 28,955 | 18,300 | 2.81% | 4.22% | 74.96% | 12.46% | 12.58% |
| Tripura | 11.64% | 1.11 | 33,812 | 22,432 | 0.41% | 0.72% | 97.02% | 1.52% | 1.46% |
| Utarakhand | 10.58% | 1.36 | 38,339 | 24,923 | 1.93% | 2.50% | 78.01% | 16.04% | 5.95% |
| MP | 10.56% | 1.39 | 29,373 | 18,780 | 2.30% | 3.40% | 63.28% | 19.31% | 17.41% |
| Maharashtra | 9.52% | 1.49 | 29,284 | 18,455 | 2.94% | 4.34% | 67.15% | 17.62% | 15.23% |
| Sikkim | 8.77% | 1.19 | 42,835 | 29,896 | 2.46% | 4.76% | 96.99% | 1.74% | 1.27% |
| Kerala | 8.48% | 1.59 | 30,797 | 20,461 | 0.57% | 0.98% | 49.00% | 33.56% | 17.44% |
| Meghalaya | 7.30% | 1.21 | 36,970 | 23,756 | 10.30% | 7.85% | 88.64% | 7.59% | 3.77% |
| Bihar | 7.19% | 1.26 | 27,094 | 17,198 | 0.89% | 1.36% | 74.70% | 13.94% | 11.36% |
| Chhattisgarh | 6.06% | 1.20 | 29,563 | 18,178 | 3.42% | 4.50% | 56.72% | 18.72% | 24.55% |
| Gujarat | 5.85% | 1.47 | 37,171 | 23,498 | 2.89% | 5.31% | 72.90% | 17.96% | 9.15% |
| UP | 5.26% | 1.30 | 30,790 | 20,115 | 1.44% | 2.24% | 62.18% | 19.69% | 18.13% |
| Haryana | 5.10% | 1.20 | 36,294 | 23,959 | 2.08% | 4.04% | 80.70% | 13.53% | 5.77% |
| Jharkhand | 4.87% | 1.46 | 28,458 | 17,934 | 3.22% | 4.16% | 69.94% | 16.95% | 13.11% |
| Punjab | 4.83% | 1.34 | 46,808 | 29,390 | 2.60% | 4.48% | 78.35% | 16.65% | 5.00% |
| Manipur | 4.04% | 1.05 | 13,696 | 8,038 | 0.06% | 13.78% | 49.14% | 18.75% | 32.11% |
| Rajasthan | 3.65% | 1.53 | 41,045 | 25,006 | 3.15% | 4.41% | 72.09% | 18.81% | 9.10% |
| Goa | 3.56% | 1.43 | 65,672 | 33,932 | 4.17% | 5.30% | 70.19% | 16.48% | 13.33% |
| Himachal | 1.30% | 1.23 | 21,224 | 13,797 | 2.50% | 3.01% | 76.73% | 19.17% | 4.10% |
| Chandigarh | 1.06% | 1.43 | 27,469 | 17,053 | 0.43% | 1.15% | 74.39% | 18.90% | 6.71% |

*Source:* CRIF Highmark (2015).

**APPENDIX 9.7**
**Credit bureau data as of June 2015 categorised on districts as per the number of borrowers**

| Districts sorted by number of borrowers | Unique borrowers/ economically active women | No. of active loans/ unique borrower | Loan amount disbursed/ unique borrower (₹) | Loan outstanding/ unique borrower | Overdue percent (amount) | Overdue percent (accounts) | % clients in cycle 1 | % clients in cycle 2 | % clients in cycle 3+ |
|---|---|---|---|---|---|---|---|---|---|
| Top 50 districts | 15% | 1.46 | 30,224 | 19,036 | 2.64% | 3.78% | 65.42% | 18.43% | 16.15% |
| 51–100 | 13% | 1.50 | 30,975 | 19,697 | 1.86% | 2.95% | 63.31% | 19.28% | 17.41% |
| 101–150 | 11% | 1.38 | 30,259 | 19,195 | 2.13% | 3.46% | 64.33% | 18.51% | 17.16% |
| 151–200 | 8% | 1.39 | 32,273 | 20,831 | 2.32% | 3.52% | 67.15% | 18.20% | 14.65% |
| 201–250 | 7% | 1.32 | 29,784 | 19,142 | 3.23% | 4.95% | 69.53% | 16.36% | 14.11% |
| 251–300 | 5% | 1.31 | 33,081 | 21,636 | 2.51% | 4.77% | 70.90% | 16.38% | 12.72% |
| 301–350 | 4% | 1.27 | 32,292 | 21,008 | 2.63% | 4.43% | 73.41% | 15.03% | 11.56% |
| 351–400 | 3% | 1.25 | 31,565 | 20,497 | 2.45% | 4.41% | 73.20% | 15.36% | 11.44% |
| 401–450 | 2% | 1.23 | 28,078 | 18,425 | 2.39% | 5.16% | 73.02% | 15.48% | 11.50% |
| 451–473 | 1% | 1.19 | 21,662 | 15,124 | 3.63% | 5.58% | 66.18% | 20.11% | 13.72% |

*Source:* CRIF Highmark (2015).

**APPENDIX 9.8**
**Credit bureau data as of June 2015 categorised on districts as per the number of MFIs in a district**

| Districts by number of MFIs | Unique borrowers/ economically active women | No. of active loans/ unique borrower | Loan amount disbursed/ unique borrower (₹) | Loan outstanding/ unique borrower | Overdue percent (amount) | Overdue percent (accounts) | % clients in cycle 1 | % clients in cycle 2 | % clients in cycle 3+ |
|---|---|---|---|---|---|---|---|---|---|
| >30 | 12.5% | 1.37 | 28,428 | 18,068 | 2.60% | 3.75% | 66.46% | 18.38% | 15.15% |
| 26–30 | 13.0% | 1.58 | 32,678 | 20,611 | 1.94% | 3.34% | 64.57% | 19.71% | 15.72% |
| 21–25 | 10.6% | 1.49 | 31,495 | 19,638 | 2.59% | 3.51% | 65.11% | 17.86% | 17.03% |
| 16–20 | 8.7% | 1.40 | 29,949 | 19,159 | 2.24% | 3.46% | 65.11% | 18.19% | 16.70% |
| 11–15 | 7.1% | 1.34 | 30,175 | 19,568 | 2.59% | 4.35% | 64.86% | 18.62% | 16.52% |
| 6–10 | 6.9% | 1.27 | 32,035 | 21,048 | 2.62% | 4.63% | 72.33% | 16.36% | 11.31% |
| 1–5 | 5.9% | 1.12 | 34,175 | 22,819 | 1.15% | 2.31% | 89.25% | 6.03% | 4.72% |

*Source:* CRIF Highmark (2015).

## REFERENCES

Kumar, Gaurav (2015). Personal Communication with the author. Chennai.

MCril (2014). *The MCril Microfinance Review 2014*. Gurgaon: Micro Credit Ratings International Limited.

RBI (2014). *Master Circular 'Non-Banking Finance Company—Microfinance Institutions' (NBFCMFIs) Directions*. Department of Non Banking Supervision. Mumbai: RBI.

# New institutional initiatives

## CONTEXT

The financial sector has had two broad categories of institutions—the banks and NBFCs.

There have been sub-categories of banks classified as:

(a) Old private sector banks (set up before nationalisation of banks in 1969)
(b) State Bank group
(c) Nationalised public sector banks (nationalised in two phases once in 1969 and later in 1980)
(d) Cooperative banks

In addition, based on the policy of the central government a new set of institutions were initiated by the state. These were banks with limited areas of operations and greater focus on inclusion. These were jointly promoted by the federal and state governments in association with a public sector bank as a sponsor bank. This category of banks was called the RRBs and it started in 1975.

In 1993, the RBI opened up the banking space to offer new banking licences for the first time. Later this was followed up by opening up for licences to the new private sector banks twice in 1993 and 1995. The first round of licences was issued for private sector banks based on the guidelines issued in 1993; the thrust was to sub-serve the larger financial sector reforms that were underway and it was also expected that these banks would lead the way in upgradation of technology and innovate in business practices (RBI, 1993). The next set of licences was issued almost a decade later in 2003 when two banks were licenced, and the guidelines did not lay any special emphasis.

In 1996, the RBI opened up the space for private sector banks to operate within a limited area as LABs (licenced in the period 1999–2002). While these banks were expected to function as a private sector alternative to the RRBs, they neither grew in numbers because of the RBI's policy on putting licencing on hold; nor were they able to scale up because of their restricted area of operation. However, as of now four LABs are operating in the country (for a detailed review of the performance of LABs, see Sriram and Krishna, 2015).

One attempt to set up a niche commercial bank was made in 2013 when the GoI set up the Bharatiya Mahila Bank (BMB) focussed on women. This bank enjoys a special category as a public sector bank under the companies act, licenced by the RBI, but not categorised as a nationalised bank.

In addition to the above, more licences were issued in 2014 for two new private sector banks. This licencing process had a long prelude—starting with the discussion paper issued in August 2010, followed by draft guidelines for new banks in August 2011 and the final guidelines in February 2013. While there were more than 20 applicants for opening up new banks, the decision of the grant of licences to two players stood out. IDFC which was a company largely into infrastructure financing got a licence to become a universal bank at one end and at the other an MFI—Bandhan—got the other licence. The year 2015 will see both these new initiatives start their operations on the ground (discussed later in this chapter).

From these initiatives, it is apparent that the RBI was envisaging most of these as full banks with restriction only on certain specialised activities or restrictions on geographical spread. The categorisation of NBFCs, on the other hand, has been more dynamic. Ever since the requirements for licencing of NBFCs came into being in 1997, the regulation has been tightened on deposit-taking activities of NBFCs, and they have largely been restricted to carrying out specialised functions including credit. The niche deposit taking residuary NBFCs have since removed as a category and existing institutions have been systematically closed down.

## INSTITUTIONAL INTERVENTIONS AND INNOVATIONS

The year 2015 can be termed as a significant year from the perspective of financial inclusion. It is significant not only because of the achievements in this area, but also because of the promise it holds out. While at the one end, we can celebrate the fact that this report is the 10th in the series of the inclusive finance reports, celebrating a decade of reviewing, assessing and reporting on the happenings in the financial inclusion space, at the other end this is also a year of celebration for all the bold initiatives that have been taken up in this niche space.

The interventions in the financial inclusion space have traditionally happened at two levels. At one level there are the interventions in the institutional design space and at the other level the interventions are in the policy space. The year 2015 is also exciting because of the bold new steps taken in institutional intervention and innovation.

The role of the state has been oscillating between that of a by-stander and applauder to an oppressive regulator. The performance of MFIs during the initial phase was exemplary in terms of the geographical spread and in reaching a number of clients—particularly women. The slowdown in the MFI sector happened due to regulatory intervention in Andhra Pradesh, and later due to a regulatory tightening by the RBI, following the implementation of the recommendations contained in the Report of the Sub-Committee of the Central Board of Directors of Reserve Bank of India to Study Issues and Concerns in the MFI Sector (Malegam Committee). However, by all accounts it appears that the MFI sector has overcome the slowdown and it grew at an aggressive pace this year.

However, 2015 will be termed as a very significant year in the agenda of financial inclusion not only because of the renewed policy thrust towards inclusion but also because of three new institutional initiatives that are getting ready to be rolled out.

The government also announced its plans to set up the MUDRA Bank with a corpus of ₹200 billion. In anticipation of the necessary statutory bills being passed, the activity of the proposed MUDRA Bank is being undertaken by a subsidiary company of SIDBI under the scheme Pradhan Mantri MUDRA Yojana. This mezzanine organisation, which will both undertake refinance activities and build the ecosystem, will operate in the space that could be called the 'missing middle'. It would go beyond the classic MFI where the loan ticket sizes are restricted to ₹100,000 to ₹1 million, thereby addressing the needs of micro enterprises. The RBI reclassification of PSL guidelines making it mandatory for banks to lend 7.5% of the ANBC to micro-enterprises will provide a strong reason for the existence of MUDRA.

The RBI invited applications for the new differentiated banks—PBs and SFBs. While the draft guidelines were put up in the public domain last year, this crystallised into the licencing process this year. The RBI finally issued in-principle approvals for 11 PBs and 10 SFBs during the year.

This was the first time that the RBI was according the status of a 'Bank' to an activity that would provide niche financial services. While the initial draft guidelines for the SFBs (then called only as Small Banks) indicated that they would have a limited (but possibly wider) footprint than the LABs, the final guidelines have opened up a nation-wide footprint, thereby paving the way for not only new players to come into the sector, but also opening the possibility for MFIs to morph into more comprehensive services. From the self-promoted market-based institutional interventions with only policy thrust, this year has seen a shift to direct institutional intervention by the state, as well as a framework for the private sector to participate in the larger inclusion agenda through differentiated banks.

There was some movement on the urban cooperative banks as well, with the High Powered Committee on cooperative banks submitting its report, which had the potential of changing the way cooperative banks are licensed and administered. The committee amongst other recommendations also suggested that the large urban cooperative banks move towards a joint stock company and apply for an SFB licence.

In addition to the above-mentioned initiatives, last year, India Post in a surprising move applied for a licence to open a universal bank when the RBI opened up the space for new players. But India Post was not granted a licence for a universal bank, and the RBI preferred to offer in-principle licences to only two new players—IDFC Limited and Bandhan. The move by India Post was surprising, as it could have approached the central banker outside of the regular licencing process, being an arm of the government. However, the move showed certain boldness as far as India Post was concerned. It was a strong statement made by India Post on their readiness to expand their presence in the financial inclusion space. India Post in its second attempt to enter the inclusion space is getting a licence to set up a PB. The importance and the promise of India Post are discussed in a separate chapter.

---

**Box 10.1 Governor Rajan on institutional approach to inclusion**

*Professor Sriram:* On the institutional front, I have seen a shift in the approach taken by the RBI. In case of LABs and even when the draft guidelines for the SFBs were put up, it appeared that the RBI had a geographic focus. But the final guidelines opened up the space for SFBs to have a nationwide foot-print …

*Dr Rajan:* Possibly, but not necessarily.

*Professor Sriram:* But that possibility is real. With LABs or SFBs with a restricted geography we would have been able to achieve a regional penetration much better. When it is open to a nationwide footprint, then it encourages functional penetration. Instead of targeting some regions, we target certain types of customers.

*Dr Rajan:* Yes you are absolutely right. My hope is that we will also get some local players. When we put up the draft guidelines, the Microfinance Institutions (MFI) represented to us and said 'look we are already national, we are able to make these small loans because we have a certain structure that decentralizes decisions locally. So why do you want to penalize us?' There is also a stability issue with these small local entities. I mean, one firm focussed in say Andhra Pradesh may be subject to both the political environment and a hurricane and so on.

*Professor Sriram:* Yes, there is the geographical concentration risk. If we look at the growth of banking post-nationalisation when we had the 1:4 rule for rural branches, and later the rule of 25% branches being in rural and semi-urban areas. But these measures have not taken away the geographical mismatch. North-east, east and centre continue to be under-banked despite these efforts. So what do we do?

*Dr Rajan:* That leads us to the real question: what comes first, industry or finance? And I think that in these areas, typically the missing factor is not primarily finance, it is only partly finance. Primarily it is industry. Unless the real sector flourishes, which means fixing all the issues that are associated with the real sector, banking itself cannot be the prime mover. So people say credit-deposit ratio is low, it could be because there is no demand for credit. Of course, you can always find somebody who says, 'I wanted a loan, I didn't get it'. That does not negate the basic point.

---

## ACTION ON THE INITIATIVES

### New private sector banks and what they mean for financial inclusion

#### IDFC Bank

IDFC Bank has already started its pilot operations in Hoshangabad district with its inclusion customers. It has called its rural strategy as 'Bharat Banking operations' and the strategy is to fully use the extant architecture and leverage technology to the optimum. The overall approach is to look at the conviction with which they would do the business with the smaller customers. While IDFC is clear that this vertical will not lose money, they are also not looking at milking profits from this business. The idea is to look at the inclusive business as a long-term customer acquisition strategy, with a decentralised focus on the districts. IDFC's overall strategy is still under wraps, but it promises to be a disruptive model fully leveraging on the new developments happening in the financial sector (PBs and SFBs) and also leveraging technology to the hilt (including mobile-based payments systems).

Unlike the other licensee Bandhan, IDFC has not been in the inclusion space significantly and the bank does not come with any past baggage. Therefore, it is expected that IDFC Bank might have some out of the box strategies that look at the art of the possible within the regulations, within the obligatory requirements but totally disruptive at the customer interface level. Much of the details of IDFC's strategy are to be seen and there would be something significant to report the next year.

#### Bandhan Bank

Bandhan has been an MFI operating in the inclusive finance space almost from the time the microfinance industry evolved in India. Bandhan has gone through all the waves of organisational and business model transformation—starting as a not-for-profit entity, collaborating with ASA of Bangladesh and then moving into a commercial model of microfinance by morphing its activities into an NBFC-MFI. Now its journey would be complete with it moving in the financial sector as a full-fledged bank. Bandhan is more articulate about its journey, and what it intends to do. Unlike IDFC, Bandhan's challenge would be to manage the space that is beyond its core strength of inclusion. Bandhan is also a bank that needs to be watched carefully because the most significant presence is in an area that has been traditionally underbanked (east and north-eastern regions). The journey of Bandhan is captured in Box 10.2.

---

### Box 10.2 The journey: Bandhan to Bandhan Bank

#### From Bandhan Financial Services Private Limited to Bandhan Bank

One of the most significant events during the year was the coming of age of the microfinance major Bandhan. Bandhan, over the years, has been one of the fastest growing MFIs focussing its operations in the eastern and north-eastern parts of the country, which have traditionally been underbanked. There was much excitement when Bandhan received its in-principle approval to set up a universal bank in April 2014 and this financial year will witness a roll-out of Bandhan as a universal bank, thus being a pioneer in completing the loop that mainstreams the excluded customers into the mainstream financial systems.

Having started as a not-for-profit entity, it grew into an NBFC) and then registered itself as a specialised MFI under the new regulations passed in 2011. By becoming a universal bank in 2015, the loop is now complete and the clients and employees of Bandhan can now claim to be completely integrated into the financial system.

Bandhan will have many other firsts to its credit, which are quite unlike for the other private sector banks that have been set up in the country after the RBI started granting licences to the private sector players in the decade of 1990s. While some of the private sector banks came from the background of being in the mainstream financial sector as DFIs such as ICICI Bank and IDBI Bank, niche players such as HDFC Bank (Housing) and Axis Bank (Mutual Funds and asset management companies), or greenfield projects (Yes Bank), none of the new banks have a Bandhan-like story to narrate. The Bandhan to Bandhan Bank journey is summarised in Table 10.1.

**Table 10.1  Bandhan to Bandhan Bank: the journey**

| Bandhan to Bandhan Bank: the journey | June 2015 | August 2015 |
| --- | --- | --- |
| Number of states | 22 | 27 |
| Branches | 2,022 | 500 new full-fledged branches<br>2,022 doorstep service centres |
| Borrowers | 6.8 million | 6.8 million |
| Customer profile | 100% small clients through branches | 70% small clients through doorstep service centres and 30% clients serviced through branches |
| Loans outstanding | ₹102.42 billion | ₹102.50 billion+ |
| Depositors | 0 | 10 million |
| Deposits | 0 | ₹10.00 billion |
| Staff | 13,067 | 4,000 staff for the banking vertical<br>14,500 staff for the doorstep service centres |

*Source:* Conversations with Chandra Shekhar Ghosh, CEO and MD of Bandhan Bank.

From the time Bandhan received the in-principle licence to the day the bank commenced business on 23rd August 2015 they have been preparing hard for a big-bang launch. Bandhan Bank created history of sorts by being the first bank to be launched with a ₹100.00 billion loan book, with a hundred million depositor base having, on an average, deposited ₹1,000 to provide a deposit base of ₹10.00 billion, and with 500 new branches rolled out on a single day, while converting all the erstwhile branches into door-step service centres. Each one of the clients of Bandhan Bank would have a full-service account with a debit card that is interoperable in the entire banking system.

The challenge for Bandhan has been reorienting the employees and customers to operate under a new setting that is regulated and that needs specialist professionals to man certain divisions, while retaining the ethos of an MFI. The transition has been achieved through constant messaging, training programmes and orientation. For instance, in order to raise a deposit base of ₹10.00 billion on the day of the commencement of the bank, Bandhan has worked hard to ask its borrowers to save small amounts in a piggy bank over the past 16 months to be ready to deposit at least ₹1,000 on the day the bank opened. Bandhan has traditionally been in the underbanked regions of eastern and the north-eastern parts of the country. While a significant portion of the 600 new branches (500 that were set up at the time of commencement plus 100 that are planned to set up in a few weeks) are in West Bengal, it is important to note that Assam would have 63 branches, Tripura 23 branches and all the other north-eastern states will have at least one branch. Bihar would start with 77 branches. Bandhan would have 380 (63%) of its branches in rural and semi-urban locations, as against the required stipulation of 25%. Also 255 (41%) of its branches will be located in unbanked locations.

As of the beginning date, 100% of the portfolio of Bandhan Bank will qualify for priority sector and over a period of time Bandhan Bank will build up a portfolio that addresses the needs of small businesses, small housing, commercial vehicles and other segments. While a significant portion of the portfolio of Bandhan Bank will continue to be unsecured, it has adequate capital (₹32.00 billion to start with representing a capital risk adjusted ratio of 34%). Bandhan intends to continue serving the unserved segments and will build up robust internal rating systems and monitoring mechanisms to meet with the Basel and other prudential norms.

In preparation for rolling out the banking operations, the MFI was put completely under a CBS platform with the branch operating as a hub. Each of the 600 branches is expected to serve as a hub, which would be attached with 3 to 4 doorstep service centres. The new bank does not intend to aggressively expand on the loan side in states where other MFIs are already present. The plan for the southern states of Karnataka, Kerala, Tamil Nadu, Telangana and Andhra Pradesh is largely to open branches that would cater to the larger 30% clients, while catering to the savings needs of the 70% population that can be considered small customers.

Bandhan Bank is something that the inclusive finance sector will watch out for as a leader. Its experience will not only help the proposed SFBs in their transition, but will also provide a road map for the future transitions that might happen.

### Payments banks

Following the recommendations of the Nachiket Mor Committee, the RBI issued guidelines for setting up of PBs and accepted applications till February 2015. The idea of a PB was that they would accept small savings, particularly of low-income households, manage remittances which would be of particular use to migrant workers and distribute third-party products. It was envisaged that the PBs will operate with cutting-edge technologies, and potentially they could operate as BCs for existing banks. The eligible promoter list was fairly liberal—as there was no credit risk involved in the envisaged organisation. The RBI received a total of 41 applications. A significant number of the applicants were organisations working in the payments space as well as in the telecom space. After referring the applications to an External Advisory Committee, the RBI finally granted an in-principle licence to 11 players as listed below. As can be seen from the list, nine of the in-principle licences have been awarded to three distinct types of players—telecom players with a strong distribution network; technology players; traditional finance companies with retail presence.

**Telecom companies**

1. Aditya Birla Nuvo: The Birla group has a presence in the financial services space and has a

telecom service company in the group—Idea Cellular, which has a mobile wallet service.

2. Airtel M Commerce Services: Owned by telecom operator Bharti Airtel and with participation from Kotak Mahindra Bank. The group has also acquired a mobile payments start up YTS Solutions. It has more than 1.6 million outlets selling airtime, which would be tapped.

3. Vodafone M-Pesa: Vodafone has international experience in the mobile money space with it M-Pesa brand. It has been operating in the space in India as well.

4. Reliance Industries: Reliance is readying its ambitious telecom launch through R-Jio. In addition, Reliance has tied up with India's largest bank State Bank of India for this venture.

### Technology companies

1. Fino PayTech: The Company was one of the earliest players to be a Corporate BC and has been a pioneer in this space.

2. Vijay Shekhar Sharma: Sharma set up Paytm—one of India's most significant mobile payments companies. They are already in the mobile wallet space and this will enhance the business of Paytm significantly.

3. Tech Mahindra: Mahindras are strong players in both the technology space and financial services. Their financial services also extend very strongly in rural areas and they have a network. Tech Mahindra has MoboMoney—a mobile payments platform.

### Finance companies

1. Cholamandalam Distribution Services: The firm is a part of the Chennaibased Chola group which has diversified interests and is a significant player in the financial services space.

2. Department of Posts: The licence for India Post, which is the largest player in the retail savings market, was much awaited and their details have been covered in a separate chapter.

### Others

1. National Securities Depository Limited (NSDL): It is a depository and handles securities that are held electronically.

2. Dilip Shantilal Shanghvi: Shanghvi, the promoter of Sun Pharma, has obtained the in-principle licence in his personal capacity.

As can be seen, the list contains a diverse set of players and these have another 18 months to roll out their businesses. Since most of the players do not come from the traditional banking background, it is expected that the roll-out would be innovative and disruptive.

Since it is envisaged that the maximum balance in any account will never exceed ₹100,000 at any point in time (as against the limit of ₹450,000 for India Post), this initiative is expected to reach the smaller segment of the customers. Moreover, the RBI in its guidelines specified that it does not expect PBs to adhere to the quota of 25% branches in villages with less than 9,999 populations, but instead indicated that it expects that at least 25% of its access points are in such locations, thereby placing a great reliance on vertical specialisation and technology. As this form of organisation has not been very widely tried, it would be interesting to watch how the revenue model for PBs will pan in times to come.

### Small finance banks

The draft guidelines had indicated a limited area of operations for SFBs. This attracted widespread response, because a large number of MFIs—institutions that were naturally interested in morphing into SFBs—had a larger footprint than what was envisaged in the guidelines. While a limited area would give a geographic focus to the inclusion agenda, a national footprint would give a functional focus. There were even suggestions that the RBI might specify limited number of districts, but leave the choice of specific districts to the banks, without the condition that the presence of bank branches has to be in a contiguous geography. However, the final guidelines differentiated the SFBs from the universal banks with three important differences: (a) a lower start-up equity; (b) a higher requirement of PSL at 75%—a proportion much larger than the requirement for RRBs and (c) restricting 50% of the loan accounts to a size lower than ₹2.5 million.

In all, the RBI received 72 applications for SFBs. A large number (more than 20) were from registered NBFC-MFIs. In addition, there were NBFCs and specialised finance companies that had applied for a licence. Two of the old LABs also applied for a licence, thereby indicating that this was a much better design and showed greater promise than LABs.

After processing the applications and referring them to an External Advisory Committee, the RBI finally granted 10 licences to players as listed below:

1. Au Financiers India Limited
2. Capital Local Area Bank Limited
3. Disha Microfin Private Limited
4. Equitas Holdings Private Limited
5. ESAF Microfinance and Investments Private Limited

6. Janalakshmi Financial Services Private Limited
7. RGVN (North-east) Microfinance Limited
8. Suryoday Microfinance Private Limited
9. Ujjivan Financial Services Private Limited
10. Utkarsh Microfinance Private Limited

In the above list it can be seen that eight are erstwhile MFIs and the players represent a wide footprint. For instance, Ujjivan has operations in 24 states and Janalakshmi in 17 states. Utkarsh works in the hill regions of Uttarakhand, RGVN in northeast, and Capital LAB has its focus on Punjab. All the players have been given a period of 18 months to convert the in-principle licence to a full licence and commence operations. The MFIs that are moving to the banking space including Bandhan represented a GLP of ₹214.76 billion representing 53.5% of the NBFC-MFIs. The licensees represent the largest players in the market. The next year would be interesting to watch on how this space evolves.

With the RBI indicating that the licencing for SFBs, PBs and commercial banks would be opened up and made on-tap, there is scope of many more institutions to aspire to be a bank. Given the recent developments in the MFI and the UCB space, the trajectory may be to start as an NBFC-MFI or a UCB and move to become an SFB en route to be a universal bank. That RBI has also indicated that over a period of time SFBs can morph into universal banks makes it a distinct possibility with SFBs. This is not allowed for the PBs.

### MUDRA

One more significant initiative the GoI announced is the setting up of Micro Units Development and Refinance Agency (MUDRA) Bank. This announcement was made in the budget speech of the finance minister where he said:

> Our government firmly believes that development has to generate inclusive growth. While large corporate and business entities have a role to play, this has to be complemented by informal sector enterprises which generate maximum employment. There are some 577 million small business units, mostly individual proprietorship, which run small manufacturing, trading or service businesses. 62% of these are owned by SC/ST/OBC. These bottom-of-the-pyramid, hard-working entrepreneurs find it difficult, if not impossible, to access formal systems of credit. I, therefore, propose to create a Micro Units Development Refinance Agency (MUDRA) Bank, with a corpus of ₹200.00 billion, and credit guarantee corpus of ₹30.00 billion. MUDRA Bank will refinance Micro-Finance Institutions through a Pradhan Mantri Mudra Yojana. In lending, priority

will be given to SC/ST enterprises. These measures will greatly increase the confidence of young, educated or skilled workers who would now be able to aspire to become first generation entrepreneurs; existing small businesses, too, will be able to expand their activities. Just as we are banking the un-banked, we are also funding the un-funded. (Jaitley, 2015, Paragraph 34)

While on the one hand the government did not accept the Usha Thorat Committee report for a DFI for SHGs, it quickly identified a gap in the micro enterprises sector. The concept of MUDRA was announced in the budget and the functions envisaged for MUDRA were going beyond what was seen and defined as inclusion. While MFIs working with loan size limit of ₹50,000 (subsequently raised to ₹100,000) were traditionally seen as the players in the inclusion market outside of the banks, with MUDRA the scope is getting expanded to fill in the middle space of the micro entrepreneurs. MUDRA would cover the space for business credit up to ₹1 million. As of now, MUDRA has announced three products—Shishu that refinances loan sizes up to ₹50,000; Kishor covering loans from ₹50,000 to ₹0.5 million; and Tarun covering loans from ₹0.5 million to ₹1 million. The design of MUDRA is evolving. The current functions of MUDRA are detailed in Figure 10.1.

In addition, it has been envisaged that the agency will have supervisory and regulatory functions as well. The thought process in ascribing the regulatory and supervisory role to the agency is in recognition of the fact that the segment that has been identified by MUDRA has not been served effectively by the formal financial sector, particularly the commercial banks. The MFIs have remained at the smaller individual client level both for reasons of specialisation and regulation. MUDRA intends to fill the gap through innovative institutional interventions. This would possibly mean working with agencies that are not regulated by the RBI—including societies, trusts, NGOs and other agencies. Therefore, it is envisaged that MUDRA would have a regulatory role as well. This particular issue has to be sorted out and will evolve as the bill is drafted. For instance, the Governor of the RBI was unequivocal when he said, 'Firstly, it [MUDRA] is not going to regulate incorporated MFIs. That will stay with us. That has been established with the government'. (See Box 10.3.) This fact was reconfirmed by Secretary Financial Services when he said:

> When we make a Bill we will reconcile it. We will talk to RBI. We will reconcile it. Right now the idea is that we don't want to disturb the existing arrangement.

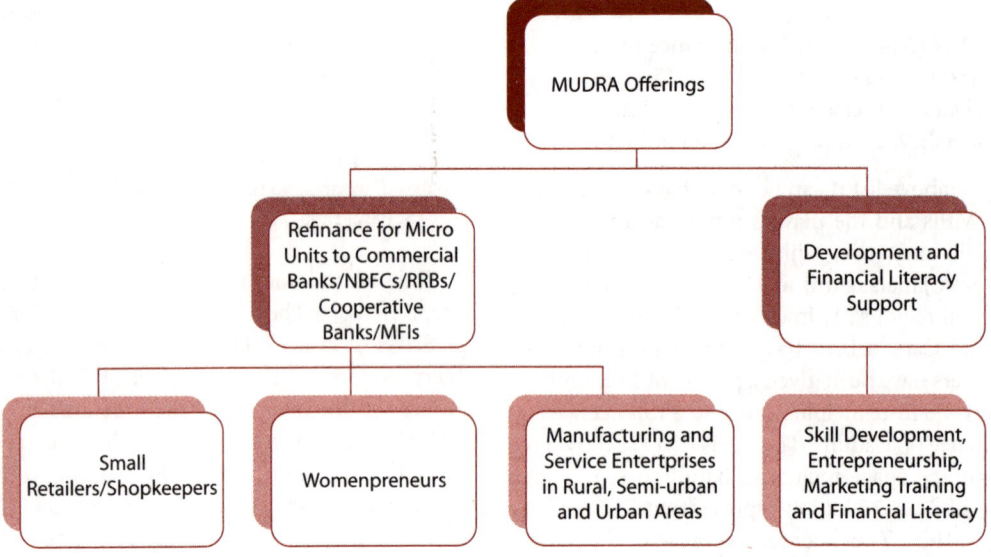

**Figure 10.1** Functions of MUDRA

*Source:* Website of MUDRA http://www.mudra.org.in/offerings.php

If corporate, NBFC, MFIs are regulated by RBI let it be so. No problem. But the other entities which are not registered with RBI but they are operating in the field. Now we want to bring them into the formal net of Mudra. (Adhia, 2015)

---

**Box 10.3 Governor Rajan on MUDRA**

*Professor Sriram:* On MUDRA, what is your view? Do you want to talk about it at all?

*Dr Rajan:* I am happy to talk about it. Firstly, it is not going to regulate incorporated MFIs. That will stay with us. That has been established with the government.

We need to bridge the gap in credit, but it will take hard work, new frameworks and better systems. The MUDRA Bank will have to work on all these dimensions. We just had a bunch of people come to the RBI and represent that small guys aren't getting credit. Yes, tell me what's new? Small guys haven't been getting credit across the world since time immemorial. The real issue is you don't solve this problem by pushing more credit in their direction. You try and figure out what are the ways in which you can bridge the gap between the financier and the small guy. Often the gap is informational and enforcement.

Informational because if you are sitting in a nationalised bank you may not know much about villages and what's going on and who is what, etc. And for a variety of reasons it may be too costly to enforce anything. So you depend on the borrower being willing to pay back. If he isn't willing to pay you back, you have no willingness or ability to go and enforce.

MFIs overcome this with their various social collaterals. And because they are closer they know what's going on. So unless you create the institutions that get closer to the borrower, you're not going to bridge that gap. It's not a question of cost of finance.

*Professor Sriram:* Yes, that is another thing....

*Dr Rajan:* No, you can always offer subsidised finance to somebody. But, unless it is sustainable, it will never scale. Now a new institution, lending to the informal sector, is not a complete answer because what are you going to do, how are you going to monitor them? You take the local money lender, there is a belief that if you lend to him, he'll offer cheap loans to the people. Perhaps he will. Or perhaps he won't.

I think this is one of those things we'll have to think outside the box and experiment a little bit. Do it at a small scale so we don't do too much damage and see what happens. So refinancing, we've tried that. I don't think that's the complete answer. Securitisation, maybe. If you can, you know, see some way of creating the necessary infrastructure, fine. If you can do some hand-holding, fine. Maybe the MUDRA Bank will do a little bit of all these. The diagnosis of the problem seems to be that nobody is lending to these informal MFIs so therefore let us create an institution to lend to them. But we have to be careful we put in place adequate frameworks and systems, else we could incur substantial losses.

However, there is much space beyond incorporated MFIs that the government is trying to bring in to make credit accessible at this level and the agency is addressing this space on an urgent basis. Pending the passage of the Bill, MUDRA has been set up as a subsidiary of the Small Industries Development Bank of India (SIDBI).

Beyond the above functions of providing refinance and eventual supervision and regulation, the plan for MUDRA also envisages creating an ecosystem for the credit market to emerge. The elements of the ecosystem include a guarantee fund, increased ease and flexibility of use of a part of the finance through a MUDRA card. In the long run, through its competitive pricing, MUDRA will also bring down the cost of finance to this segment of the borrowers significantly.

While the design intent of MUDRA is ambitious, the roll-out would be calibrated and it would certainly help in expanding the scope and definition of inclusion.

Clearly the year 2015 has been an exciting year as far as the new initiatives are concerned. This is a year where there was an institutional intervention after a gap of more than three decades. The ambitious initiative of MUDRA is looking at bridging the missing middle in the inclusion story. In addition, the RBI has issued in-principle licences to two distinct forms of differentiated banks—PBs which is totally a new concept and dramatically different and potentially impactful SFBs. The SFBs take the LAB initiative to a much higher level and this initiative shows potential of scale. With large players interested in this space, the inclusion agenda is getting addressed not only by the direct intervention of the state, but also by creating an environment for the private sector to participate in this endeavour.

## REFERENCES

Jaitley, Arun (2015). *Budget 2015–16*. New Delhi: Ministry of Finance, Government of India.

RBI (1993). *Guidelines on Entry of New Private Sector Banks*. Mumbai : RBI.

——— (2014). *Draft Guidelines for Licencing of 'Small Banks' in the Private Sector*. Mumbai: RBI.

Sriram, M.S. and Krishna, Aparna (2015). Review of Local Area Banks and Policy Implications for Narrow Banks in India. *Economic and Political Weekly*, Vol. L, 11, pp. 52–60.

# Interview with Governor Raghuram Rajan

## APPROACH TO FINANCIAL INCLUSION: PMJDY

*Professor Sriram:* Thank you for agreeing to speak to us for the annual Inclusive Finance India Report.

The first issue that we would like to discuss is the approach to financial inclusion. We have both the Reserve Bank of India (RBI) and the Government of India (GoI) being interested in this agenda in a big way and the objectives of both the RBI and GoI are converging. However, while the objectives may be converging, are the paths really converging? If they are not, then how do we manage this? I ask this in the backdrop of the ambitious announcement that the GoI made about the PMJDY and the caution that the RBI has tried to exercise on the scheme.

*Dr Rajan:* Historically, if we outline the paths of the government and the RBI, we implicitly believe that a push is needed and given a sufficient push, it can become self-sustaining. Now, over time we have discovered that it hasn't become self-sustaining. So, either the push hasn't been enough or that the notion that sufficient push will create self-sustainability itself is wrong. There is something else that needs to be done and we unfortunately have not found what it is thus far.

With PMJDY the government is giving yet another push and saying let us cover everybody to the extent possible. There is some virtue in this approach. This is because some programmes like DBTs are intended to be linked to these accounts. These programmes can work well if everybody is covered. If something like Aadhaar is also universal and linked to these accounts, it also helps in measuring the extent of indebtedness. If the coverage is partial, it does not quite work. So, the thrust on universal accounts, Aadhaar and DBT is good.

At the same time, I think we need to reconsider and examine if the gaps are in the institutional framework and the nature of institutions that are participating in this endeavour. So we are basically saying: We need local institutions that have lower costs and employ local labour that will not go the RRBs way and then demand the terms and pay scale that is national. For that we need to empower local institutions like SFBs. We should see whether we can get cooperatives to be governed better (some of them already are), or move them into a joint stock structure where they will be regulated like the SFBs. We have set up a committee to see the possibilities for cooperative banks.

The other issue is whether we can tap into the last mile. So the SFBs would be for small credit, whether it is retail credit or rural credit or rural industry or urban industry, but as far as bank accounts and financial services go, they can be created in a PB. For example, just yesterday in a remote village in Sikkim, where there is no bank, I saw an outlet selling mobile airtime. That point can be used as a cash point operated by any mobile company. So that is where PB comes in. Can we include everybody by including cash in-cash out points, which can be a BC of a variety of banks? I am very hopeful that this way we can cover much more ground.

## APPROACH TO INCLUSION: INSTITUTIONAL INNOVATION

*Professor Sriram:* On the institutional front, I have seen a shift in the approach taken by the RBI. In case of LABs and even when the draft guidelines for the SFBs were put up, it appeared that the RBI had a geographic focus. But the final guidelines opened up the space for SFBs to have a nationwide foot-print....

*Dr Rajan:* Possibly, but not necessarily.

*Professor Sriram:* But that possibility is real. With LABs or SFBs with a restricted geography we would have been able to achieve a regional penetration much better. When it is open to a nationwide footprint, then it encourages functional penetration. Instead of targeting some regions, we target certain types of customers.

*Dr Rajan:* Yes you are absolutely right. My hope is that we will also get some local players. When we put up the draft guidelines, the MFIs represented to us and said 'look we are already national, we are able to make these small loans because we have a certain structure that decentralizes decisions locally. So why do you want to penalize us?' There is also a stability issue with these small local entities. I mean, one firm focussed in say Andhra Pradesh may be subject to both the political environment and a hurricane and so on.

*Professor Sriram:* Yes, there is the geographical concentration risk. If we look at the growth of banking post-nationalisation when we had the 1:4 rule for rural branches, and later the rule of 25% branches being in rural and semi-urban areas. But these measures have not taken away the geographical mismatch. North-east, east and centre continue to be underbanked despite these efforts. So what do we do?

*Dr Rajan:* That leads us to the real question: what comes first, industry or finance? And I think that in these areas, typically the missing factor is not primarily finance, it is only partly finance. Primarily it is industry. Unless the real sector flourishes, which means fixing all the issues that are associated with the real sector, banking itself cannot be the prime mover. So people say credit-deposit ratio is low, it could be because there is no demand for credit. Of course, you can always find somebody who says, 'I wanted a loan, I didn't get it'. That does not negate the basic point.

*Professor Sriram:* Though RRBs did equalise this balance a little bit, possibly at the cost of the viability of some of the RRBs themselves, but if you look at the 1960s' data when it was predominately south and west, north has caught up over these decades and largely when I was looking at the data, the deeper penetration of rural branches has been much more of RRBs than commercial banks.

*Dr Rajan:* This is why we are trying to foster these new institutions. Locally managed institutions have a great incentive to give local loans. We have to ensure that they are viable and are not unstable because of their local dependency. That is why, we are willing to see a variety of them, and also maybe look at strengthening the urban cooperatives as well as the RRBs, including changes in their mode of governance. But the other thing is that we also have to look at the financial infrastructure that supports these. Today, we have credit information bureaus; can they penetrate more fully in the rural area? Can Aadhaar be used every time a loan is made so that everybody knows the extent of indebtedness? Today, somebody who wants a loan needs to get a no-objection certificate from everybody else.

*Professor Sriram:* But MFIs are also part of the Credit Information Bureaus.

*Dr Rajan:* Exactly! It is not linked with Aadhaar as yet, but it is linked to some address that seems to be working reasonably well. But can we do this in a more systematic way? The second is collateral registries for bigger players. Can we register collaterals with (some entity) and say you have borrowed once against this you cannot go re-hypothecate it somewhere else? If these kinds of structures are put down (credit information bureaus, collateral registries), as well as more rapid action by the small courts, I think credit will flow more easily.

*Professor Sriram:* This has always intrigued me, both on the LABs and the SFBs, you've always had a higher CRAR at 15%. But you know that the problem is on the assets side, because of either geographical concentration or functional concentration. With a high CRAR that risk doesn't go away. So how does a higher CRAR help, apart from the fact that it keeps the depositors a little safer? It does not attract capital because the Return on Equity (ROE) will not be great unless you have leveraged enough.

*Dr Rajan:* Presumably if you are taking on more risk, you'll have to charge a premium. This notion that somehow you're going to charge the riskier guys lower interest rates and still serve them rates doesn't make a good argument.

*Professor Sriram:* Is there any other way in which the assets side itself can be diversified by allowing them to do a lot more treasury and things like that?

*Dr Rajan:* You can do securitisation of loans. The only problem is you need to have adequate skin in the game to collect because you cannot securitise loans and then not be around to collect.

*Professor Sriram:* With Basel III kicking in, do you think all the banks including RRBs, SFBs and Co-operative Banks be covered under the norms? How does that pan out?

*Dr Rajan:* Eventually some version of Basel will be there. I think apart from capital ratios, we have to have some notion of liquidity for all these entities, but the counter-cyclical capital buffers, this that, we'll have to see how to apply them across the board. But let us see.

*Professor Sriram:* Do you think RRBs should further consolidate?

*Dr Rajan:* I think there is a process by which this is taking place. There is some talk of one RRB per state rather than two.

*Professor Sriram:* That is right. That is what the ministry was pushing a couple of years ago.

*Dr Rajan:* Yes, I would say we need to maintain the local character of these institutions, rather than make them so big that policies are made in Delhi or in Mumbai, and not locally. I think when we get to that point we have created too big an RRB.

*Professor Sriram:* Let us look at the public sector banking architecture. Would it be a good idea to break them up functionally and say that you specialise and have a set of institutions, which penetrate into functional specialisation, given that we are talking of tradable PSL notes?

*Dr Rajan:* I think that could emerge, could be a regional specialisation as well as functional. But I don't think we should force it from Delhi or Mumbai. It should be something that is driven by the banks primarily.

*Professor Sriram:* But you need to provide a framework which allows that to happen.

*Dr Rajan:* We need to decentralise decision making to the banks themselves. Which means we need to create strong boards as the government has suggested. And let them be free, let them decide what the policy is. And as you free up independent boards they will say we cannot all be doing the same thing.

*Professor Sriram:* Actually, if you go to a public sector bank and do a blind test, you will not know which bank it is.

*Dr Rajan:* Exactly! So let them differentiate themselves, but it can't be driven by the Ministry or the RBI. It has to be done by the bank itself.

*Professor Sriram:* In the inclusion space we also have a lot of unregulated entities, registered but unregulated, like Trust, Societies and possibly section 8 companies. What is the RBI's outlook on such entities?

*Dr Rajan:* As far the unincorporated entities go, including your local money lender, I mean we do have a huge number of those but we cannot do much about it unless it gets to a size that it starts creating a systemic concern. So our current view is that we will help coordinate the regulation of these entities through State Level Coordination Committees (SLCCs). Many of them are more of a law-and-order issue rather than a systemic stability issue.

*Professor Sriram:* Therefore, are you saying that the RBI should not be too concerned?

*Dr Rajan:* No, no, we should be concerned about them. When somebody loses money they are going to say that I was taken for a ride by this financial institution, where were the regulators? We have had enough adverse mentions by various judicial and investigative agencies. Clearly, even if it is not our baby, the public will hold us responsible. So what we are doing is activating these SLCCs in every state which has the Chief Secretary, the Criminal Investigation Department, the Director General of Police, etc. which will come together to exchange information about who these operators are or where there is a possibility of public harm.

*Professor Sriram:* … and also are of a size that could cause concern.

*Dr Rajan:* Yes, the size will cause concern. For the tiny guys we are trying to say that if you take deposits, or what are deemed deposits, without having the regulatory permission, then it will essentially be a cognisable offense. So before you default on a deposit, even the act of taking it without licence should be seen as a cognisable offense. Otherwise you have these guys who are running Ponzi schemes and until they disappear they are fine, they are legal. So I think we need to make unlicensed deposit taking an offense. So those are two areas where we are pushing harder.

## MICROFINANCE

*Professor Sriram:* The next thing I want to talk to you is about MFIs. Prior to 2010 they were growing at a very fast pace. Then the Andhra Pradesh episode happened and then the RBI set up the Malegam Committee. I think the RBI announcement came on the same day as the Andhra Pradesh ordinance. So, possibly the RBI was anticipating a crisis because if you look at the date it was the exact same date as the Chandigarh board meeting. Based on the report of the committee, there are stringent norms laid out on MFIs. Some of these possibly are still necessary, but some of these are difficult to implement like income, asset size and number of loans. The number of loans is, of course, possible to monitor.

*Dr Rajan:* That I have said that there has been some substantial improvement in monitoring the over-indebtedness of the individual.

*Professor Sriram:* That is true, but there are a couple of things—85% of the qualifying assets (portfolio) has to be in a defined category of households with ₹60,000 income in rural areas and ₹120,000 income in urban areas. Such norms lead to a large amount of misreporting. It also becomes worthless data for their own data mining purposes.

*Dr Rajan:* What we need to do is liberalise. We are trying to develop a norm for NBFCs as a whole. See, the problem comes when some NBFCs get regulatory preferences. For example, lending to NBFC-MFI counts as priority sector. If we say that lending to any NBFC against microfinance loans should count as priority sector, then the entire privilege for NBFC-MFI vanishes. So, that is probably something that we could examine. And that will alleviate this problem of having to micro-manage the structure of the MFIs.

*Professor Sriram:* Yes, because 85% is also a difficult ratio to maintain, given that some of these clients actually graduate and there is a fair mid-level market developed.

*Dr Rajan:* Yes I know. We are trying to move away from creating these silos for NBFCs, to make it continuous. If you are 95% in equipment financing, you are treated as thus and such. But if you are 70% into MFI financing … so you should get privileges based on what you do, rather than because of the institution you are categorised as. That is all. We shouldn't have 0/1 categories.

## MUDRA

*Professor Sriram:* On MUDRA, what is your view? Do you want to talk about it at all?

*Dr Rajan:* I am happy to talk about it. Firstly, it is not going to regulate incorporated MFIs. That will stay with us. That has been established with the government.

We need to bridge the gap in credit, but it will take hard work, new frameworks and better systems. The MUDRA Bank will have to work on all these dimensions. We just had a bunch of people come to the RBI and represent that small guys aren't getting credit. Yes, tell me what is new? Small guys haven't been getting credit across the world since time immemorial. The real issue is you don't solve this problem by pushing more credit in their direction. You try and figure out what are the ways in which you can bridge the gap between the financier and the small guy. Often, the gap is informational and enforcement.

Informational because if you are sitting in a nationalised bank, you may not know much about villages and what is going on and who is what, etc. And for a variety of reasons it may be too costly to enforce anything. So you depend on the borrower being willing to pay back. If he is not willing to pay you back, you have no willingness or ability to go and enforce.

MFIs overcome this with their various social collaterals. And because they are closer they know what is going on. So unless you create the institutions that get closer to the borrower, you're not going to bridge that gap. It is not a question of cost of finance.

*Professor Sriram:* Yes, that is another thing....

*Dr Rajan:* No, you can always offer subsidised finance to somebody. But, unless it is sustainable, it will never scale. Now a new institution, lending to the informal sector, is not a complete answer because what are you going to do, how are you going to monitor them? You take the local money lender, there is a belief that if you lend to him, he'll offer cheap loans to the people. Perhaps he will. Or perhaps he won't.

I think this is one of those things we'll have to think outside the box and experiment a little bit. Do it at a small scale so we don't do too much damage and see what happens. So refinancing, we've tried that. I don't think that is the complete answer. Securitisation, maybe. If you can, you know, see some way of creating the necessary infrastructure, fine. If you can do some hand-holding, fine. Maybe the MUDRA Bank will do a little bit of all these. The diagnosis of the problem seems to be that nobody is lending to these informal MFIs so therefore let us create an institution to lend to them. But we have to be careful we put in place adequate frameworks and systems, else we could incur substantial losses.

## PRIORITY SECTOR LENDING AND AGRICULTURE

*Professor Sriram:* Would you like to talk about the PSL norms and the changes that are on the anvil?

*Dr Rajan:* Yes, we are increasing the small and marginal farmer support and the micro support. Our approach was, let us figure out who really needs access, because we have mixed up access and priority and national importance together. In some cases we don't know where it ends up. So these are the customers who desperately need access. Let us push here. For the rest, these are broadly national priorities, we'll put it broadly and you can choose between one and the other. Agriculture target is still 18% but 7% (going up to 8%) to small and marginal farmers is the harder target. Those are people who truly need credit. Once we achieve the marginal farmer and the micro enterprise category, the rest are probably going to be relatively easy to achieve. And therefore, it won't become that binding, but these two essentially become binding.

*Professor Sriram:* That brings me to the agriculture portfolio. It is a wicked problem in a typical public policy sense. When you are talking of trading of PSL notes, the report recommends trading of obligations without moving the portfolio and restricts this to banks. So there is no regulatory arbitrage. Does it make sense for us to think of actually encouraging a regulatory arbitrage? Say, NBFCs lend at a higher interest rate for agriculture and the banks achieve their targets by purchasing this portfolio? If that is possible then possibly there will be a specialised institution marked which actually caters to the needs, but banks also achieve their targets, in a lazy way.

*Dr Rajan:* The problem with that is it makes it too easy and the banks themselves will back off lending to the priority sector. The NBFCs that have been doing this lending will come into the market and sell. You will not get incremental lending to the priority sector, and maybe even a decline. Basically NBFCs will crowd out the banks and sell priority sector loans to them. So unless we impose targets on the NBFCs also, it will not serve the purpose.

*Professor Sriram:* With the recommendations of the internal working group on tradability of PSL obligations, do you think it may morph into a larger trading platform across structures in future or you want to keep it limited to the banking system?

*Dr Rajan:* As of now banks. But let us see how it goes.

*Professor Sriram:* Is there no other way, with which we can do anything about this subvention and make lending to agriculture inherently attractive?

*Dr Rajan:* No. Subvention doesn't necessarily imply that you have to lend at 9%. That is not so much the subvention than the fixed price. The subvention actually tries to make lending a little more attractive.

We have said to the government that they should eliminate fixed price. Otherwise what happens is that you get an excessive focus on gold loans. We have this policy of saying do 'A' but you cannot either charge the appropriate interest rate or take collateral. In that case banks are basically saying 'Why should I do "A"?'

*Professor Sriram:* That is right. Then they'll do the minimalist thing required.

*Dr Rajan:* Or find somebody who looks like 'A' but is not really 'A'. I have pledged my gold, I get a gold loan. And that counts as agriculture.

*Professor Sriram:* But the banks still don't get the return and that is the problem. Even if they look at the total adjusted cost of funds, agriculture has to become a loss-making portfolio because of the interest rate cap.

*Dr Rajan:* It does not have to be that way. But we do worry about cases where the same guy who borrows from the bank goes back and re-deposits, because he is charged effectively 4% and earns 8% on fixed deposits.

## POST BANK

*Professor Sriram:* Can we talk about the Post Bank. I am not sure what happened but they had applied for a licence as a mainstream bank, the Finance Minister announced in the budget that they will be a PB. Any reasons why they were not considered for a universal bank?

*Dr Rajan:* At that time we did not proceed with the universal bank application because it had not been sent with government approval. With the PB application announced in the budget, we are examining the proposal for a PB.

*Professor Sriram:* Do you think it would have been a good idea to grant a universal bank licence?

*Dr Rajan:* I would say it would be appropriate for them to first start as a PB.

*Professor Sriram:* But they are already a PB in one sense.

*Dr Rajan:* Yes, well they say that. But it would be nice to segregate all that properly into a structure, have a clear accounting, have a sense of who is in the structure, who is not. There is a need for transparency about the banking operations. What kind of a relationship do they have with the postal department? That needs to be clarified substantially. Once that is clear, the separation is clear.

*Professor Sriram:* Postal department had a consultant's report which had a road map, basically saying that every post office will not have a bank branch but in 6–7 years every district head-quarter will have a banking outlet.

*Dr Rajan:* See, our worry about credit to any untested organisation, especially if the organisation can, in a span of a year or two, generate ₹2 trillion in deposits, how will that be deployed? What kinds of loans will be made? Where is the credit evaluation capacity? We need to have a greater comfort with that.

*Professor Sriram:* One of the arguments made was that they don't have credit experience. That is an oxymoronic argument. But you are saying size is the argument....

*Dr Rajan:* Exactly, but let us first get the bank management, cash management and the structure together. Once we have confidence that all those things are working well and there are no operational risks then we can start slowly seeing how we can move the Post PB towards more. In a number of countries the postal bank is just cash in-cash out, no lending. It doesn't make loans. Some advocates are basically saying the postman knows the local area and can make loans. But the postman has no financial experience. He can only do know your customer (KYC) at best. He can't make the loans objectively, because his friends are there. So, in what sense is he going to make loans and collect them?

## COOPERATIVES

*Professor Sriram:* You are moving towards converting cooperatives into mainstream banks. But the form of the organisation doesn't permit you to do that in one sense, because there is no residual claim on liquidation income as far as cooperatives are concerned. There is only residual claim on current income. With all these large banks, what route would you take?

*Dr Rajan:* There are two options for cooperatives that we regulate. They could morph into the kind of structure that the Malegam Committee has proposed, which gives us a little more regulatory confidence. The other is to transform into the joint stock bank. In the United States when it went through this, they did basically give the equity rights to the existing depositors. We'll have to worry about how the membership of the cooperative will get rights to the equity.

*Professor Sriram:* Particularly since these banks are largely controlled by borrowers rather than depositors.

*Dr Rajan:* Exactly!

*Professor Sriram:* So, that is a tougher problem and much more gradual issue.

*Dr Rajan:* We'll have to figure out how to do it. So we'll have to make sure that members are involved in the proportion they share the cost of subscription. Maybe the appropriate proportion would be one member, one equity share. And so, that way we don't get an excess concentration of the surplus value in a few hands.

*Professor Sriram:* What do you do with the accumulated reserves and the surpluses?

*Dr Rajan:* So it would be divided up equally across the membership. That would also accord with the cooperative nature. However, all this needs to be thought through in discussions with stakeholders.

## LAST MILE DELIVERY

*Professor Sriram:* On the last mile delivery of financial services, the last big idea that we tried was BC and that has had mixed response and mixed results. Are there any other big ideas you have on this?

*Dr Rajan:* I think BC has to go together with connectivity and with mobile transfers. BC has to be perhaps cash in-cash out. But having agents who do other functions acting as a BC may also allow for recovery of cost.

*Professor Sriram:* That is the State Bank of India model, where they have put this CSP very near the branch in most of the places so they divert small ticket traffic to the CSP. It is safe in the sense that the exposure of the CSP is backed up by a fixed deposit. As the point is near the branch, anytime CSP runs out of limits they can go top it up. They have given limited access to CBS. It is a very interesting model but not many banks have picked it up.

*Dr Rajan:* Well some have, but I was thinking more in terms of he is doing another business, and the BC is on the side. So, the other business which is not a banking business, like he is running a shop and he does BC also on the side.

*Professor Sriram:* Yes, these guys also do photocopying, selling insurance products and other small services.

*Dr Rajan:* In some states they are doing government business.

*Professor Sriram:* Yes the Sahaj is doing that, wherein you share the sunk costs across.

*Dr Rajan:* Exactly! The fixed costs are shared; so, that I think would work. We are trying to figure out what we can do with white label BCs. So allow them to do business for multiple banks. Now there the problem right now is which bank controls them. Let them have one bank which they do primary business with, but let the bank not make it disadvantageous to work with other banks.

## CONCLUDING QUESTIONS

*Professor Sriram:* One last personal question, you've been outside the system, you've been extensively writing, including your Hundred Small Steps and so on. Has your outlook, having occupied the office, changed a little bit with the internal constraints kicking-in? In a way you have cautiously advocated the markets approach and deepening of the markets.

*Dr Rajan:* I have broadly moved in the direction of that report in a number of dimensions. I just saw the currency markets; trading has increased substantially over the past few months and interest rate futures markets have increased; so this notion that somehow we are against markets is wrong. Where I have become a little more cautious is that, post financial crisis, the notion that market participants are fully responsible is hard to hold. A variety of problems plague them.

Take, for example, External Commercial Borrowings (ECBs). Should we, as the Sahoo Committee suggests, allow unbridled ECB, regardless of who you are, so long as you hedge? I am uncomfortable because I don't think the only problem is lack of hedging. I think there are a number of players who basically are willing to take on dollar loans and remain unhedged because they pay one and a half per cent. They basically say that if the dollar appreciates substantially against the rupee, I am in deep trouble. But then I go to the bank and say take a hit, so I am not really in trouble, my banker is in trouble. And if the dollar stays where it is, I make a ton of money.

*Professor Sriram:* So there is an upside but there is no downside. Downside goes back to the public.

*Dr Rajan:* Exactly! That is the game the unhedged promoter could be playing. In that game if we don't have proper bankruptcy, the moral hazard involved is tremendous. So this notion that we liberalise and just require hedging may be optimistic.… First, they don't hedge, and second, I cannot monitor what they hedge. Banks tell us they cannot monitor, obviously because he hedges the first day he undoes it the second day. How do you know if he undid it? You have no idea. I think there is a value here to being reasonably conservative. Of course, you don't want to be so conservative that you hold back necessary change. So I am open to change, but I, precisely your point, want it explained and I want to understand whether it is an ivory tower view of participants or a reasonable view.

The banks have a constraint because some bank managers also have a short horizon and are desperate to find everywhere which way to off-load the problem to the future, so the next manager can take care of it. So in that kind of an environment, the kinds of outcomes can be quite different from what you get in a well-functioning capital market. Even in a well-functioning capital market we have the experience of 2008. So basically, I am cautious. I'd like to see markets work better, I'd like to bring more of them into the picture, but let us be a little more careful about how much we rely on them.

# Acknowledgements

1. Access Development Services
   Vipin Sharma, CEO
   Radhika Agashe, Executive Director Access Assist
   Lalitha Sridharan
   Anshu Singh
   Sayantani Mukherjee
2. Aquarius India
   S.N. Subramanya
3. APMAS
   C.S. Reddy, CEO
4. Bandhan-Bandhan Bank
   Chandra Shekhar Ghosh, CEO and MD
5. Bharatiya Mahila Bank
   Usha Ananthasubramanian, Chairman and Managing Director
6. Bill and Melinda Gates Foundation
   Pawan Bakhshi
7. CAFRAL
   G. Gopalakrishna, Director
   Smita Aggarwal, Senior Programme Director
8. Canara Bank
   S.S. Bhat, Chief General Manager
9. CRIF Highmark
   Parijat Garg, Vice President, Business Development
10. HDFC Bank
    Ashey Aggarwal, Vice President, Strategic Projects and Financial Inclusion
11. IBA
    M.V. Tanksale, CEO
    Rema Menon, Officer on Special Duty
12. ICICI Bank
    Avijit Saha, General Manager, Rural and Inclusive Banking
13. IDFC
    Rajiv Lall, Executive Chairman
14. India Post
    Kalpana Tewari, Member, Postal Services Board (since retired)
    Sandhya Rani Kanneganti, Post Master General
    Sachin Kishore, Director CBS
15. IndusInd Bank
    Bonam Srinivas, Head Inclusive Banking Group
16. IFMR
    Bindu Anant, President IFMR Trust
    Sharon Buteau, Executive Director, IFMR Lead
    Amulya Krishna, IFMR Lead
    Vaishnavi Prathap, IFMR Finance Foundation
    Parul Agarwal, IFMR Lead
    Gaurav Kumar, Senior Partner and Head-Origination, IFMR Capital
    Ganesh K.V., Deputy CEO, IFMR Rural Channels
    Anup Roy, Associate Director, IFMR Lead
17. MCril
    Alok Misra, CEO
18. Microfinance Institutions Network
    Alok Prasad, Ex-CEO

Ratna Viswanathan, CEO

Nikhil Chandra, Associate Vice President

19. MicroSave

Manoj Sharma, Managing Director

Bhavna Srivastava, Specialist

20. Ministry of Finance, Department of Financial Services

Hasmukh Adhia, Secretary, DFS

Alok Pandey, Director DFS

21. Ministry of Rural Development

Amarjeet Sinha, Additional Secretary

22. MUDRA

Jiji Mammen, CEO

23. National Bank for Agriculture and Rural Development

Harsh Bhanwala, Chairman

H.R. Dave, Deputy Managing Director

G.R. Chintala, CGM, MCID

Dhirendra Routray, GM, MCID

Subrata Gupta, CGM, DFIBT

M.V. Ashok, CGM, DEAR

P.K. Misra, ex-CGM, IDD

D.M. Magar, CGM, IDD

A.G. Das, GM, IDD

A.K. Singh, GM

24. National Payments Corporation of India

M. Balachandran, Chairman

A.P. Hota, Managing Director and CEO

25. Omidyar Network

Ameya Upadhyay

Anuradha Ramachandran

26. Prime Minister's Office

Anurag Jain, Joint Secretary

27. Reserve Bank of India

Raghuram Rajan, Governor

Pallavi Chavan, Assistant Adviser, DEPR

28. Sa-dhan

P. Satish, Executive Director

Saibal Paul, Senior Manager

Somesh Dayal, Associate Director

29. Sampark

Smita Premchander

30. SKDRDP

Dr L.H. Manjunath, Executive Director

31. Small Industries Development Bank of India

Umesh Chandra Gaur, General Manager

Surendra Srivastava, DGM

Veena Padia, Consultant

32. UIDAI

V.S. Madan, Director General

33. Sector Experts

S. Ananth

Brij Mohan, Former Executive Director, SIDBI

Y.C. Nanda, Former Chairman, NABARD

V. Puzhalendi

B. Sambamurthy

N. Srinivasan

Usha Thorat

# Technical Partner

**CRIF High Mark (CHM)** (www.crifhighmark.com) is India's most comprehensive credit bureau with coverage for retail, rural/agriculture, microfinance, small and medium-sized enterprise and commercial borrowers. CHM provides information-based risk management solutions to all types of lenders, including microlenders, for checks at the point of origination and during servicing of loans. It also offers analytics, data management and related software solutions, which support lenders in decisions related to markets, customer segments, products and so on as well as in automating credit processes.

CHM pioneered India's first microfinance bureau and today operates the world's largest microfinance credit bureau database. The bureau coverage for microfinance sector has supported the sector to increase access to credit to hitherto under-penetrated borrower segment, while controlling multiple financing. CHM's work for microfinance sector has been recognised through a Grand Jury Award at Manthan South-Asia Awards 2014, a Silver Award at SKOCH Digital Inclusion Award 2012 and coverage in industry reports such as State of Sector Report, Bharat Microfinance Report and so on.

CHM's sophisticated technology capabilities allow it to accurately pinpoint the geographical location of a borrower despite the existence of inherent contradictions in the address reported into the credit bureau. This allows CHM to create geo-insight reports (market insights, competitive benchmarking, etc.) that are based on not only more data but also more accurate data. Its customers (MFIs, other organisations engaged in micro-credit, lenders to the sector, etc.) have benefitted from using its services for their market entry or market review exercises.

CHM is now part of CRIF SpA, a global end-to-end knowledge company operating in over 50 countries with expertise in credit bureaus, insurance data pools, analytics, scoring and decision solutions. CHM's other investors include State Bank of India, Punjab National Bank, SIDBI, Shriram City, Edelweiss and a group of 26 MFIs. For more information, please write to info@crifhighmark.com.

# About the Author

**M.S. Sriram** is Professor at the Centre for Public Policy, Indian Institute of Management (IIM) Bangalore. In addition, he is currently a Distinguished Fellow of the Institute for Development of Research in Banking Technology—set up by the RBI. In the past, he was the ICICI Bank Lalita D Gupte Chair Professor of Microfinance, and Chairperson Finance and Accounting Area at the IIM Ahmedabad; on the faculty of IRMA, and Vice President of Basix. He has also taught at IIM Udaipur, SP Jain Centre for Management in Dubai and Singapore, the Solvay Brussels School of Business and Economics and the Azim Premji University Bengaluru.

Sriram is a coauthor of three Books—*Beyond Micro-credit* published by SAGE-Vistaar and two books on flow of credit to small and marginal farmers.

Sriram has served on several committees set up by GoI, RBI and NABARD. He was till recently on the External Advisory Committee of the RBI for granting licences to small finance banks. He is also on the board of NABFINS, NDDB Dairy Services and Centre for Budget and Policy Studies, and a Trustee of Pratham Books and Dastkar Andhra.